EMERGENT TOKYO

DESIGNING THE SPONTANEOUS CITY

JORGE ALMAZÁN+
STUDIOLAB

T0364167

ORO
Novato, California

1 INTRODUCTION: WHY TOKYO?   004

1.1   The city that inspires the world
1.2   Tokyo at a dangerous crossroads
1.3   Glimpsing Tokyo's future through its postwar past
1.4   A field guide to several different Tokyos
1.5   The urban fabrics that nurture emergent Tokyo
1.6   Beyond exotic mystery and glamorous chaos
1.7   Emergence: a new lens for understanding Tokyo

2 YOKOCHŌ ALLEYWAYS   018

2.1   An alleyway that's designed to be explored
2.2   What defines a yokochō?
2.3   Clandestine origins, uncertain future
2.4   The yokochō revival
2.5   The world's densest bar district: Golden Gai
2.6   Shibuya's hidden Nombei Yokochō
2.7   Yanagi Kōji in Nishi-Ogikubo
2.8   Learning from yokochō alleyways

Case 01   Golden Gai   036
Case 02   Nombei Yokochō   044
Case 03   Yanagi Kōji   052

3 ZAKKYO BUILDINGS   060

3.1   The iconic buildings that no one talks about
3.2   What makes a building zakkyo?
3.3   How does a building become a zakkyo building?
3.4   The iconic zakkyo of Yasukuni Avenue
3.5   Kagurazaka's zakkyo buildings have an Edo legacy
3.6   The Karasumori zakkyo block in Shimbashi
3.7   Learning from zakkyo buildings

Case 04   Yasukuni Avenue   080
Case 05   Kagurazaka Street   086
Case 06   Karasumori Block   092

4 UNDERTRACK INFILLS   098

4.1   What lies beneath
4.2   A century of undertrack spaces
4.3   Ameyoko: old-school shopping under the railways
4.4   Kōenji: finding the slow life in a fast city
4.5   Ginza Corridor: courtship under the expressway
4.6   Learning from undertrack infills

Case 07   Ameyoko   112
Case 08   Kōenji   118
Case 09   Ginza Corridor   124

5 ANKYO STREETS

130

5.1 The flowing streets of Tokyo
5.2 The campaign to make Japanese street life boring
5.3 Ankyo river streets in history
5.4 Mozart-Brahms Lane: Harajuku's linear oasis
5.5 Yoyogi Lane: portrait of a communal backstreet
5.6 The inclusive Kuhombutsu Promenade
5.7 Learning from ankyo streets

Case 10 **Mozart-Brahms Lane** 144
Case 11 **Yoyogi Lane** 150
Case 12 **Kuhombutsu Promenade** 156

6 DENSE LOW-RISE NEIGHBORHOODS

162

6.1 An ocean of houses
6.2 How dense, how low? A working definition
6.3 The joys of dense, low-rise neighborhoods
6.4 The origins of a delicate balance
6.5 Higashi-Nakanobu: ordinary in the best sense
6.6 Tsukishima: spontaneity in the grid
6.7 North Shirokane: the beauty of urban diversity
6.8 Learning from dense low-rise neighborhoods

Case 13 **Higashi-Nakanobu** 182
Case 14 **Tsukishima** 186
Case 15 **North Shirokane** 190

7 TOKYOLOGY

194

7.1 A chronology of thinking about Tokyo
7.2 Self-orientalism: nihonjinron in Tokyology
7.3 Charting a new critical approach to Tokyo

8 A TOKYO MODEL OF EMERGENT URBANISM

206

8.1 Tokyo's rising corporate-led urbanism
8.2 Tokyo's corporate urban centers: what fails and why
8.3 Safety as a pretext for homogenization
8.4 Emergent urbanism versus corporate-led urbanism
8.5 Designing the conditions of emergence

Endnotes 218

1 INTRODUCTION: WHY TOKYO?

1.1   The city that inspires the world

Is it possible to design a city that possesses Tokyo's best qualities? This book was written to answer this question in the affirmative—both by explaining how Tokyo became one of the most vibrant and livable cities on the planet, and by distilling those experiences into a practical program of action for the world's cities to learn from. But grappling with this question begets an even simpler question in turn, one that has vexed urbanists for generations: Can a city truly be designed at all?

Urban design is a mixture of art and science, with many competing schools of thought and few absolute truths. Times change, new ideas about cities come into prominence, and previously dominant ones fall out of favor. The result is that young planners and architects have a habit of exploring new approaches that horrify their elders. The modernist urban planners and architects of the 1950s, for example, would tell you that a city could be designed top-down out of whole cloth. But after watching that approach crash and burn, many of their successors swung the pendulum in the opposite direction, abandoning maximalist dreaming and resigning themselves to letting so-called market forces shape the evolution of the city. Their market-dominated development decisions have made cities across the globe more sterile and exclusionary, driving the next generation of young urbanists to push back and dream big once again.

This new wave of urbanist thinkers is disenchanted with market fundamentalism and stepping up to champion architecture and public policy as meaningful tools for shaping our cities. Unlike the modernists of old, however, they try to avoid top-down, heavy-handed techniques. On their watch, cities across the globe are developing a new inventory of spatial and aesthetic possibilities, marrying global thinking to their particular local contexts. At their best, they embrace the dynamic energy of their inhabitants rather than letting opaque bureaucracies and profit-focused corporate interests sweep them aside.

For many of these urbanists, Tokyo stands out as an aspirational ideal of what a city can be, even if they don't fully understand how the city works or how its best aspects came into being. To those who have visited Tokyo, this admiration won't be surprising. There is nothing quite like encountering the city for the first time; its gleaming commercial cityscapes and its intimate residential neighborhoods each inspire their own sense of wonder. But to use Tokyo as a source of inspiration, one must move beyond the awed gaze of the tourist and begin to ask questions about the *why* and *how* of the city. That, in a nutshell, is the purpose of this book.

Tokyo's greatness as a city stems from its wide variety of inclusive and adaptive urban spaces. It is a cityscape shaped in ways big and small by the daily micro-scale choices and actions of its residents; its unique patterns and urban eco-systems take on a life of their own beyond the limitations of government master planning and corporate profit-seeking. This book examines five of Tokyo's most striking patterns: *yokochō alleyways* (Chapter 2), multi-tenant *zakkyo buildings* (Chapter 3), *undertrack infills* (Chapter 4), flowing *ankyo streets* (Chapter 5), and *dense low-rise neighborhoods* (Chapter 6). These patterns form the core of *emergent Tokyo*, a city of intimacy, resilience, and dynamism built from the bottom up by its ordinary inhabitants.[1] Emergent Tokyo cannot be copied wholesale, but it has much to teach anyone who hopes to build a better city.

1.2 Tokyo at a dangerous crossroads

Today, however, Tokyo is on the verge of dramatic change. Drastic rede-velopment is currently underway throughout the urban core, in some cases over-whelming the city's traditional fabric and transforming its low-rise residential areas. Although Tokyo has the image of a mega-city in the popular imagination, until recently high-rise buildings were few and far between, with concentrations mainly around Shinjuku in the west and Marunouchi in the east. The new devel-opments aren't confined to any specific area, and in the decades to come they may reach a tipping point, shifting not only the city's population but also its mode of urban life. Tokyo's thriving present may give way to a very different future.

Tokyo has always been a dynamic, ever-changing city, but these new redevelopments are something else entirely—we call it *corporate-led urbanism*. They consist primarily of variations on a single building typology: super-high towers of luxury apartments and offices perched on top of shopping center-style commercial podia. It's easy to imagine one even if you've never been to Tokyo, since they look identical to the similar luxury mixed-use complexes found in nearly every other global city. These new redevelopment projects are sleek yet inorganic; they inadvertently highlight Tokyo's key urban qualities—the aspects of the city we explore in this book—by showing just how much is lost when those qualities disappear.

The process of covering Tokyo with skyscrapers began slowly in the 1980s, but it accelerated dramatically in 2002 with the passage of the Law on Special Measures for Urban Renaissance. Japan's legal system has long upheld strong property rights, frustrating the real estate industry's dreams of large-scale redevelopment while at the same time helping local communities preserve their socio-economic fabric. The 2002 law stepped around this system by designating specific areas of the city as special zones where existing urban regulations were suspended, allowing private-sector developers to negotiate case-by-case deals with local government officials that the old system never would have permitted. In practice, this gifts enormous powers to mega-developers that previously rest-ed in the hands of the state. Clusters of new skyscrapers now define the skylines of Tokyo neighborhoods like Shiodome, Shinagawa, Marunouchi, and Roppongi, and major transit hubs such as Shibuya Station are also seeing radical increases in density through large-scale development projects.

Glimpsing Tokyo's future through its postwar past

Is Tokyo doomed to be overtaken by the charmless sterility of corporate-led urbanism? We hope not, and in this book we aim to offer an alternate path: one that draws lessons from both the city's unique history and its present strengths. But what should our emergent alternative look like in practice? We are not historical preservationists seeking to freeze or 'museum-ize' the city, nor do we want to plan the entire city from the top down like the hubristic modernists of yesteryear. Instead, our approach draws on the vitality of Tokyo's early postwar period, which laid an enduring foundation that defines much of Tokyo even today.

As the Japanese government attempted to rebuild their devastated capital city, they initially drafted a comprehensive reconstruction plan, but soon concluded that they lacked the budget to carry it out. And so, in areas where neither the government nor the country's real-estate and transportation mega-corporations could properly fund reconstruction efforts, whole neighborhoods instead rapidly rebuilt themselves. Working on a small scale, residents rebuilt homes and shops using scraped-together funds while relying on little more than their collective grit and inventiveness, and black markets full of micro-entrepreneurs sprung up around the city's major train stations. These neighborhoods were not initially planned, per se—they *emerged*, and their ramshackle, spontaneous spirit can still be felt today when walking Tokyo's backstreets.

This approach was adopted out of harsh necessity, but the resulting neighborhoods have a striking charm: intimate townscapes with exceptional vitality and livability, featuring a fine-grained urban fabric comprised of numerous small buildings. Before long, Tokyo's postwar spontaneity gave way to more methodical planning measures designed to impose at least some measure of order on the city's development, but in doing so they invested little effort in changing the character of these postwar neighborhoods. For those abroad, Tokyo offers an alternative paradigm of urban planning—one that combines light planning from above and self-organizing emergence from below. That said, weak planning also brings a range of challenges. Tokyo's classic neighborhoods have historically lagged behind the rest of the city in terms of open spaces and infrastructure, and have been less prepared when major natural disasters have struck. If our goal is to discover ways of constructing a city that reflect the best of Tokyo, understanding the key features of these emergent postwar neighborhoods is an excellent place to start.

Our goal in this book is to explain these features in a way that respects the city's complexity, resisting the temptation to reduce Tokyo down to a mere collection of architectural phenomena or construct simplistic just-so theories that paper over the city's messy reality. Tokyo is full of exceptions to any generalization—spaces and architecture where the question "How did this come to be?" has no single, easy answer. Explaining even a single building can require a tale of various top-down and bottom-up processes across history, real estate economics, public policy, and culture. But amidst the city's complexity, we see a constellation of phenomena that collectively form *emergent Tokyo*, and we believe it can serve as a source of inspiration for the future—not only for Tokyo, but for many cities around the world.

1.4 A field guide to several different Tokyos

As the struggle between emergent Tokyo and corporate-led Tokyo demonstrates, not all of Tokyo's cityscape is particularly Tokyo-esque. Tokyo's intimate old neighborhoods and dynamic commercial districts are full of the vibrancy and life associated with the best aspects of the city, but other areas are now dominated by grids of generic skyscrapers and corporate developments. What's more, the majority of Tokyo's daytime population lives in railway suburbs full of mundane apartment blocks and suburban tracts, much the same as can be found on the outskirts of many other cities. How can we champion Tokyo's superlative aspects in light of the fact that so many of its citizens live and work in areas that bear little resemblance to our Tokyo ideal? And even aside from that, how could any single model of Tokyo encapsulate all of the city's radically different districts, with their wide range of histories, internal dynamics, and future possibilities?

Instead of reducing the city's diversity to a singular Tokyo model, we conceive of Tokyo as having multiple neighborhood models or archetypes, each with its own distinct urban fabric—areas which are similar in terms of land use, street patterns, and building types, even if they're on opposite ends of the city. This, in and of itself, is not a novel observation by any means. Both Tokyo's intellectual class and its common citizens have long drawn these conceptual divisions themselves, most notably the centuries-old division between the genteel *yamanote* or 'high city' and the *shitamachi* or 'low city' of merchants, artisans, and laborers. However, new insights are possible when we look at Tokyo's neighborhoods through a more concrete, modern lens: the power of data science.

Tokyo's metropolitan government now offers a wealth of quantitative information about every building, road, and plot of land in the city, data which can be analyzed algorithmically to lay bare the differences between Tokyo's diverse neighborhoods. By poring through government databases, we have pinpointed several key characteristics of Tokyo neighborhoods that strongly predict their other contours, enabling us to compare and contrast at the scale of the city in concrete, quantifiable terms. For example, neighborhoods with a similar building scale and mix of land use often resemble each other in subtler metrics as well, such as their permeability to the public, accessibility for pedestrians, and the intimacy and vibrancy of their communities. Through this analysis, one can begin to grasp a common pattern language across Tokyo neighborhoods and gain a sense of how their essential characteristics give them a distinctive tenor and daily rhythm.

One difficulty with this approach is that the boundaries between Tokyo neighborhoods are often rather ambiguous. How can we compare neighborhoods if we don't know where one ends and the next begins? To solve this problem, we've turned to a distinctly Japanese way of dividing up the city: the

Fig. 1-1   Tokyo's neighborhood archetypes across the city's 23 wards.

The distribution of these different neighborhood archetypes throughout Tokyo has been deeply shaped by the city's overall superstructure. Village Tokyo is the most common fabric, but it mostly appears outside of the Yamanote loop train line, which loosely marks the boundaries between Tokyo's urban core and its suburbs. A dense network of commuter train lines radiates outward from the Yamanote loop into suburbia, creating areas of urban intensity around their stations in the style of Local Tokyo. Office Tower Tokyo, meanwhile, has traditionally centered on the Marunouchi district in front of the Imperial Palace, but redevelopment around the main stations along the Yamanote Line is bringing one skyscraper after another to major transit hubs like Ikebukuro, Shinjuku, Shibuya, Shinagawa, and Shimbashi. In between these two extremes lies a rich diversity of mix-use and mix-scale urban neighborhoods, primarily matching our Mercantile Tokyo and Pocket Tokyo.

———	train and subway lines	
	Fig. 1-2	Village Tokyo
	Fig. 1-3	Local Tokyo
	Fig. 1-4	Pocket Tokyo
	Fig. 1-5	Mercantile Yamanote Tokyo
	Fig. 1-6	Mercantile Shitamachi Tokyo
	Fig. 1-7	Mass Residential Tokyo
	Fig. 1-8	Office Tower Tokyo
	Other:	Chōme with low residential and commercial land usage (the Imperial Palace grounds, major parks, campuses, industrial districts, etc.)

0   5   10km

chōme system.[2] Tokyo has been administratively slicing up Tokyo into mini towns known as chōme since the Edo period; each chōme often has its own local neighborhood associations and a cohesive character. Within the 23 wards that comprise Tokyo's urban core, the average chōme is only about 0.2 km² in size (or roughly ten Manhattan blocks), allowing for reasonably granular analysis.[3] By observing Tokyo chōme by chōme, we can take the city on its own terms rather than imposing an arbitrary rubric from the outside.

Through our mathematical analysis, we've sorted Tokyo's wide variety of cityscapes into six major archetypes Fig. 1-1.

Village Tokyo Fig. 1-2 encompasses Tokyo's vast *kōgai* or 'suburbs.' Village Tokyo has a consistently low-rise fabric and is almost exclusively residential in nature, with commercial activity typically limited to convenience stores and local shopping promenades (known as *shōtengai*) for daily products.[4] In addition to Tokyo's suburbs, Village Tokyo also appears in some pockets inside the Yamanote Line. Most of Village Tokyo is tied to the city's rail transit network, giving it a very different feel from the car culture of American suburbia (and much of Japan).

Local Tokyo Fig. 1-3 combines the small-scale housing of Village Tokyo with concentrations of mid- or high-rise buildings, often around important suburban train stations. The result is a low-rise, fine-grained urban fabric with a mix of residential and commercial buildings. A general lack of wide arterial roads in Local Tokyo discourages vehicular traffic in favor of pedestrian access, leading to a more intimate communal feel that fits well with the globally popular notion of Transit Oriented Development (TOD). These areas tend to have a longer urban history than Village Tokyo, and many have developed their own unique character that can attract visitors to even remote suburban locations. Examples of Local Tokyo include the neighborhoods of small independent shops that

Fig. 1-2   Village Tokyo: A continuous fabric of densely packed two-floor, single-family houses south of Hatanodai Station in Shinagawa Ward. Some mid-rise buildings, like schools and housing blocks, are scattered throughout the area (1:7,500).

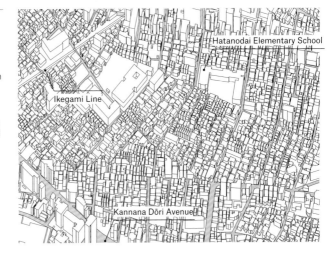

surround Tōyoko Line stations like Jiyūgaoka or Gakugeidaigaku, as well as the famously lively carousing districts found along Chūō Line stations like Nakano and Kōenji.

Pocket Tokyo Fig. 1-4 appears when intimate residential areas are ringed by larger, sturdier buildings around the major roadways on their periphery that serve as both a barrier against fires and a neighbordhood boundary. This creates a pocket neighborhood within the block, jam-packed with older, lower-rise buildings and narrow, winding streets. The larger commercial buildings on the periphery also provide a daytime consumer population, as their workers patronize the smaller mom-and-pop businesses in the residential interior. Pocket Tokyo tends to appear in in-between areas connecting major commercial districts, such as between the commercial districts of Shibuya, Ebisu, and Gotanda Stations. Some Pocket Tokyo neighborhoods in prestigious central Tokyo locations have become highly desirable addresses, such as chic Minami Azabu or Hiroo.

Mercantile Tokyo consists of neighborhoods with major commercial aspects that also integrate a range of housing. However, not all instances of Mercantile Tokyo are cut from the same cloth. Unlike other archetypes, these neighborhoods tend to look very different depending on whether they derive from West Tokyo's *yamanote* high city or East Tokyo's *shitamachi* low city. This distinction does not always align neatly with history and geography; for example, some West Tokyo neighborhoods have taken on a more shitamachi style feel.

Yamanote Mercantile Tokyo Fig. 1-5 generally pairs large-volume commercial buildings with lower-rise housing and complex patterns of narrow streets, often surrounding a railway station. At first glance, this is not so different from Pocket Tokyo. However, the sheer scale of commercial development and architecture is often higher, and both commercial and residential buildings tend to cluster together, creating a gap between the commercial cityscape and the needs of residential life at human scale. Depending on the specific neighborhood, this can sometimes have negative repercussions for the livability of the area, but there are plenty of success stories as well. The leafy, well-to-do environs of Shibuya and Ebisu are typical examples of the Yamanote Mercantile Tokyo.

Shitamachi Mercantile Tokyo Fig. 1-6, meanwhile, tends to have wider, more regular streets with buildings lined up neatly along them, allowing for greater car traffic. However, the buildings are predominantly mid-rise, with fewer height differences between buildings on major roads and those on backstreets. Another key difference is that buildings in Shitamachi Mercantile Tokyo often have several different uses at once. A two-story residential house, for example, might feature an artisan workshop or small shop on the first floor, with the proprietor living directly above his workspace. This fluid mixing of uses lends these neighborhoods an organic, anything-can-happen feel. In Yamanote Mercantile Tokyo, by contrast, buildings tend to be devoted to single uses, with a range of commercial and residential buildings scattered across the area. East Tokyo contains most of these neighborhoods, including famous old commercial districts such as Asakusa or Ningyōchō. However, they can also be found in central areas like Ara-

Fig. 1-3 **Local Tokyo:** Commercial and residential buildings surround Jiyūgaoka Station at the intersection of Meguro and Setagaya Wards, fading out gradually into low-rise single-family houses (1:7,500).

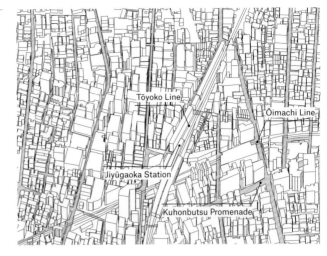

Tōyoko Line

Ōimachi Line

Jiyūgaoka Station

Kuhonbutsu Promenade

Fig. 1-4 **Pocket Tokyo:** High-rise commercial and residential buildings along Sakurada Avenue and the Yamanote Line tracks in Shinagawa Ward enclose interior neighborhoods of narrow alleys and low-rise buildings (1:7,500).

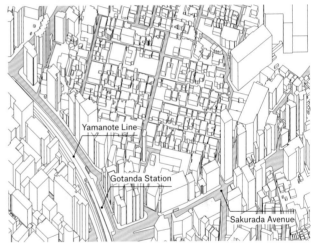

Yamanote Line

Gotanda Station

Sakurada Avenue

Fig. 1-5 **Yamanote Mercantile Tokyo:** The commercial district around Ebisu Station in Shibuya Ward. The area concentrates businesses of diverse scales, from shops on the ground floors of houses to office towers (1:7,500).

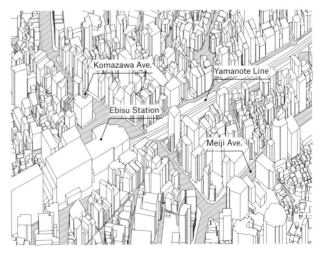

Komazawa Ave.

Yamanote Line

Ebisu Station

Meiji Ave.

kichō and Kagurazaka, as well as newer areas of West Tokyo such as the globally famous youth culture enclave of Shimokitazawa.

Mass Residential Tokyo Fig. 1-7 has a singular focus: to pack an incredibly high number of residents into a relatively spread out, mid- to high-rise residential fabric. The high-volume buildings of Mass Residential Tokyo tend to be apartments and condominiums surrounded by large open spaces, often constructed on a scale that separate them from the rhythm of ordinary street-level life. As with Village Tokyo, these areas are often somewhat disconnected from the non-residential life of the city, requiring their residents to commute elsewhere for commercial and professional activities. The pioneering *danchi* public housing projects of the 1960s and 1970s and the recent clusters of residential towers (or *tower mansion*) along Tokyo Bay are both exemplars of this workhorse archetype, which achieves a population density rarely seen in Tokyo's inner wards.

The final type, **Office Tower Tokyo** Fig. 1-8, represents the closest thing Tokyo has to a 'central business district' archetype. It consists primarily of large-volume, high-rise commercial buildings, which Tokyo's central government has historically tried to spread around the city's major transit hubs in order to prevent the over-centralizing of big business in a single portion of the city. These districts' underlying real estate often commands astronomical prices, and as a result every corner of their plots are given over to some profit-generating purpose. Office Tower Tokyo neighborhoods often take on outsized importance in local politics due to their economic prominence, an influence which is all the more unusual since they have very few nighttime residents. This archetype includes the city's most important commercial centers, such as West Shinjuku, Marunouchi, and sections of post-redevelopment Shibuya. Shibuya's changes exemplify how Tokyo's public policies and development efforts are transforming the city; as it has undergone massive redevelopment in preparation for the 2020 Olympics, the area's fabric is shifting from Yamanote Mercantile Tokyo toward yet another instance of Office Tower Tokyo.

1.5 The urban fabrics that nurture emergent Tokyo

Within the grand sweep of Tokyo each of these archetypes has their role to play, and our goal is not to paint any of them as inherently better than the other.[5] Mass Residential Tokyo may be unsightly, for example, but it successfully houses a large percentage of the city's residents. Marunouchi may be crammed with generic skyscrapers that could just as easily be from any other city in the world, but it ably suits Tokyo's role as a global business capital and has been the site of increasing mixed-use development in recent years. There is a different Tokyo for every season, and even the most humdrum neighborhoods can evolve in new directions over time.

That being said, certain urban fabrics stand out for their uncanny ability to make Tokyo feel dynamic and intimate at a human scale. For example, Local Tokyo has produced a wide variety of distinctive, beloved neighborhoods across very different locations, time periods, and sociopolitical circumstances. Pocket

Fig. 1-6 **Shitamachi Mercantile Tokyo:** The east side of Ueno Station in Taito Ward. With predominantly mid-rise commercial buildings on narrow plots, these districts offer a tight-knit community of small and mid-scale enterprises (1:7,500).

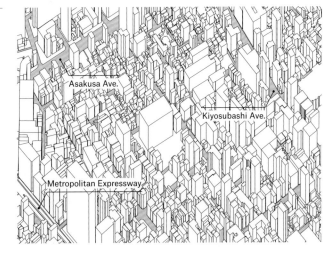

Fig. 1-7 **Mass Residential Tokyo:** Slab housing blocks from the 1960s in the Tatsumi district of Kōtō Ward to the left, new super-high-rise apartment towers from the 2000s onward in the Shinonome district to the right (1:7,500).

Fig. 1-8 **Office Tower Tokyo:** A skyscraper district on the west side of Shinjuku Station, planned in accordance with modernist principles in the 1960s (1:7,500).

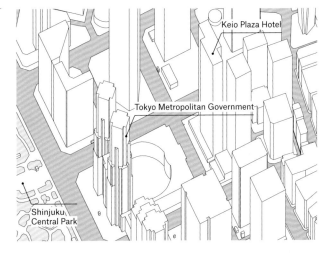

Tokyo in particular offers hope that development can still be compatible with human-scale living. By examining the urban fabric of these neighborhoods, we can discover not only how to build a better future for Tokyo, but also how to export the lessons of Tokyo to the world.

The emergent urban patterns discussed in this book, such as zakkyo buildings and dense low-rise neighborhoods, are not scattered at random throughout Tokyo; there is a clear rhyme and reason to where and when they emerge, and thinking in terms of archetypes helps illuminate that underlying logic. Emergent Tokyo manifests in different ways across the city, and specific urban fabrics create the right ecosystem to nurture these phenomena and give them context. Zakkyo buildings, for example, mostly appear within Yamanote Mercantile Tokyo, whereas dense low-rise neighborhoods emerge within Village Tokyo and Local Tokyo.

In short, the key elements of emergent Tokyo only emerge when the conditions are right—neighborhood conditions, economic conditions, regulatory conditions, and even historical and social conditions. In some parts of the city, they are conspicuously absent; the relative homogeneity and low foot traffic of Mass Residential Tokyo can't support them, and redevelopment has pushed them out of the sleek-but-sterile cityscapes of Office Tower Tokyo. For urbanists elsewhere in the world who would like to make their cities more Tokyo-esque, the goal cannot be to copy and paste Tokyo's urban features onto a new landscape, but rather to think creatively about how these conditions for emergence can be recreated in other contexts.

1.6 Beyond exotic mystery and glamorous chaos

Understanding that there is no single Tokyo and distinguishing its multiple and diverse fabrics is crucial if we want to learn from the city. But one should also be aware of two dominant myths perpetuated by much of the writing about Tokyo: the idea that Tokyo is a mysterious city that can only be understood as a product of Japanese culture, and that it is uniquely a city of chaos.

Works of academic and essayistic writing on Tokyo—referred to collectively in this book as *Tokyology* (see Chapter 7)—often take for granted that Tokyo's peculiarities are the product of Japanese cultural proclivities, rather than doing the hard work of finding concrete explanations and making empirically testable claims. There is a definite element of Euro-centric *orientalism* to this phenomenon—after all, one rarely sees a similar approach taken when major Western cities are under the microscope. To make matters worse, this orientalism is mirrored within Japan by homegrown cultural-essentialist theories collectively known as *nihonjinron* that also seek to explain Japan's social phenomena as the result of 'uniquely Japanese' cultural qualities.[6]

At first glance, all this emphasis on cultural difference is understandable, given the stark visual differences between Western cities and Tokyo. However, looking beyond the urban core, such easy assumptions rapidly fall apart. Japanese suburbia has the usual landscape of highways, drive-in franchises, and big-box shopping malls one sees across the world, with not a speck of exotic Japan in sight. When stepping outside the tourist-trafficked areas of Tokyo can produce such a dramatically different impression, that suggests something more than 'Japaneseness' is at work. Serious urbanist writers would never attempt to describe life in New York City, say, via the experience of visiting Times Square as a tourist. But when Western writers and journalists find themselves in Tokyo, somehow this basic truth is 'lost in translation.' To learn from a city, one must step past its façade and into its residents' everyday reality.

In this book, we've attempted to dig deeper into phenomena that are often portrayed as the inevitable result of Japanese culture, revealing how they grew out of more prosaic causes: a mélange of government policies, community choices, and so many other socio-historical processes. Culture has its place in our discussions of the city, but orientalism and nihonjinron offer only a flattened, essentialized version of culture as a one-size-fits-all explanation.

The second inescapable cliché is that Tokyo is uniquely chaotic, unlike Western cities that are ostensibly more rigid and orderly. This is generally not meant as a criticism. Architects such as Ashihara Yoshinobu describe Japanese cities as comparatively "ugly" but cast this state of affairs in a positive light, arguing that a city being ever-changing and "chaotic" has its upsides by enabling economic and social vitality in a postmodern world and denigrating the Western insistence on conceiving the city as a consistent whole.[7] When Western scholars of Japanese urbanism (such as the pioneering Barrie Shelton) praise Japanese cities as being particularly suited to contemporary urban life, they often root their arguments in a similar chaos essentialism to what Ashihara offers.[8]

This viewpoint, while meant benevolently, miscasts a global phenomenon as something uniquely Japanese. The depiction of Tokyo as a city full of 'the good kind of chaos' originated in the 1980s, when urbanist thinking based on chaos theory came into vogue worldwide. Western architects and planners became enthralled with the city's uncontrollable and fragmentary aspects, rejecting earlier modernist notions that one could ever truly control a city. But Western writers generally don't treat Dallas or Los Angeles as exotic cities of chaos; as Western cities under the Western gaze, they are simply cities.

For Tokyo, however, the clichéd image of chaos is still dominant today in the global imagination, even as it flies in the face of the city's quaint, convivial neighborhoods and clockwork-efficient transportation. A label that began as jargon used in architectural discussions of the 1980s has been essentialized into something that stems from Tokyo's immutable Japaneseness, positioning the city again as an exotic Other that stands apart from Western metropolises and preventing a nuanced discussion of commonalities and differences. Pretending Tokyo is utterly different from Western cities quickly becomes an excuse to reject Tokyo's example as a comparison case or a source of practical wisdom.

This book is our best attempt to understand Tokyo without relying on stereotypes and first impressions. We've attempted to avoid both a patronizing Euro-centric orientalism and its Japanese nihonjinron equivalent. In doing so, we wish to put Tokyo on par with other cities that have inspired architects and urbanists to imagine new possibilities for designing built environments around the world. New theories in architecture and urban design often first arise from examinations of real-world urban phenomena that are highly specific to a particular time and place, but are later found to fit much broader contexts. For example, Jane Jacobs's famous "eyes on the street" and Rem Koolhaas's "culture of congestion" emerged from their respective studies of New York but are now referenced worldwide.[9] We acknowledge Tokyo's distinct cultural character without essentializing or fetishizing it, in the hopes that architects, urban policy practitioners, and visitors to the city alike will come away with a better, truer understanding of the city.

1.7   Emergence: a new lens for understanding Tokyo

Over the past century, every major philosophy of urban planning has eventually faced challenges it could not overcome. Modernism fell out of favor as the sheer difficulty of controlling all the fragmentation and chaos of a modern city became increasingly apparent. Post-modernists followed them with unsuccessful attempts to recreate urban life using historical models, which in practice generally involved ham-fistedly layering past forms of the cityscape over current social and economic realities. More recently, many urbanists have decided to simply embrace the chaos, abandoning any duty to lay out a cohesive vision of the city's future and writing off attempts to critique and control urban development as naïve—in some cases even glamorizing their own lack of control. However, the approach of these "post-critical" urbanists ultimately failed as well.[10] The vacuum created by post-criticality was filled in practice by an over-reliance on market forces and commercial developers. Their ascendance since the 1980s echoes a broader shift across the globe toward neoliberal austerity economics and increased corporate political influence which has accelerated social segregation, privatized public spaces, and homogenized our cities.

Where does this leave us? The damage of these failures is real, and extends beyond cities themselves into architecture as a profession. Faced with a decline in public commissions and increasingly constrained by their financial reliance on corporate interests, architects have gradually lost much of their role as independent public figures. How can we overcome this blithe acceptance of corporate-led urbanism that has taken root in both Japan and the West? How can we reconstitute the city as a collective project of its inhabitants, rather than simply leaving the future up to market forces? How can we fight for an idea of the city as a coherent whole while also avoiding top-down, hierarchical planning visions that have already failed?

Tokyo's cityscape offers a bold alternative to these past approaches. However, understanding Tokyo requires that we expand our thinking beyond the sphere of architecture and into the interdisciplinary realm of complex systems theory: in particular, its concept of *emergence*. Emergence is the spontaneous creation of order and functionality from the bottom up. The classic example is the flocking behavior of birds; large groups of birds in flight are often strikingly synchronized, adopting aerodynamic formations or changing directions in unison to avoid a predator. This is not the result of a leading bird somehow transmitting orders with a mysterious animal telepathy; the flock's coherent behavior simply *emerges* from each bird responding to the movements of its neighbors. As a result of these micro interactions, the flock becomes a coherent macro entity, with aerodynamic and defensive skills far beyond those of any individual bird. Through emergence, the whole is greater than the sum of its parts.

What's true in the animal kingdom can also apply in the context of a city.[11] The public spaces and neighborhoods of a city are *socio-material entities*—that is, they simultaneously have both a physical reality and a social context. A neighborhood is not just a built landscape, nor is it just the group of people who inhabit it. Just as in a flock of birds, the properties of the neighborhood as a whole emerge organically from all the interactions between its social and material parts. Treating urban spaces as emergent ecosystems can help us understand how so many of Tokyo's districts have developed such robust, idiosyncratic identities.

The five urban phenomena profiled in this book are an excellent place to start. Trying to explain any given Tokyo neighborhood's unique character requires delving into a complex web of interactions between buildings, infrastructure, local culture and practices, legal codes, and numerous other factors, including the choices of its individual inhabitants. By taking in their full complexity without trying to flatten it or abstract it away, we can use that understanding as inspiration in other cities and contexts.

The goal of looking at emergent Tokyo is not to develop some grand theory of the city that would render consideration of its individual parts unnecessary. In emergent systems, the individual components of the system do not disappear permanently into a homogenous whole. Just as with birds of the flock, individual residents of a neighborhood will inevitably act in ways that surprise and confound planners and policymakers. In a city that listens to its inhabitants, there will always be a messy, complex role for the individual in shaping public life.

Contrary to the persistent cliché of Tokyo as the epitome of glamorous chaos, the best parts of the city have a strong sense of cohesive identity even without a centralized, hierarchical authority dictating what that identity should be. This character endures and evolves over time, even as people move or individual buildings change. Tokyo's urban social fabric is not indestructible, but it is remarkably resilient; in many corners of the city, the local sense of place has survived generations of natural disasters, global war, economic transformation, and radical political upheaval. Its study can not only help us to understand Tokyo but also empower us to design Tokyo-esque adaptability and spontaneity into cities around the world.

2 YOKOCHŌ ALLEYWAYS

横丁

Fig. 2-1   Golden Gai in Shinjuku as of July 2019.

2 YOKOCHŌ ALLEYWAYS

2.1 An alleyway that's designed to be explored

One of Tokyo's hallmarks are its classic commercial clusters known as *yokochō*—warrens of lively, micro-scale bars and restaurants centered around tiny alleys and backstreets Fig. 2-1. Yokochō are often found in the shadow of established commercial districts around the railway stations of Local and Mercantile Tokyo. Some think of them as being old-fashioned, unsafe, crowded, or populated with dubious characters, but yokochō are widely beloved as prime settings of informal public life thanks to their small scale and relaxed yet intimate atmosphere. How did they come to be, and what will they become next?

As with so many other unique aspects of Tokyo's modern cityscape, yokochō originated from the black markets that appeared around major train stations after Japan's wartime defeat. Many small-scale black market entrepreneurs eventually became squatters, building makeshift structures on any unoccupied space they could find. At the end of the black market period these spaces were regularized and often relocated as part of the city's redevelopment, with thousands of former black market sellers gaining formal property rights to new spaces in cramped commercial warrens. Illegal market stalls transformed into bars and restaurants (and sometimes brothels and gambling parlors), and through the government's relocation policies these micro-commerce districts shifted outward from the city's station-fronts and into surrounding neighborhoods.

In Tokyo there is an increasing interest in yokochō as a phenomenon, not only among architects and urbanists but also among ordinary citizens. They are regularly featured in print and online media as either "unknown" spaces of interest to be "explored," beckoning the city's unassuming residents to "discover" the "dark" or "deep" side of Tokyo, or alternately as nostalgic relics from the Shōwa period, catering to a burgeoning desire among Tokyo's youth for a taste of 'Shōwa retro' atmosphere and aesthetics.[12] In academic research, yokochō are considered an archetypal urban morphology that epitomizes many of the transformations that Japanese cities underwent in the postwar period.[13] When US occupation forces issued an order in 1949 to uproot the black markets, street stalls were removed and converted into four different types of architecture, all of which still exist in Tokyo today: *kaikan* (literally meaning 'assembly halls'), which are essentially multi-story warehouses subdivided into numerous rooms where each room sports a separate small business; *department stores* (though more small business-oriented than either their Western equivalents or longstanding Japanese conglomerates such as Isetan); *underground passages* with spaces allotted for small shops; and *nagaya*, long row houses typically paired with narrow alleyways. Nagaya are the architectural cornerstone of most of Tokyo's historic yokochō.[14]

This chapter delves into the socio-spatial qualities of yokochō and their diverse contributions to Tokyo's cityscape.[15] The influential Shōwa-era publication *Nihon no hiroba*[16] included yokochō as a characteristic example of a particularly Japanese approach to public space, but our aim here is not to continue the interminable debate on their Japaneseness. Instead, we aim to better understand why they so often create flourishing urban ecosystems, spaces where small-scale actors collectively produce a vibrant patchwork of city life through their web of interactions.

2.2   What defines a yokochō?

Originally, the term yokochō[17] referred to a type of secondary street in the highly organized urban structure of Edo (*yoko* means 'side' and *chō*, 'street, block, or town') before organically arriving at its current meaning over time. Yokochō are a frequent presence in the entertainment districts (*sakariba*) found around major transit hubs in urban Japan. The typical yokochō is an area of alleys filled with small bars and restaurants, forming a semi-hidden nightlife location not immediately visible from the main streets and station areas.

For the purposes of this study, we have chosen to avoid the artificial yokochō that developers sometimes install inside malls and other commercial projects—glorified food courts that attempt to profit from the cachet of the term. Instead, we prefer to focus on genuine yokochō that fit squarely within Tokyo's architectural and cultural legacy.[18] Specifically, we have chosen and mapped micro-bar clusters comprised mostly of low-rise buildings of three stories or less with footprints under 50 m², connected by alleys of less than 4 m in width.

Fig. 2-2   Clusters of yokochō alleyways across Tokyo's 23 wards (1:375,000).

•   Yokochō
——— Yamanote Line
——— Other train lines

Yokochō fitting this description can still be found all across Tokyo Fig. 2-2, although many of them have disappeared. Most of them are close to train stations or main streets but are hidden behind taller buildings or inside urban blocks. In many cases yokochō were built on illegally or informally occupied plots, and ownership ambiguities create challenges for real estate companies eyeing these districts for redevelopment possibilities. Many of the remaining yokochō are popular enough to be economically sustainable, making them resistant to developer pressure so long as their owners collectively wish to continue. In most cases, yokochō have kept their old original wooden buildings. They exist in a wide range of different spatial configurations, from straightforward linear arrangements to complex self-contained street networks.[19] In many yokochō, shared toilets facilitate the hyper-specialization of space, allowing the smallest microbars to operate with little more than a proprietor behind the counter and a seat for a customer.

Yokochō are a major setting of informal public life in Tokyo, a "third place" beyond home and work.[20] Yokochō bars have an incredible ability to facilitate communication among customers, and between the owner (who is usually also the bartender) and the customers.[21] The rise of yokochō as a popular tourism destination poses new challenges to maintaining this atmosphere, since the presence of foreigners who do not speak Japanese and possess only a limited understanding of Japanese social mores is often felt particularly deeply in such an intimate social environment. As discussed below, however, prominent yokochō such as the Golden Gai have proven that the model's inherent flexibility and adaptability can be a strength in Tokyo's age of mass tourism.

2.3   Clandestine origins, uncertain future

As mentioned above, most yokochō began as temporary black markets during the postwar rationing period. At that time Tokyo contained an estimated 60,000 black market stalls,[22] with nearly every station along the commuter lines having at least a small market of illicitly acquired foreign goods. By the late 1950s, however, Japan's meteoric economic recovery had rendered the black markets obsolete. In order to cater to the changing needs of the times, from the late 1940s onward the market stalls began gradually transforming into bars for snacks and drinks.

Efforts to rid the black markets of street stalls first began in 1949 via the issue of the Stall Clean-up Order by the American occupation forces.[23] Notably, these measures did not treat black market merchants as a criminal element to be pushed out of society, but rather as a group worthy of reasonable accommodation that could be integrated into plans for the next stage of postwar development. Under the new law, many merchants were relocated from the land immediately surrounding their respective stations to other nearby areas. From the start of Japan's rapid economic growth in the late 1950s and through the 1970s, land plots around stations were developed into large office and commercial buildings whenever possible. The fragmented ownership situation of former black market land made redevelopment difficult, since every last one of the many proprietors had to be convinced to sell their lots if the goal was to form a unified plot of land to build upon. Many of them disappeared nevertheless, but some, like the famous Golden Gai, have miraculously survived despite intense redevelopment pressure by mounting a well-organized resistance through their local business owner associations.[24]

Yokochō are facing a range of serious challenges beyond being pressured to sell their land for profit. Their disproportionately wooden structures built in the 1950s are inevitably deteriorating, despite structural reinforcements and renovations. Their family businesses often lack successors willing to devote themselves to continuing a parent's labor of love for long hours and little pay. Regular customers, many of them members of Japan's postwar baby boom generation, are hitting retirement age en masse, which also often means retirement from late night drinking. The popular image of cramped spaces, dirtiness, and danger adds to the challenge.[25]

2.4 The yokochō revival

Despite these very real problems, there is a growing interest in yokochō and their potential as agents of urban regeneration.[26] Areas like Golden Gai have managed to attract a younger generation of bartenders and customers, demonstrating that the yokochō is not a generationally fixed phenomenon and is not at risk of extinction—so long as redevelopment can be kept at bay. For example, although the year 2008 saw the demolition of the famous *Jinsei Yokochō*,[27] which had anchored the Ikebukuro Station entertainment district since 1950, it also saw the opening of a brand new yokochō-style space in the fashionable district of Ebisu. This *Ebisu Yokochō* reproduces not only the visual atmosphere of the old postwar yokochō but also their unique management structure, with the space hosting multiple young chefs each in charge of their own tiny bars and restaurants. The small size of each stall allows for lower rental fees than usual for a prime location and affords each entrepreneur the opportunity to develop their own independent business.

There are more of these modern yokochō initiatives springing up in Tokyo and across the country.[28] For both chefs and diners, the yokochō model has clear economic, managerial, and creative advantages. In the restaurant trade, up-front initial investment costs are high, and new establishments tend to fail within their first few years. As a result, chefs around the world are searching for ways to lower start-up costs and risk that fit with their own local context, such as the rising use of mobile food trucks in the United States. Yokochō spaces enable the sharing and outsourcing of infrastructure and equipment in a way that minimizes the investment for each individual. Floor areas are small, and consequently rental fees are low. For instance, in Ebisu Yokochō shops have an area of about 10 to 16.5 m² (3–5 *tsubo* in the Japanese measurement system).[29] Since the shops are small and run independently, they naturally tend to attract and incubate young restauranteurs and thus serve as a base for innovation in the sector.

For individual restauranteurs, the yokochō model offers an alternative to options such as franchised dining that lessen risk but also compromise the potential for creativity. Perhaps most importantly, the allure of a yokochō space offers a competitive advantage at attracting customers in a city with the most numerous dining and drinking options in the world. Tokyo has many times more bars and restaurants than New York City or Paris, and in its *sakariba* entertainment districts their density is among the highest on the planet; for a new restaurant without an established clientele of regulars, standing out is essential for survival. Yokochō districts, even modern ones, become distinct destinations in their own right, with a character and attractive power separate from any given restaurant that happens to inhabit them. Ebisu Yokochō, for example, has grown into a famous meeting spot for the city's young singles, with romance (or its more temporary equivalent) in the air on weekend nights and some restaurants posting explicit rules regarding attempted flirtation with other customers. The sections of Golden Gai that cater to Japanese customers, by contrast, cultivate a slower, more contemplative vibe. The yokochō format offers a diversity of atmospheres, an ease of interaction among customers, and a low-profile sense of intimacy that enables everyone to find their own particular niche.

We have chosen to analyze three yokochō alleyways in greater detail, with the goal of understanding both their commonalities and what makes each distinctive in its own right. Two of them are located by major transportation hubs: Shinjuku's Golden Gai, a bar neighborhood that boasts the densest collection of drinking establishments in the world Figs. 2-3, 4, and Shibuya's Nombei Yokochō, a tiny and compact cluster of two-story micro-bars sandwiched between the district's towering redevelopment projects Figs. 2-5, 6. The third, Nishi-Ogikubo's Yanagi Kōji, is a more local yokochō that sits in the suburbs along the famed Chūō Line Figs. 2-7, 8. While many of Tokyo's remaining yokochō sit near major transit hubs and some have even become international landmarks, Yanagi Kōji still has a local, relaxed character and serves as a prime example of how neighborhood yokochō still play an important role in informal public life.

2.5

Case 01

The world's densest bar district: Golden Gai

Tokyo's most famous yokochō is East Shinjuku's Hanazono Goldengai, popularly known as Golden Gai. Covering only 3,265 m²—about half of a soccer field—it contains over 250 late-night drinking establishments connected by a web of alleyways, as well as a few eateries and subcultural art and performance spaces. Alley widths range from 1.7 to 2.7 m; in some sections, both walls can be touched by extending one's arms Figs. 2-9, 10. These alleys are not public land, but rather shared private property among all Golden Gai landowners that is maintained by the area's bar owners.

Within footprints ranging from 10 to 15 m², each bar's interior is highly idiosyncratic and creative, displaying the personal world of its owner with different musical styles and decorations. Golden Gai offers a cozy environment for social encounters and night conversation, and its proprietors take pains to preserve the atmosphere of intimacy and creativity that has historically attracted artists and bohemians, drawing both locals and an increasing number of foreign tourists Figs. 2-11 to 14.

Golden Gai originated from the postwar black market stalls located on the east side of Shinjuku Station. After the forced removal of stalls began in 1949, the market residents were relocated en masse into newly built nagaya row houses in Golden Gai's current location half a kilometer away. The new site quickly became famous for prostitution, as many of the row house establishments offered bars on their first floor with private rooms conveniently located on the second. After authorities began tightening their regulation of the sex trade with the Prostitution Prevention Law of 1958, the area converted into a bar district.

According to histories of the district, the evolution of Golden Gai can be split into four periods.[30] During the first period (1965–1984), the district acquired its fame as a pub area. In 1965 the area was renamed the Shinjuku Golden Gai (literally 'Shinjuku Golden Street'), and a growing number of intellectuals and artists frequented the area's bars while the number of establishments increased.

The decade from 1985 to 1995 marked a period of tension and uncertainty. Land prices skyrocketed as a result of the economic bubble, and Golden Gai became the target of *jiage*, the practice of real estate agents aggressively or even violently harassing small landowners into selling their plots to a developer hoping to consolidate them into a bigger plot. Golden Gai saw frequent fires during this period under suspicious circumstances, with rumors often declaring them jiage-related arson. In 1986 some bar owners created a dedicated group to protect themselves from jiage, but the pressures of the era nevertheless led many bars to close.

Eventually the economic bubble burst, easing the *jiage* pressure as Tokyo real estate speculation cooled off, and Golden Gai returned to some semblance of normalcy. The late 1990s saw a major movement led by the bar owner's associations to revitalize the district, with serious effort put into improving the state of its collectively owned lanes and utilities infrastructure. Over time, prosaic quality of life increases laid the groundwork for Golden Gai's longer-term sustainability.

The district also successfully weathered a critical generational transition. From 1992 onward, several changes to Japan's Law on Land and Building Leases made it easier for aging proprietors of Golden Gai bars to lease their properties out to new tenant businesses without selling the land itself, enabling a new generation of younger managers who admired Golden Gai's culture to launch their own establishments.[31] Although many yokochō have disappeared or shrunk due to the retirement of shop owners, Golden Gai shows no signs of slowing even as its originators age out of their bartending years. Currently there is a healthy mix of old and new establishments as well as veteran and young managers.

Today, rather than the decline and abandonment that many yokochō face, the success of Golden Gai poses a new challenge, perhaps marking a fifth era of the district: it has become a popular tourism destination. Tourism to Tokyo has quadrupled in a span of five years. Foreigners are now as common as Japanese among Golden Gai's nighttime lanes, sparking fears that the intimate and countercultural character of the district could be lost. However, the small and distributed nature of Golden Gai's many establishments appears to be allowing for a sustainable equilibrium. Golden Gai's bars have always been diverse in their niche themes and range of clientele, and the district's bars now sharply differentiate themselves according to their approach to foreign tourists. Everything from the language of signage to varying cover charge systems allows bar owners to subtly modulate their approach. Roughly half the district's bars are either tourist-friendly or actively prefer an international clientele, whereas the other half range from indifferent and unaccommodating toward non-Japanese speakers to posting Japanese-speaking requirements or even requiring an introduction from regulars to enter (a policy referred to as *ichigen-san okotowari*). Many bars are finding increasingly creative ways to split the difference and accommodate the expectations of both locals and outsiders. In a growing number of Golden Gai bars, for example, only Japanese patrons pay a cover charge and receive the traditional *otōshi* appetizer, a standard Japanese drinking custom that tourists often find confusing and off-putting; to compensate, foreign guests are charged higher drink prices.

At the macro level, the tourism boom has created a shared awareness among owners of the importance of cultivating and maintaining the area's identity. The influx of tourists into Golden Gai has even helped drive a yokochō boom among Tokyo twenty-somethings, many of whom grew up hearing Golden Gai referenced as a dangerous and foreboding place but who decided the neighborhood was worth exploring after seeing the foreign enthusiasm for it. Whatever the future holds for Golden Gai, the owners and indeed the area itself have displayed a collective resilience and ability to adapt.

Fig. 2-3   Night view of Golden Gai as of June 2019.

Fig. 2-4   The evolution of Golden Gai (1:4,000).

0   40m

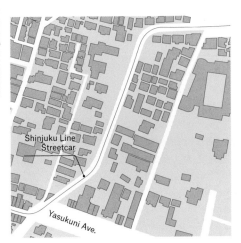

1933   Before the war, the area was still predominantly residential. What is now Golden Gai was crossed by the Shinjuku Line of the Tokyo City streetcar system, and Yasukuni Avenue's western stretch had not been widened yet.

Source: *Kasaihoken Tokushuchizu* (Toshiseizusha, 1933).

1962   By this point, the postwar black markets have been dismantled for over a decade, and their vendors relocated. One of the relocation sites is the current Golden Gai, hidden behind the recently widened Yasukuni Avenue.

Source: *Tōkyō-to Zenjūtaku Annaizuchō* (Jūtaku Kyōkai, 1962).

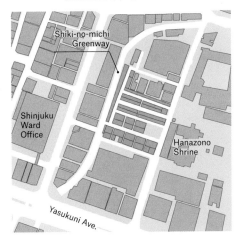

2018   The old streetcar line was dismantled and converted into the Shiki-no-michi Greenway in 1970. Golden Gai has survived redevelopment, but most of the surrounding land plots have been merged to construct large commercial buildings.

Map source: *Jūtakuchizu* (Zenrin, 2018).

Shibuya's hidden Nombei Yokochō

Nombei Yokochō (or 'drunkard's alley') sits in a privileged but hidden location Fig. 2-15. This alley of tiny ramshackle bars is a few short minutes' walk from Shibuya Station, a major transportation hub and tourist hotspot. And yet it sits relatively unnoticed between giant modern skyscrapers, a pocket of local life in the midst of the global city.

Nombei Yokochō's composition is fairly simple; four nagaya row houses along two parallel alleyways. One alleyway sits under the shadow of the Yamanote railway tracks, and the other runs between the nagaya, measuring only 1.5 m wide Fig. 2-16. This tiny strip boasts 38 active bars, most of them with footprints of only 2.1 m width by 2.3 m depth. Their 4.8 m² average ranks Nombei Yokochō's bars among Tokyo's tiniest, but the minuscule scale is nevertheless used very effectively, as it allows for a counter and around five seats on the first floor, as well as a table for five other guests on the second floor Figs. 2-17 to 20.

Nombei Yokochō's origins are much as one would expect. After the war, countless unlicensed street stalls sprang up around Shibuya Station, especially along Dōgenzaka Street and what is now Bunkamura-dōri Street. Following the 1949 push for stall removal, the ward administration planned the street vendors' relocation into permanent buildings, which they called *maaketto* ('markets'). They established a lottery system, and winners were assigned in groups to relocation districts.[32]

Nombei Yokochō was one such destination. Located behind the existing Shibuya Central Market, it was concealed yet conveniently located. The permanent buildings that gradually transformed into today's Nombei Yokochō were built in 1951. Initially one story high, their owners incrementally converted them into the district's current two-story configuration.[33] The relocated vendors formed an association that bought the land from the ward in 1965.[34] According

Fig. 2-5   The internal alley of
Nombei Yokochō as
of July 2020.

Fig. 2-6   The evolution of Nombei Yokochō (1:5,000).

0   50m

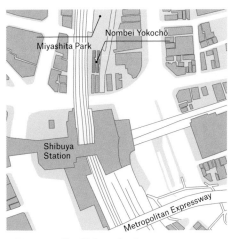

1951   The site of what is now Nombei Yokochō was little more than an urban gap sandwiched between the Shibuya River and the Yamanote Line. It sat behind the Shibuya Central Market, one of the first postwar markets created in Shibuya to relocate street vendors.
Source: *Kasaihoken Tokushuchizu* (Toshiseizusha, 1949, 1951).

1970   The Shibuya Station area was transformed during the high economic growth period, but Nombei Yokochō and the Shibuya Central Market remained unchanged. On the north side of Nombei Yokochō, Miyashita Park was redeveloped in 1964 on human-made land above a parking lot.
Source: *Jūtakuchizu* (Zenrin, 1970).

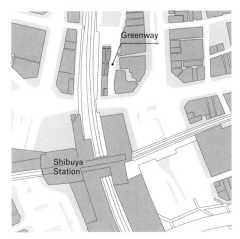

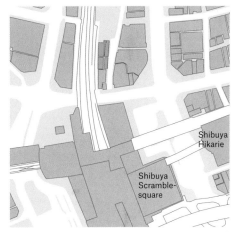

1991   The Shibuya River along the yokochō has been covered and converted into a greenway (*ryokudō*) managed by the ward. Shibuya Central Market has been redeveloped into two multi-tenant zakkyo buildings.
Source: *Jūtakuchizu* (Zenrin, 1991).

2019   Starting with the Hikarie tower's completion in 2012, the surrounding area is undergoing a drastic transformation full of new shopping spaces and office skyscrapers. In 2020, the former Miyashita Park was redeveloped into a combined shopping mall and hotel. Nevertheless, Nombei Yokochō survives in its tiny urban gap.
Source: *Jūtakuchizu* (Zenrin, 2019).

to the rules of the association, which is still operating today, the actual land of Nombei Yokochō belongs to the association and each store owner owns only the building and the right to run their business.[35]

Japan's high growth period from the mid-1950s to early 1970s saw a radical transformation of Shibuya. As the district became a commercial hub, land plots were merged and ever larger buildings erected. Nombei Yokochō, however, remained largely unchanged with only minor utility improvements. As in Golden Gai, the yokochō managed to resist the *jiage* threats typical of the bubble period, and even today the old wooden structures survive amidst the radical transformation of Shibuya's station area.[36]

The Tokyū Corporation—the owner of the suburban line that connects Shibuya with Yokohama as well as much of Shibuya's prime real estate—has embarked on a large-scale effort to redevelop Shibuya, constructing over half a dozen new office and shopping super-high rise towers around and on the station. Shibuya Ward has for its part transformed Miyashita Park, formerly the last free and open public space remaining near Shibuya Station, into a high-rise hotel and four-story shopping mall, offering only a modest green space on the rooftop as a mea culpa for the park's destruction.[37]

Amidst this cataclysmic redevelopment, the remaining 38 bars and restaurants of Nombei Yokochō have not only survived but thrived. Sandwiched between Shibuya River, the JR Yamanote train line, and the shopping mall usurping Miyashita Park, the association that controls the yokochō's land rights have spent nearly half a century refusing astronomical buy-out offers from Shibuya developers, and they are unlikely to be tempted into selling any time soon. As in Golden Gai, many members of the association are getting old, but in recent years an increasing number of owners and customers are young and enthusiastic for the district's future. Nombei Yokochō is more active than ever, and the heady lure of Shibuya to tourists has ensured a strong customer base.

2.7 Yanagi Kōji in Nishi-Ogikubo

Case 03

Yanagi Kōji (or 'willow alley') is a thriving local yokochō located close to the south exit of Nishi-Ogikubo Station on the Chūō Line, which connects Tokyo's central Yamanote loop line with some of the city's most cultured and bohemian residential suburbs Figs. 2-21, 22. Unlike Golden Gai and Nombei Yokochō, Yanagi Kōji is not a tourist hot spot, but rather a center of local neighborhood life. Comprised of 45 small restaurants and bars housed in wooden buildings along two alleys, its buildings are two stories high and range in footprint from 14 to 30 m² Figs. 2-23 to 26. Yanagi Kōji's central alley, about 3 m wide, is closed to traffic and usually occupied by pedestrians dining and drinking outside, creating a lively and open street.

Although its independence from Tokyo's tourist economy has spared it some of the challenges felt by other yokochō, Yanagi Kōji has its own threats to face. As in other West Tokyo neighborhoods, such as Shimokitazawa, Nishi-Ogikubo's success at cultivating local culture has attracted interest from real estate developers. Local activists fear that ostensibly innocuous municipal projects such as road widening are designed to facilitate redevelopment, as has already happened nearby in the bohemian yet gentrifying neighborhood of Shimokitaza-wa. Yanagi Kōji is owned by a real estate company, not by an owners' association; if Nishi-Ogikubo undergoes extensive redevelopment in the future, it remains to be seen how much of this exuberant yokochō will survive.

The neighborhoods around Nishi-Ogikubo and other Chūō Line stations grew rapidly after the 1923 Great Kantō Earthquake, as large swathes of the city's population abandoned cramped central Tokyo in favor of more expansive living quarters to the west. Unlike other suburban neighborhoods, however, Nishi-Ogikubo suffered considerable bombing during World War II due to its location near an aircraft factory.[38] During the war, authorities created open evacuation spaces around the train station. As with so many other Tokyo stations, these evacuation spaces were rapidly occupied after the war by black marketeers.[39] When the black markets were finally shut down, long wooden nagaya houses were hastily constructed to consolidate their unlicensed vendors into proper market stalls, and today's Yanagi Kōji is the successor to one such nagaya market.

In Yanagi Kōji as in other yokochō, prostitution spread like wildfire amidst the hardships of the postwar period—earning it a reputation as a "blue line zone." Until strict measures against prostitution were enforced in 1958, Tokyo's sex trade was divided between officially designated prostitution areas (referred to as "red line zones") and areas where prostitution was not legally permitted but was available nevertheless ("blue line zones").

From its earliest days, Yanagi Kōji has continuously featured an economy of sex and intimacy, although its form has shifted over time. After the prohibition of prostitution, most of Yanagi Kōji's more dubious establishments converted into 'snack bars,' late-night drinking establishments typically owned by or employing female staff who serve male customers. The concept of a snack bar is rather specific to Japan, largely because it arose out of a peculiar Japanese legal loophole. When the Japanese government banned vice businesses from operating late at night, an explicit exception was carved out for late-night dining. And so thousands of the city's companionship-oriented bars began to offer customers light snack foods in order to legally qualify as restaurants, providing female attention while escaping being tarred with the label of vice. Windowless and hidden, these bars tend to be favored by middle-aged and elderly men; when the young embrace them, they generally do so in a spirit of retro kitsch. A night at a snack bar typically consists of conversation and karaoke singing with a female bartender or *mama-san*.

For decades through the 1980s, snack bars dominated Yanagi Kōji, with a few family run izakaya and noodle shops also in the mix.[40] In 1969 this section of the Chūō Line was elevated, and the north row of the yokochō's wooden buildings were demolished and rebuilt larger in concrete. Today this north row shares Yanagi Kōji's atmosphere but does not match the intimate human scale of the remaining central row of wooden nagaya.

Fig. 2-7   Yanagi Kōji as of July
2020.

Yanagi Kōji started to become more international from 2001 onwards, when a Japanese owner opened the area's first Thai cuisine restaurant, *Hansamu shokudō* ('handsome restaurant'), attracting an increasing number of young people and a larger share of women. A Bangladeshi restaurant, *Miruchi*, opened the following year. Since then, Yanagi Kōji's bar scene has diversified with new generations of customers, owners, and nationalities.[41] Although some older snack bars still remain, the alley took on a more open atmosphere; the façades changed to become more visible from the outside, and owners started to put chairs and tables outside.

Despite its suburban location, demolition and redevelopment are still threats here. Stores in Yanagi Kōji are rented by a single real estate agency, and that offers fewer possibilities for resistance against displacement than other yokochō where land is collectively owned. Recent concerns revolve around Suginami Ward's decades-old plan to widen the adjacent Kita-Ginza Street by 5 m.[42] From 1966 onward, any new buildings constructed along Kita-Ginza Street have faced strict spatial limitations in accordance with these plans. However, the road itself has never actually been widened, and the general small scale of the area has remained intact.

In 2016, after 50 years of inaction, the Tokyo government finally decided to act on the road widening plans. This plan implies the demolition of any buildings not complying with the setback, which would mainly affect the area south of the station where Yanagi Kōji and numerous other small businesses are located. Local activists see this road widening plan as not only unjustified but openly destructive, and many suspect that the government plan's revival is driven by the interest of developers in redeveloping Nishi-Ogikubo.[43] Under Japanese zoning laws, the road widening would in turn allow for the construction of taller buildings. And as has already happened in many other areas of Tokyo, the high-rise buildings and condominium towers that accompany road-widening projects

Fig. 2-8   The evolution of Yanagi Kōji (1:2,500).

0   30m

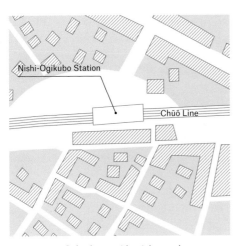

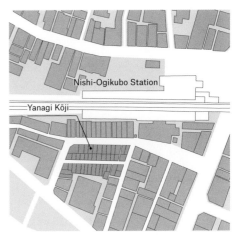

1929   Suburban residential areas have developed on both sides of the newly built Chūō Line. There is no trace yet of the markets that would appear after the war.

Cluster of buildings

Source: Dainipponteikoku Rikuchi Sokuryō-bu, 1929.

1959   Yanagi Kōji remains as a successor of one of the nagaya markets built on the south side of the station. The equal subdivision into small plots has been kept. At this point, most stores have been converted into snack bars.

Source: *Kasaihoken Tokushuchizu* (Toshiseizusha, 1959).

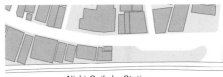

1981   The train lines have been elevated and widened. The buildings adjacent to the tracks have been demolished and rebuilt as larger concrete structures. The land subdivision has barely changed, but family run eateries start to appear, mixed with the snack bars.

Source: *Jūtakuchizu* (Zenrin, 1981).

2018   Several land subdivisions have been merged to create bigger bars, but the overall configuration remains. The yokochō has become a bar cluster deeply rooted in the local community. However, the planned widening of the Kita Ginza Street might trigger redevelopment and change the whole area, including Yanagi Kōji.

Source: *Jūtakuchizu* (Zenrin, 2018).

would likely threaten the neighborhood's existing urban fabric and social ecosystem. The neighborhood activists opposed to road widening consider Yanagi Kōji a core space of the community and an area worth protecting.

Yanagi Kōji's success makes one thing clear: in Tokyo, today's yokochō are not merely theme parks for tourists. Its roots in a multicultural suburb give it a surprisingly international character, but Yanagi Kōji thrives with almost no income from foreign tourism, and its deeply rooted community has helped it survive through occasional downturns in the Japanese economy. Yanagi Kōji's central 3 m wide alley plays host to women and men of diverse ages and nationalities. Despite its narrowness, the alley feels welcoming, with windows and doors open and tables and chairs set outside. Nishi-Ogikubo, as a neighborhood, has managed to incubate a strong community full of beloved small businesses and quirky shops, and its yokochō plays a central role.

2.8 Learning from yokochō alleyways

How can a rusty area of tiny, run-down wooden buildings survive in the midst of Tokyo's most expensive real estate? What makes them so attractive for artists, intellectuals, and tourists alike? When we peer into a yokochō, we see an agglomeration of both social and spatial relationships that creates synergistic effects. Yokochō offer an ecosystem of shared interests, supported by an architecture of extreme compactness and smallness. What are the design principles that we can take from them?

2.8.1 Foster communication and character through smallness

Smallness is the most striking characteristic of yokochō bars. Most are staffed by a single person and can only serve 5 to 10 customers, with common floor plans areas ranging from 7 to 15 m². Interviews with owners show that they see advantages in this smallness, as it enables genuine communication between staff and customers as well as among customers.[44] Owners also appreciate their manageability and economy, since a bar can be operated by one person (often the owner themselves), rents are cheap, and facilities such as toilets are sometimes shared by the whole street. This gives independence to each owner, who can act boldly and give their bar a distinct and personal character without being forced to target a mass audience. Most yokochō bars are highly idiosyncratic and creative, displaying the personal world of the owner through music, decoration, and other aesthetic choices. The small scale enables personalization and fosters diversity and individual expression. Unlike the homogenization of shopping malls and chain stores, yokochō are an example of the capacity of neighborhoods to generate incredible diversity when the broader structure of the city gives their residents the opportunity.

2.8.2 Keep things informal and low profile to create a sense of belonging

In yokochō bars, modest size and interior decor can facilitate an overall atmosphere of informality. To paraphrase the renowned social theorist Ray Oldenburg, they function as a "third place" where one can feel a sense of belonging outside of both work and home. In a city full of sleek, modern restaurants with astonishing interior designs, low profile design choices and spatial informality have become the key to a relaxed environment. Interior spaces are generally simple, but they convey the human touch of the owner.

2.8.3 Create spaces that can host numerous independent owners and operators

The liveliness of a yokochō seems difficult to reproduce or plan. However, in reality Tokyo's yokochō were often the result of a strict planning process. Authorities accommodated former black-market merchants inside newly built construction, including the nagaya compounds which we now think of as yokochō. When vendors were transferred to new compounds, they were allocated an equal floor area within the new space. The results of this process are still visible in today's yokochō. Land ownership is sometimes collective (like in Nombei Yokochō), with only buildings owned individually. In most cases, the system allows owners and managers to customize their spaces, invest in them as a long-term project, and get involved in decision making affecting the yokochō as a whole. This emphasis on smallness and fragmented egalitarian ownership has fostered an emergent sense of community and shared responsibility.

2.8.4 Build resilient and creative communities via economies of agglomeration

Yokochō bars may strictly speaking compete with one another, but in the broader sense they cooperate in order to collectively attract customers. Bar hopping in yokochō is common, with customers visiting several establishments in quick succession to enjoy a diversity of drinks, music, ambiance, and company. This refreshingly compact and finely subdivided spatial configuration enables the emergence of a localized micro-economy of agglomeration, a third place full of third places, that can retain its popularity through the years no matter the fortunes of any of its individual establishments.

2.8.5 Let experimentation and innovation produce emergent identity

Each yokochō naturally tends to develop its own clear identity. Although Golden Gai has seen several iterations—a black market, a red-light district, a drinking spot for intellectuals and countercultural types, a global tourist attraction—it has kept a liminal urban identity all its own. This pervasive atmosphere is facilitated by its specific physicality and configuration: an urban morphology of hiddenness, smallness, compactness, and low-profile spaces. It is an identity that has emerged naturally through the years, and although it was not established by a top-down process, it has been nurtured and defended through difficult periods by the collective conscientiousness of its owners. In a period of unitary corporate mega-redevelopments with top-down, mass-market branding, yokochō offer a valuable example of how intentional choices can foster the emergent identity of a space.

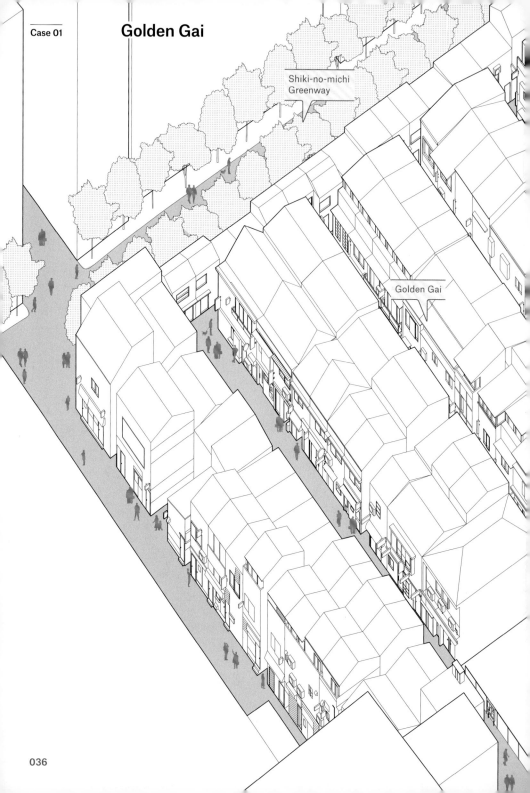

Case 01

Golden Gai

Shiki-no-michi
Greenway

Golden Gai

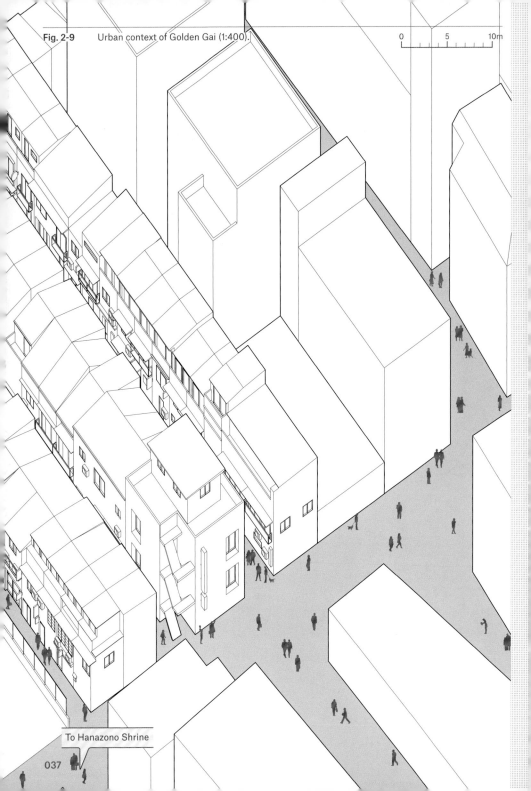

Fig. 2-9   Urban context of Golden Gai (1:400).

0   5   10m

To Hanazono Shrine

037

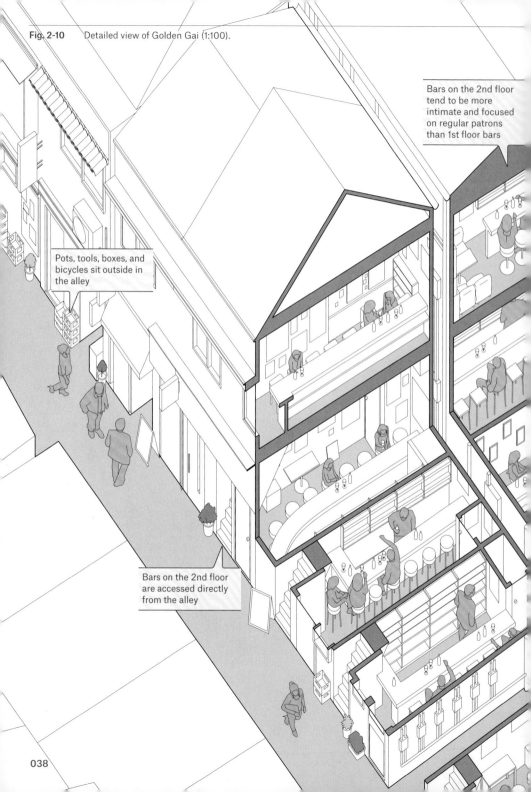

Fig. 2-10   Detailed view of Golden Gai (1:100).

Bars on the 2nd floor tend to be more intimate and focused on regular patrons than 1st floor bars

Pots, tools, boxes, and bicycles sit outside in the alley

Bars on the 2nd floor are accessed directly from the alley

Fig. 2-11 Perspective floor plan and cross-section of Bar Alpaca in Golden Gai (1:60).

EMERGENT TOKYO

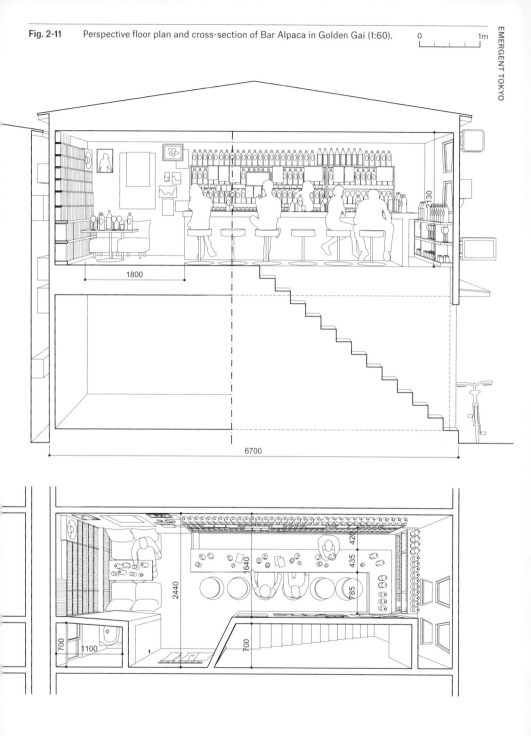

Fig. 2-12 Bar Alpaca. Alpaca stuffed animals of different sizes decorate the various corners of this bar, together with jazz disc covers, portraits, and personal mementos of the owner and clients. As in many bars in Japan, regular customers keep bottles labeled with their names behind the bar as a physical expression of their commitment to the establishment. The bar includes a reading corner for four people and a shelf densely packed with books.

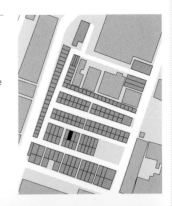

March 2019

0   1m

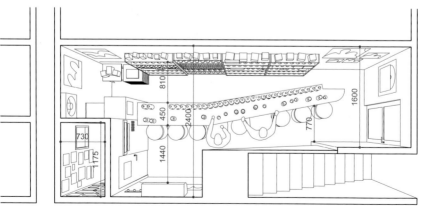

Fig. 2-14 Bar Evi. This bar is dedicated to movies and music, with film posters decorating every corner. Music CDs occupy a considerable portion of the shelf behind the counter. Diverse miniatures and posters decorate shelves and walls, many of which are presents from regular customers. Thus, the bar's ornamentation and visual atmosphere are created both by the owners and by its clientele. Beyond its more obvious function, this bar's toilet serves as a makeshift bulletin board—flyers and announcements for cultural events cover its surfaces.

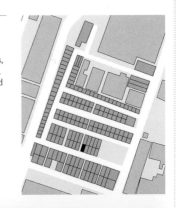

June 2019

Nombei Yokochō

Yamanote Line

Seibu Shibuya
Department Stores

Q-Front

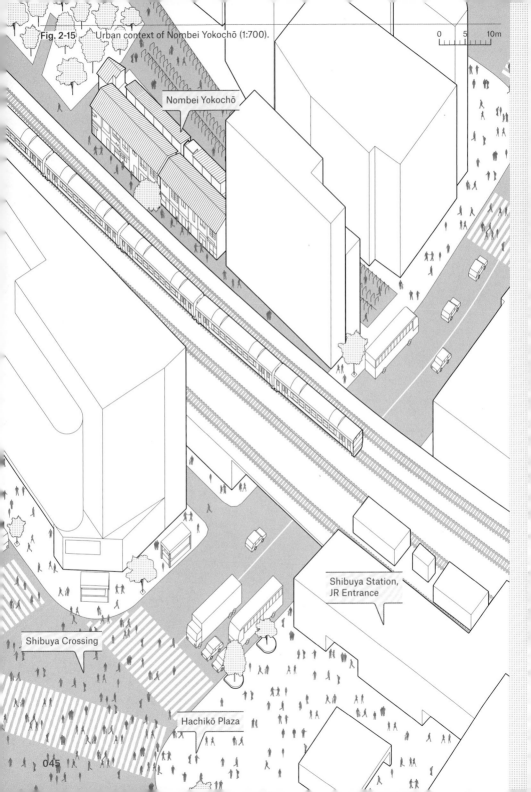

Fig. 2-15 Urban context of Nombei Yokochō (1:700).

0 5 10m

Nombei Yokochō

Shibuya Station,
JR Entrance

Shibuya Crossing

Hachikō Plaza

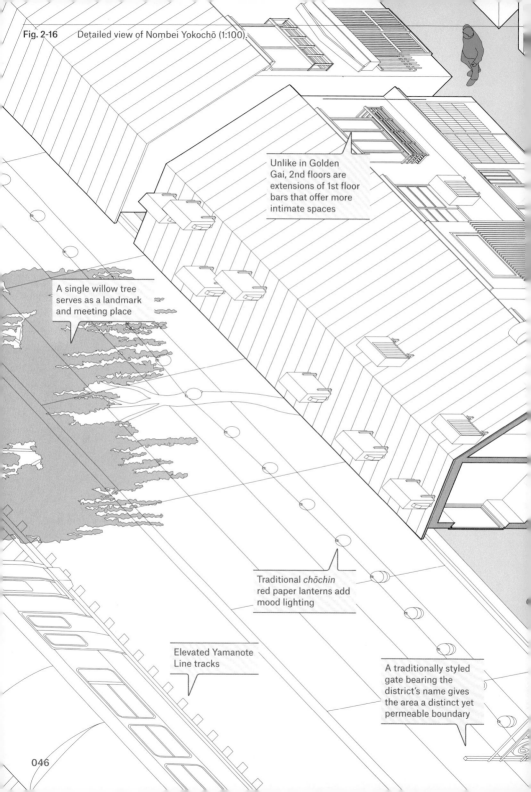

Fig. 2-16   Detailed view of Nombei Yokochō (1:100).

Unlike in Golden Gai, 2nd floors are extensions of 1st floor bars that offer more intimate spaces

A single willow tree serves as a landmark and meeting place

Traditional *chōchin* red paper lanterns add mood lighting

Elevated Yamanote Line tracks

A traditionally styled gate bearing the district's name gives the area a distinct yet permeable boundary

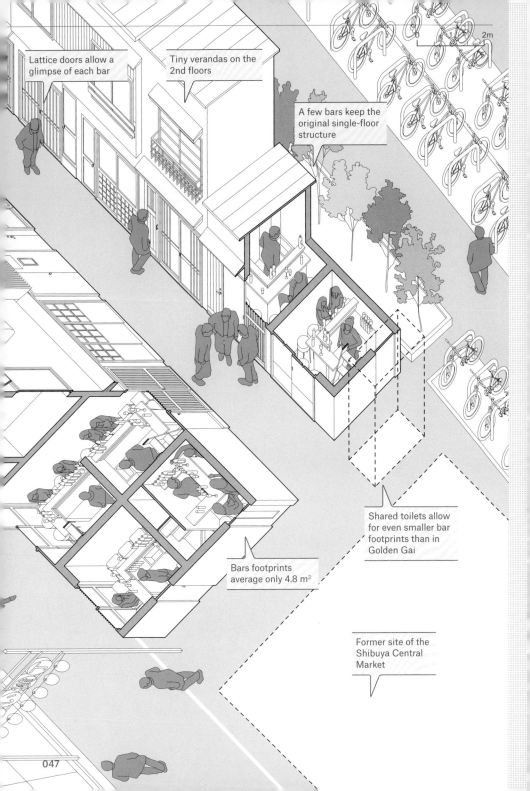

Lattice doors allow a glimpse of each bar

Tiny verandas on the 2nd floors

A few bars keep the original single-floor structure

2m

Shared toilets allow for even smaller bar footprints than in Golden Gai

Bars footprints average only 4.8 m²

Former site of the Shibuya Central Market

Fig. 2-17 Perspective floor plan and cross-section of
Bistro D'Arbre in Nombei Yokochō (1:60).

0   1m

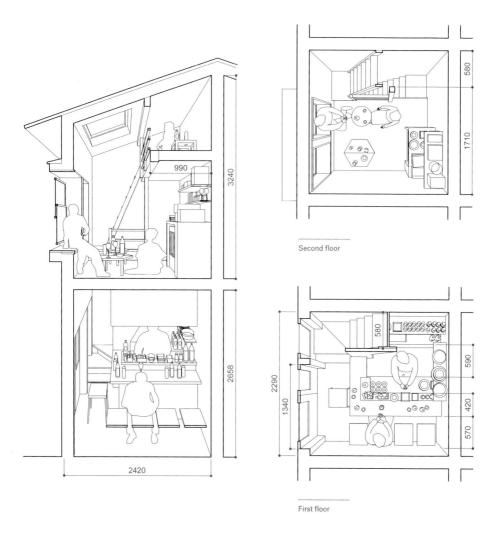

Second floor

First floor

Fig. 2-18 Bistro D'Arbre. Two independent operators run two different businesses here. During the daytime, the site hosts a milkshake and vegan taco bar. At night, it turns into a French bistro. Located on Nombei Yokochō's western row, the bar is well-positioned to attract curious pedestrians. Its doors can be opened entirely, exposing the counter and inviting passersby in. Foreign tourists have used markers to write notes on the walls marking their visit, with one proclaiming it "better than all the bars of San Francisco." The second floor is flooded with natural light and full of small spaces to relax. One can sit in the loft and see the sky through the top window, and a windowsill faces the adjacent willow tree. Many yokochō bars are diversifying their offerings and aesthetics, shedding their previous reputation as windowless late-night watering holes as they expand into daytime services and create luminous spaces.

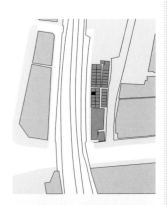

August 2020

Fig. 2-19 Perspective floor plans and cross-section of Bar Usagi in Nombei Yokochō (1:60).

0   1m

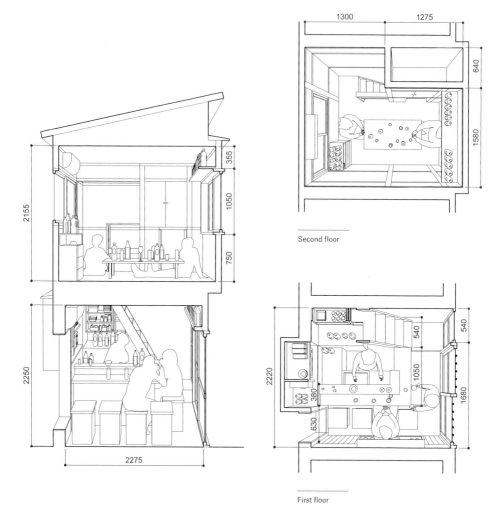

Second floor

First floor

Fig. 2-20   Bar Usagi. Opened in 2019, this bar is run by one of Nombei Yokochō's new generation of young bar owners. The first floor allows six people to sit at the counter, and the second floor offers a similar amount of floor seating. The bar has a back door, which helps clients leave the space more comfortably. In addition to the usual drink offerings, Usagi serves home-style Japanese cooking. The tiny kitchen allows cooking, serving, and washing dishes in an extraordinarily compact space. The kitchen shelves are located in an attached alcove that protrudes outward into the alley. The simple Japanese dishes and unpretentious coziness of the interior create a sense of intimacy that attracts both locals and foreign tourists, who account for half of the clientele.

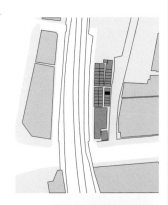

October 2019

Yanagi Kōji

To Kichijōji Sta.

Yanagi Kōji

Shinmei Ave.

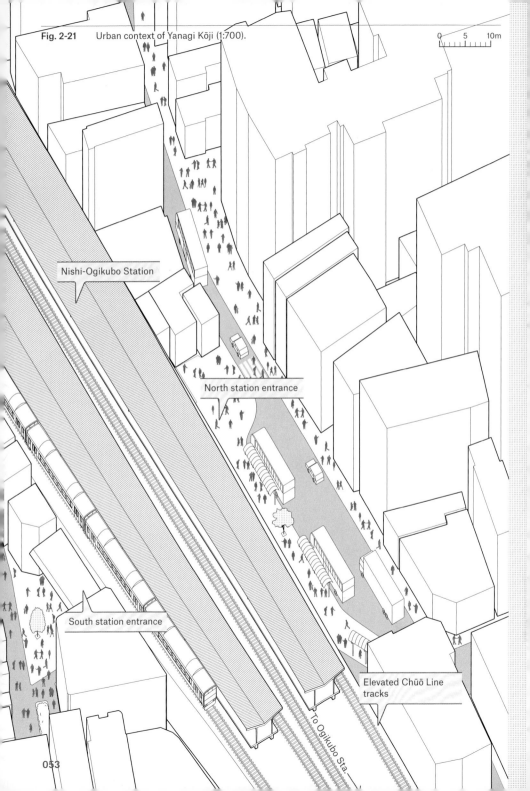

Fig. 2-21 Urban context of Yanagi Kōji (1:700).

0 5 10m

Nishi-Ogikubo Station

North station entrance

South station entrance

Elevated Chūō Line tracks

To Ogikubo Sta.

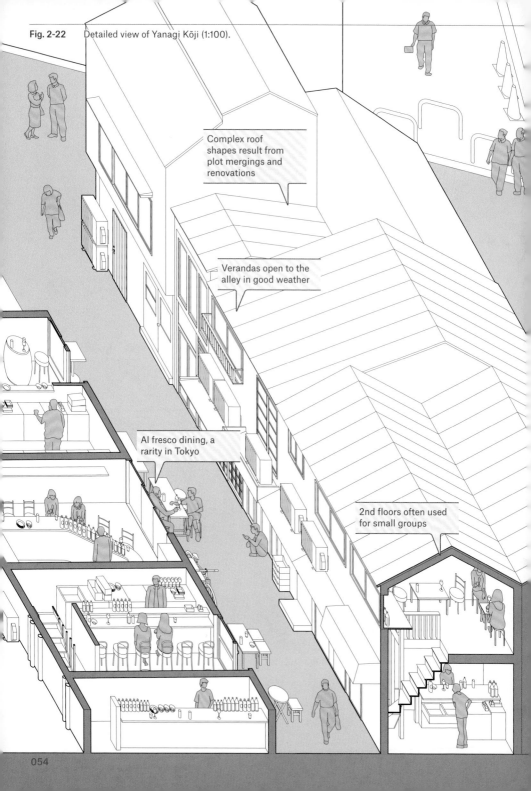

Fig. 2-22   Detailed view of Yanagi Kōji (1:100).

Complex roof shapes result from plot mergings and renovations

Verandas open to the alley in good weather

Al fresco dining, a rarity in Tokyo

2nd floors often used for small groups

Fig. 2-23   Perspective floor plan and cross-section of the Greek Bar in Yanagi Kōji (1:60).   0 ⊢⊢⊢⊢⊢⊣ 1m

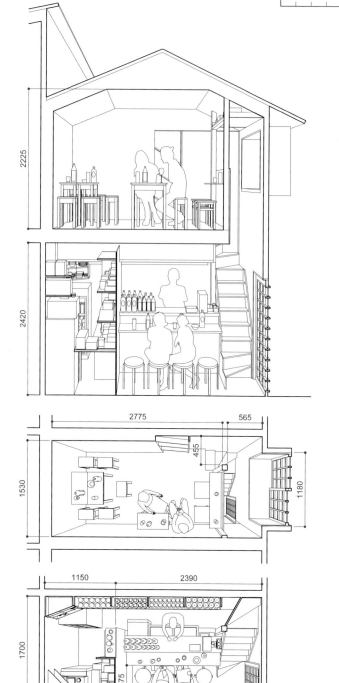

Second floor

First floor

Fig. 2-24 Greek Bar. Painted in vivid blue and yellow and decorated with Greek memorabilia, this bar is a new addition to Yanagi Kōji's multicultural bar scene. The tiny space is one of the smallest in Yanagi Kōji since it still has the original 1 *ken* wide by 2 *ken* deep footprint that most of the area's bars began with in the 1950s (a ken is a traditional unit of length corresponding to approximately 1.8 m). The owner, a young Greek chef, has correspondingly low rent and costs. The first floor contains the usual compact counter as well as a kitchen storage unit holding the ingredients and equipment for elaborate Greek cooking. As in most other bars of Yanagi Kōji, when the weather allows, a table and chairs are set out for customers in the alley.

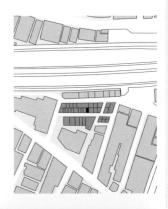

February and
August 2020

Fig. 2-25 Perspective cross-section (1:60) and floor plans (1:100) of the Handsome Bar in Yanagi Kōji.

0   1m

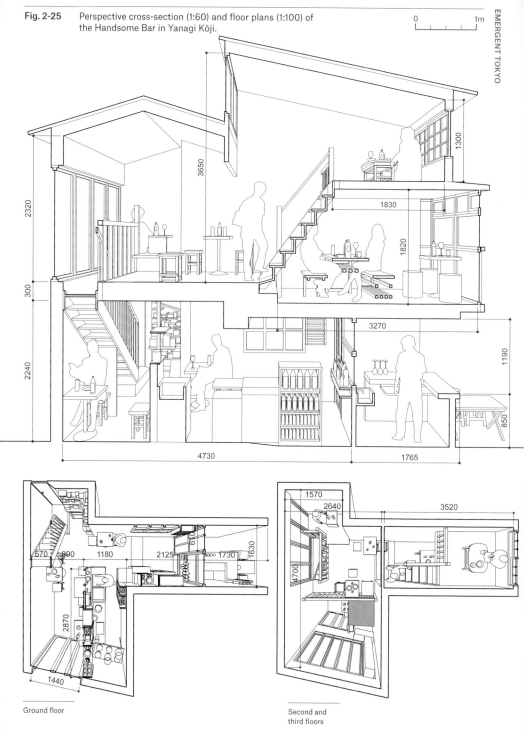

Ground floor

Second and third floors

Fig. 2-26 Handsome Bar. This Thai food bar opened in 2001 as a more modest eatery, but its popularity led the owner to expand into an adjacent building, creating a complex three-dimensional interior configuration. The entrance doubles as a bar counter open to the alley. The kitchen occupies most of the first floor, with dining tables of different sizes and designs on the second and third floors. Chairs, tables, hand railings, and other details are carefully hand-crafted in wood. This elaborate interior is connected visually with the exterior through windows of different sizes and types. By opening them in summer, the entire interior can be easily cross-ventilated.

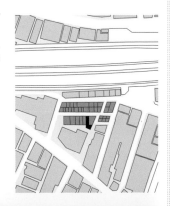

December 2019

3 ZAKKYO BUILDINGS

雑居ビル

Fig. 3-1 Zakkyo building cluster along Yasukuni Avenue as of September 2006.

3 ZAKKYO BUILDINGS

3.1 The iconic buildings that no one talks about

One of the most striking features of Japan's urban scenery is its abundance of densely packed multi-story buildings adorned with vertical stretches of neon signage—what the Japanese refer to as 'zakkyo buildings.' Their cavalcade of lights advertises that each floor of a building holds its own potential entertainments and attractions, collectively giving Tokyo a rich vertical dimension beyond mere high-rise offices and residences. Although buildings in this style are a central part of what makes Tokyo's cityscape visually iconic in the Western imagination, driving the perception of a city with nearly infinite possibilities hidden just out of the public view, few are aware of their history and urban context, to the point that the phenomenon has no corresponding name in English.

The term *zakkyo*, literally meaning 'coexisting miscellany,' primarily refers to multi-tenant buildings containing a mixture of offices with a wide range of consumer establishments. Zakkyo buildings, sometimes referred to as 'pencil buildings,' generally sit on narrow plots that dictate a slender shape Fig. 3-1. While in most cities around the world a building's commercial uses are located on its ground floors along the street, these buildings accommodate commercial functions vertically on all levels. It is possible to find a restaurant, an internet café, a health clinic, a hostess club, and a language school in the same building, without any particular hierarchy or organizing principle.

Most Japanese writings on zakkyo buildings focus exclusively on disaster prevention, especially after a fire on the 1st of September 2001 in Shinjuku's Kabukichō red-light district killed 44 people. For many Japanese architecture researchers and policymakers, these buildings represent a source of problems rather than a unique local vernacular architecture. However, some commentators, mostly Western, have begun addressing zakkyo buildings from architectural and urban viewpoints. Minoru Takeyama's Ichibankan building in Kabukichō has been highlighted as a prime example of the form, with one urbanist comparing it to an "up-ended Golden Gai alley."[45] From this point of view, zakkyo buildings are tantamount to vertical streets—a spatial arrangement rarely seen in Western countries, where commercial establishments are confined either to the ground level or to shopping centers.

A great deal of writing about Tokyo tends to focus on the neon façades of zakkyo buildings, whether to celebrate or denigrate them.[46] Discussions abound on why 'the Japanese,' who have shown a refined sensibility in their gardens and houses, accept this seemingly chaotic visual landscape. The late Japanese architect Ashihara Yoshinobu answered this question with a cultural explanation, postulating a general cultural "lack of concern" for exterior space in Japan that creates "unsightly building exteriors."[47]

This is at best an incredible oversimplification, and it neglects the historical and social diversity of Japan in a misguided attempt to shackle Japanese ethnicity to intrinsic psychological traits. It is easy to find examples of a refined and elaborate sensibility toward exterior space in many Japanese urban landscapes, both in the countryside and in cities such as Kyoto and Kanazawa. The phenomenon here is clearly happening case-by-case, rather than being the result of some general ethnic proclivity. To understand zakkyo buildings, one need not reach to pop ethnography; instead, we must examine their spatial configuration, their historical context, their relationship with their surroundings, and the combined effect on urban spaces where they cluster.

3.2   What makes a building zakkyo?

The term zakkyo denotes a hodgepodge assortment of elements that co-exist together in the same place. When referring to buildings, it describes multi-tenant buildings containing a mixture of offices and commercial businesses. Unlike large department stores and office towers, developed by companies with the patience and capital to acquire and merge multiple plots over years or even decades, zakkyo buildings are typically slender buildings on narrow plots.

Zakkyo buildings often appear in the dense commercial districts of Mercantile Tokyo that surround many train stations, where land prices are high but potential customers are numerous Fig. 3-2. Buildings tend to be taller in these districts, reflecting higher allowable floor area ratios and an economic incentive to build as densely as possible, while land plots are often small. They are also found

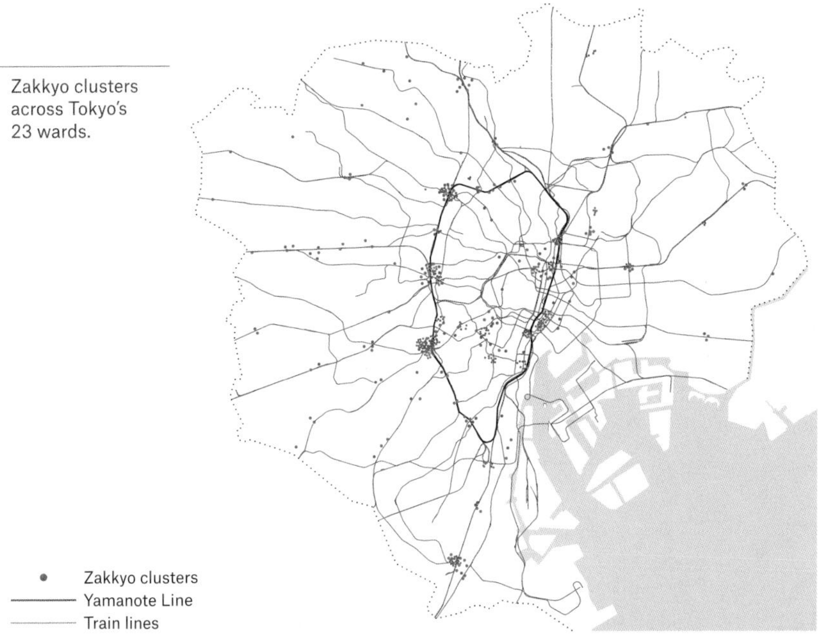

Fig. 3-2   Zakkyo clusters across Tokyo's 23 wards.

•   Zakkyo clusters
——— Yamanote Line
——— Train lines

in Pocket Tokyo neighborhoods among the mid-rise buildings that line their perimeters. These buildings have echoes across East Asia, such as in South Korea where they are known as *keunsaeng*.[48]

Zakkyo buildings are shaped by a combination of national and local legal frameworks, though architectural regulations do not employ the term zakkyo building; the nearest term is *fukugō yōto* (multi-purpose or multi-use), as they are called in disaster prevention regulations and official land use classification.[49] Japan's national regulations for building height and access to natural light determine the maximum volume of any given building, from which only small utilitarian rooftop constructions and rooftop billboards can stand out Fig. 3-3. These relatively narrow confines of law and regulation lead to a striking visual effect when zakkyo buildings begin to cluster together, a rhythmic repetition felt through the variety of bright signboards running down the sides of their slim volumes.

Although zakkyo buildings are found in virtually all commercial districts of Tokyo and other reasonably sized Japanese cities, there is no unified definition of the term and classifications can vary considerably. Nevertheless, we can point to certain qualities as reflecting the pinnacle of the form:

Central location. Zakkyo buildings tend to appear in areas zoned as commercial districts, typically near station squares or major roads. Plots of land facing onto wider streets are allowed higher floor area ratios and more building height by architectural regulations and zoning.

Public use. Zakkyo buildings are filled with establishments that are open to at least some segment of the public and collectively attract a considerable number of customers. Depending on the area, these range from daytime businesses, such as clinics or language schools, to nighttime taverns and socially tol-

Fig. 3-3 Volume restrictions in areas zoned as 'commercial districts' (*shōgyō chiiki*).

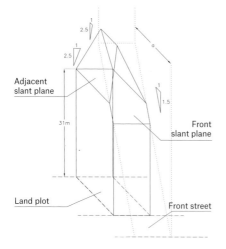

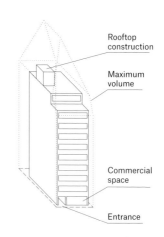

Maximum volume permitted by sunlight access regulations in areas designated as commercial districts (plot coverage ratio 80%, floor area ratio ranging from 200% to 1,000%).

A typical loft building is designed to maximize usable space within the sunlight regulations, a configuration frequently used for offices.

erated but less visible businesses selling intimacy, such as hostess bars, or even sexual services.[50] These segmented buildings often accommodate businesses with further compartmentalized interiors, such as karaoke boxes and manga cafés, that can be used almost like domestic spaces.[51]

Maximum generic loft space and minimal interior circulation. In order to optimize their rental income, these buildings make use of the maximum floor area ratio within the volume permitted by regulations. The spaces offered to tenants are generic un-partitioned loft floors that permit complete customization. Indoor staircases, corridors, and lobbies are reduced to the minimum.

A profusion of public signage. The main façades of zakkyo buildings are generally full of advertisements—almost always ads for the contents of the building, and sometimes generic advertisements as well. These advertisements are regulated by municipal ordinances and sometimes informally influenced by neighborhood advisory committees Fig. 3-4, and are arranged to be visible from different points of view: rooftop billboards for viewing from distant locations such as train platforms; protruding billboards designed to be seen by passers-by along the street; attached advertisements and information directly in front of the building for those entering.[52]

3.3 How does a building become a zakkyo building?

A large share of today's zakkyo buildings did not begin their lives as such. In many cases they were simply generic construction designed to fit the city's relevant architectural standards and regulations, occupied as multi-tenant low-rent office buildings with a commercial ground level. Over time, however, they became zakkyo buildings through a gradual vertical colonization by incoming

Fig. 3-4   Summary of regulations concerning outdoor advertising on buildings located in commercial districts.

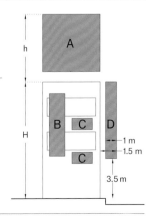

Rooftop advertising (A)
- Maximum rooftop billboard height (h) no more than two thirds of total building height (H), and at most 52 m from ground level to the top of the advertisement.
- Rooftop billboards can rise above the maximum construction volume under sunlight regulations (see **Fig. 3-5**).

Advertising attached to a façade (B and C)
- Maximum height of 52 m from ground level to the top of the advertisement.
- Above the ground floor, no blockage of windows or other openings by rigid billboards (C) is allowed, aside from hanging banners and other textile advertising (B).
- In total, advertisements can take up no more than 30% of the façade, excluding windows and the like.
- Maximum area of any single advertisement is 100 m^2.
- Billboards with identical content must be separated at least 5 m from each other.

Advertising protruding from a façade (D)
- When advertising extends from the plot boundary into the public space by 1 m or less and from the façade by 1.5 m or less, it must be raised up at least 3.5 m from the ground (2.5 m if it extends only 0.5 m or less into public space).

commercial enterprises. Their staircases and elevators, once purely functional in nature, become an extension of the street with their own commercial signage; the façade turned into an advertisement for the establishments within. This spontaneous and incremental colonization was common among the first generation of zakkyo buildings in the 1960s and 1970s.

Following this generation, a new series of zakkyo buildings were consciously designed as such with special adaptations for recreational uses. Their designers improved circulation with panoramic elevators, wider and more articulated entrance lobbies, and more orderly displays of advertisements and information about the building's establishments. Shops on the lowest floors are arranged to be easily visible from the street, and space for billboards on the façade and rooftop are integrated into the overall design Fig. 3-5.

The north side of Shinjuku's famous Yasukuni Avenue showcases this gradual transformation over the decades Figs. 3-6, 7.[53] Until the early 1960s, most of its buildings were low-rise and occupied by independent stores, eateries, and offices paired with small and straightforward advertisements. In the early 1970s there was a boom of construction with buildings reaching the maximum allowed

---

Fig. 3-5   Generations of zakkyo buildings

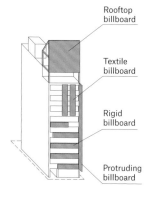

Rooftop billboard

Textile billboard

Rigid billboard

Protruding billboard

First generation (1960 through the mid-1980s): a building that was initially used for offices is gradually covered by advertisements and colonized by publicly accessible commercial establishments.

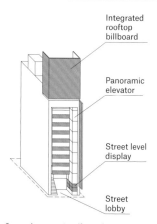

Integrated rooftop billboard

Panoramic elevator

Street level display

Street lobby

Second generation (from the 1980s onwards): Some buildings consciously designed as zakkyo buildings, including integrated advertisements and panoramic elevators designed to maximize their desirability for this purpose.

Fig. 3-6   Transformation of zakkyo building usage on Yasukuni Avenue's north side over the years. The category 'recreation' includes *manga kissa* cafés, *karaoke boxes*, game centers, *pachinko*, and *mahjong*. 'Restaurants' includes bars, izakaya, and cafés. 'Services' includes clinics, hair, nail salons, and estheticians. 'Offices' includes customer-facing offices such as banks and money lending businesses.

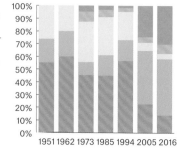

■ Recreation   ■ Services   □ Retail
■ Restaurants   ■ Offices

100%
90%
80%
70%
60%
50%
40%
30%
20%
10%
0%

1951 1962 1973 1985 1994 2005 2016

Fig. 3-7 Cross-sectional diagram showing the transformation of building usage on Yasukuni Avenue's north side over the years.

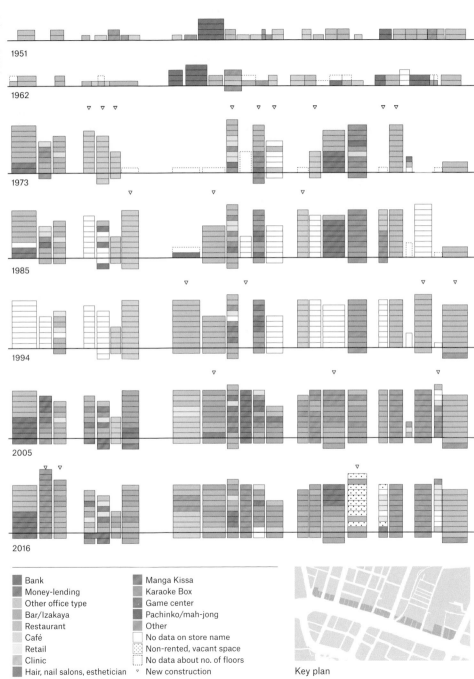

1951

1962

1973

1985

1994

2005

2016

■ Bank
■ Money-lending
☐ Other office type
☐ Bar/Izakaya
☐ Restaurant
☐ Café
☐ Retail
☐ Clinic
■ Hair, nail salons, esthetician

■ Manga Kissa
☐ Karaoke Box
☐ Game center
■ Pachinko/mah-jong
☐ Other
☐ No data on store name
▣ Non-rented, vacant space
⋯ No data about no. of floors
▽ New construction

Key plan

height of about ten stories. The types of shops inhabiting the zakkyo buildings at first remained similar to what had come before, but gradually services and entertainment businesses started to appear. Over time restaurants became the dominant use, followed by recreation businesses such as karaoke, pachinko, and manga cafés, a transition that accelerated in the 2000s Fig. 3-7. Today, half of the street's zakkyo buildings belong to the first generation from the 1970s and early 1980s, while the other half have been reconstructed in the 2000s and 2010s. This rhythm of periodic reconstruction every few decades is common in Tokyo's commercial districts. Some of the still-standing first-generation cases have housed a fantastic variety of businesses over their half decade of history, ranging from offices and restaurants to pachinko parlors and health clinics.

This diversity of uses changes the possibilities of the cityscape. Tokyo is currently beset by large-scale luxury redevelopments that require tremendous investment, leading to a narrow range of profit-maximizing uses. They create some buzz in their first years before the newest and latest development supplants them, but their blandness and sterility often casts a lingering shadow over the surrounding cityscape. Zakkyo buildings—with their capacity to grow, change their function over time, and reinvent themselves—offer a more robust infrastructure for urban self-regeneration. When zakkyo buildings cluster, their combined effect intensifies urban vitality and creates striking urban sceneries. Across Tokyo, landowners and developers continue to build new zakkyo buildings and integrate them into the city's urban fabric in a variety of ways. These clusters can take dramatically different forms, ranging from Shinjuku's flashy Yasukuni Avenue Figs. 3-8, 9 to the more intimate Kagurakaza Street Figs. 3-10, 11 and the layered cityscape of Shimbashi station's Karasumori Block Figs. 3-12, 13.

3.4   The iconic zakkyo of Yasukuni Avenue

Case 04

The most representative case of zakkyo clustering in Tokyo is found along Yasukuni Avenue, close to Shinjuku Station, a cityscape pictured in many of the most iconic global portrayals of Tokyo. In this row of zakkyo buildings on deep

Fig. 3-8   The urban landscape created by Yasukuni Avenue's zakkyo buildings as of February 2007.

Fig. 3-9   The evolution of Yasukuni Avenue's north side zakkyo buildings (1:5,000).   0   60m

1933
Shinjuku Station had already become a major transit hub, connecting the Yamanote Line with new railways that make Tokyo's Western suburban expansion possible. However, the station surroundings remain unchanged and predominantly residential.
Source: *Kasaihoken Tokushuchizu* (Toshiseizusha, 1933).

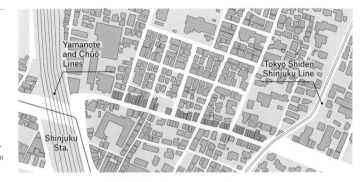

1951
As part of the postwar reconstruction, Yasukuni Avenue was widened and the Kabukichō district was created out of war-ravaged residential districts through a land readjustment project. Along the avenue, the first three-story buildings begin to appear.
Source: *Kasaihoken Tokushuchizu* (Toshiseizusha, 1951).

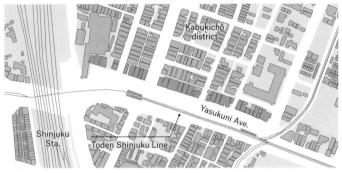

1962
Japan enters its period of high economic growth. Real estate developers begin to merge land plots close to Shinjuku Station in order to accommodate commercial buildings.
Source: *Tōkyō-to Zenjūtaku Annaizuchō* (Jūtaku Kyōkai 1962).

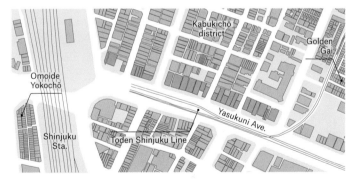

2016
Most buildings along this stretch of the avenue have become zakkyo buildings. The trend toward land merging and bigger buildings continues, but the plots along this stretch retain their small initial sizes, as does most of Kabukichō.
Source: *Kibanchizujōhō* (Kokudō Chiri-in, 2016).

and narrow plots, each building strives to be open to the street, making the transition between the street and the interior as smooth as possible. Entrances, stairs, and elevators are all directly connected to the street, making the ground floor a continuous site of pedestrian traffic. Zakkyo buildings often eliminate foyers and reception spaces entirely, writing them off as unnecessary elements. Figs. 3-14, 15.

The northern side of Yasukuni Avenue, between the Yamanote Line rail tracks to the east and Kuyakusho Avenue to the west, has become an icon of Tokyo, omnipresent in guidebooks, documentaries, and films. Invariably, foreign movies located in Tokyo include atmospheric scenes of the protagonist moving along this particular stretch—see, for example, *Lost in Translation* (2003), *Kill Bill* (2003), or *Wolverine* (2013). This stretch has the visual power of other urban symbols that evoke specific global cities, such as the Eiffel Tower in Paris, Big Ben in London, or the Empire State Building of New York. However, unlike those urban icons, this street remains an unintended symbol, an *emergent* monument. Its evocative power outstrips the few large-scale monuments, such as the Tokyo Skytree, that the city has intentionally produced.

This stretch of Yasukuni Avenue is the southern boundary of Kabukichō, one of the so-called adult entertainment districts of Tokyo. Red-light districts have a centuries-old history in Tokyo, but Kabukichō's status as such is a relatively recent development. Before the war it was a residential area, but along with the rest of Shinjuku the area was devastated during the World War II air raids. Only a portion of its reinforced concrete buildings remained, such as the famous Isetan and Mitsukoshi department stores.

After the war, government authorities rapidly embarked on urban restructuring and reconstruction with the 1946 Special City Planning Law,[54] which relied on the concept of Land Readjustment Projects or LRPs.[55] These projects were used as a method of organizing districts with irregular plots and street patterns, usually with the aim of improving urban areas that had originally emerged informally or on agricultural land and thus lacked necessary public facilities and infrastructure. Under LRPs, landowners pool their ownership, contributing a portion of their combined property for public facilities (roads, parks, etc.) as well as selling off a portion at the end of the process to pay for the costs of planning and construction. When completed, plots that have undergone an LRP typically have smaller land surfaces but higher market value, and the process gives planning authorities a means of improving public infrastructure without a substantial outlay of public funds. As Yasukuni Avenue and Meiji Avenue were widened, several LRPs were conducted in the surrounding area. Unlike in other parts of Shinjuku, Kabukichō's LRP was not driven by the government, but rather by a private association led by businessman Suzuki Kihei, who planned for the area to become an amusement area with a kabuki theater as its main attraction. The theater was never built, but the name stuck.

As the decades passed and plots in Shinjuku were merged to accommodate bigger buildings, Kabukichō's buildings retained relatively small footprints. The northern stretch of Yasukuni Avenue in particular underwent a striking transformation, evolving over the course of six decades from a low-rise array of shops and offices into a verticalized entertainment street despite almost no change in building footprint. As building heights increased throughout what the Japanese have formally termed their 'period of rapid economic growth' (1954 to 1973), their offices and retail were gradually displaced by entertainment businesses aimed at attracting an affluent nighttime crowd.

The area is often described as unsightly and chaotic, but its zakkyo buildings display a strong sense of architectural unity. This is not the result of a top-down plan; in Japan, urban ordinances and architectural regulations apply to each discrete independent building, but for the most part there aren't rules requiring the developers and owners of these buildings to treat them as a part of an overall urban composition, such as the requirements for uniformity in alignments, color palette, or window sizes often found in Western cities. Nevertheless, when multiple zakkyo buildings are built under similar conditions in terms of plot size and location, they naturally tend to develop into a larger cohesive scene Figs. 3-16, 17.

3.5

Case 05

Kagurazaka's zakkyo buildings have an Edo legacy

The sloped Kagurazaka Street (Kagurazaka-dōri) runs down the middle of Kagurazaka, a dining and shopping district in Shinjuku Ward. The intimate 10 to 12 m wide promenade is lined with burgeoning zelkova trees and a variety of zakkyo buildings that combine to create some of Tokyo's most unique scenery. Zakkyo buildings along Kagurazaka Street offer direct access from the street, creating an 'active edge' where their semi-private space meets the public sphere Figs. 3-18, 19. Their uses tend toward restaurants and bars, but there are shops and offices as well. Unlike the 42 m wide Yasukuni Avenue, in Kagurazaka Street there is no space to see billboards from a distance, and signs tend to be smaller and closer to the pedestrian Figs. 3-20, 21.

Kagurazaka Street's character has its roots in the Edo period. Like most lands located close to the former Edo castle, Kagurazaka's plots were large and owned by high-profile clans. However, at the end of the Edo period, the parcels along the street were given to low-status samurai residences and subdivided into plots with frontages of 4 *ken* (about 7.2 m). Even today, most buildings along Kagurazaka Street are not wider than 7.2 m, giving a rhythm to the streetscape.

Kagurazaka was once known for being a geisha district (known as *hanamachi* or *karyūkai*).[56] The World War II air raids reduced the district to ashes, but its hanamachi quickly reappeared after the war and remained in operation until 1948, when the passage of the Businesses Affecting Public Morals Regulation Law prohibited most operations of Kagurazaka's geisha houses. Many *machiai* (teahouses for waiting geisha) converted into restaurants while at the same time preserving some elements of their exclusive character. This hybridization produced many of the *ryōtei* (luxurious traditional Japanese restaurants) that remain along the northern side of Kagurazaka Street to this day. Locals are proud of this hanamachi character and the way in which Kagurazaka's beautifully preserved alleyways hide some of Tokyo's most exquisite traditional cuisine.

Fig. 3-10 The urban landscape created by zakkyo buildings along Kagurazaka Street as of March 2021.

Kagurazaka's main shopping promenade began to change from the 1960s onward. Newer, sturdier buildings rapidly rose in height, up to the 6 or 7 floors allowed by regulations. The bubble period accelerated this process, but plot sizes along Kagurazaka Street remained mostly unchanged.

Over time, the changes only became more dramatic. Deregulation from the 1980s onward allowed for large-scale redevelopment projects, a trend that reached its highest point in 2002 with the much-publicized Law on Special Measures for Urban Renaissance.

After the bubble burst, declining land prices made residential development feasible in central locations once again. The construction and development lobbies managed to get approval for regulatory relief under the Building Standards Law, particularly from the 'slanted plane regulation' that limits building heights according to street widths. In the 1990s the combined impact of these changes was to enable super-high-rise towers to be built in low and mid-rise neighborhoods such as Kagurazaka, prompting an aggressive inner-city residential construction boom.[57]

Kagurazaka's locals were at first not aware of the deregulation and took for granted that such construction was simply not legally possible in their neighborhood. When Kagurazaka became a hot spot for development, however, the neighbors organized an opposition group.[58] In the end, they only managed to reduce one tower from a planned 31 floors to 26, but they learned a valuable lesson. Together with the old *shōtenkai* (the merchants association of the commercial promenade) and the *chōkai* (neighborhood association), several non-profit associations and groups banded together to become a more proactive and agile force.[59]

As in many other districts, these neighbors' initiatives resulted first in agreements for shared and consensual rules in areas such as height limitations. Soon, however, the neighbors learned that those agreements—which cannot be legally enforced—did not impress developers. Even in the face of a unified and public local opposition, real estate firms continued to force their projects through as-of-right.

Fig. 3-11 The evolution of Kagurazaka Street and its zakkyo buildings (1:5,000).

0   60m

1937
Kagurazaka has already become a densely populated area known for its *hanamachi* or geisha district. Numerous *machiai* (establishments where geisha entertain patrons) and exclusive *ryōtei* restaurants appear along the back alleys.
Source: *Kasaihoken Tokushuchizu* (Toshiseizusha, 1937).

1952
Kagurazaka has been largely destroyed by the firebombing of Tokyo. The area begins to recover, although still with fewer and more scattered buildings than in the prewar period. Along Kagurazaka Street, most commercial buildings are two stories high.
Source: *Kasaihoken Tokushuchizu* (Toshiseizusha, 1952).

1982
Buildings along Kagurazaka Street have grown vertically, but their plots remain the same width. Concrete buildings have replaced the wooden houses. In 1984 the ward authorities expand its sidewalks and plant the street's famed zelkova trees.
Source: *Jūtakuchizu* (Zenrin, 1982).

2017
The construction of large buildings like the Eins Tower and Porta Kagurazaka prompted locals to demand a new district planning to preserve the urban scale and avoiding construction setbacks that erode the vitality of street life.
Source: *Jūtakuchizu* (Zenrin, 2017).

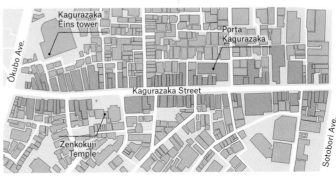

After enduring several more major new construction projects, the neighbors managed to approve two legally enforceable district plans in 2007 and 2011, which together cover Kagurazaka Street from Sotobori Avenue to Okubo Avenue and much of its hinterland.[60] This kind of district plan requires a tremendous amount of organization and landowner consensus to achieve—close to 100%, in fact. In Tokyo, only a few active and united communities have managed to successfully get them approved by planning authorities.

The Kagurazaka district plans revive the regulatory framework that existed prior to the 1990s deregulations, eliminating the changes that allowed for super-high rises. In addition to offering more protection to Kagurazaka's roji alleyways, the district plan limits height to 31 m (about ten floors) along Kagurazaka Street. By revoking the option to obtain extra height permissions by setting back buildings, the district plan promotes construction that preserves the street's existing scale and continuity. In essence, the district plans have reenacted the rules that initially produced the zakkyo buildings of the 1960s and 1970s.

Examining Kagurazaka opens a debate about the stereotypical characterization of Tokyo as a dynamic, ever-changing city. This way of looking at Tokyo is often cynically used to justify large-scale corporate redevelopments, explaining them away as yet another instance of Tokyo's continuous metamorphosis, but the Kagurazaka case shows that dynamism under the wrong conditions can destroy the fabric of a community. Large-scale corporate redevelopments, like those opposed by citizens in Kagurazaka, freeze Tokyo's vibrancy by petrifying districts into sterile, fortress-like, inward-looking, highly controlled projects with less adaptability, less diversity, less creativity, and less dynamism.

3.6 The Karasumori zakkyo block in Shimbashi

Case 06

Shimbashi Station is a major transportation hub surrounded by several of Tokyo's main business districts. Shimbashi is one of Tokyo's main *sakariba*, or nightlife districts, and attracts employees from nearby offices after the work day ends. Despite its popular depiction in the media as a 'salaryman mecca' for middle-aged men, today's Shimbashi features a more diverse crowd.[61]

In front of the station sits one of the liveliest plazas in Tokyo. A steam locomotive—or "SL," as they are called in Japan—placed on the plaza reminds passersby that Shimbashi was the birthplace of Japanese railways. The SL Plaza (SL *Hiroba*) is a popular meeting spot, but the square does not offer opportunities to sit, a result of the implicit general ban on benches in Japanese public spaces. Nevertheless, it is always full of people waiting, talking, coming, and going. SL Plaza's success directly contradicts a common talking point about Japanese cities—namely that public plazas are somehow in conflict with Japanese culture. In Japan, a well-located plaza will function much the same as in a Western city, even when benches and other amenities are scarce.

Countless zakkyo buildings surround SL Plaza. In fact, the entire west exit—together with the SL Plaza and the zakkyo building hinterland—creates an intense, tri-dimensional entertainment district. It is especially impressive at night, when the plaza and the neon-clad buildings can be seen from the elevated rails of the adjacent Yamanote Line. The block containing the Karasumori Shrine is of particular interest; it is formed by a perimeter of zakkyo buildings, encircling lower buildings and a network of alleys Figs. 3-22, 23.

Shimbashi's spatial configuration and character have accumulated over the course of decades and are shaped by the area's history. As with other locations around the former Edo castle (the current Imperial Palace), the Shimbashi district once accommodated the lands and residences of large *daimyō* (feudal lords), which were then subdivided and sold after the Meiji Restoration. In 1909, the precursor of Shimbashi Station—called Karasumori Station—was completed. The new station facilitated access to a nearby geisha district, triggering land development in front of the station.[62] As Wold War II intensified, the authorities forced a general evacuation and purchased the land in front of the station, which became vacant due to the war. A few days after the war ended, street vendors began pouring in to form one of Tokyo's first black markets of the postwar era. In 1946, their stalls were reorganized into wooden barracks, known as the Shinsei Market, which occupied most of the current SL Plaza and what is now the New Shimbashi Building, a local landmark with a yokochō-like atmosphere that contains hundreds of tiny businesses across multiple floors. The Shinsei Market had 298 shops, most of them bars and restaurants—a relatively easy business to open for those who came to Shimbashi after the war.[63] As in Kagurazaka, the restrictions enacted by the Businesses Affecting Public Morals Regulation Law of 1948 pushed the machiai and other geisha-related establishments to either close or convert into bars and restaurants.[64]

In 1961 the Tokyo government expanded the station square and built new buildings on both sides, responding to both new legislation designed to promote fire-resistant buildings and widening of public spaces[65] and the construction demands of completing the Shinkansen bullet train in preparation for the 1964 Tokyo Olympics. On the west side, the New Shimbashi Building was finally completed on the site of the former Shinsei Market in 1971, offering 11 floors and four basement floors of commercial and office space. The authorities relocated the vendors of the demolished Shinsei Market into the basement floors of these new buildings.[66]

The Karasumori Block sits in the shadow of these redevelopments. A perimeter of zakkyo buildings hides three narrow alleys lined with two-story buildings, and a Shinto shrine with its *sandō*, or approach path. The alleys and exterior streets are animated by a plethora of entrances, billboards, windows, and stairs, inviting pedestrians to dining and entertainment offerings Figs. 3-24 to 26. Building façades host advertisements at different scales: giant advertisements in the outer zakkyo buildings, lanterns and small signs along the alleyways Figs. 3-27, 28. The alleys (which have existed since the Edo period), the shrine, and the intimate character of the nightlife have all been preserved despite earthquakes, bombings, and redevelopment. The Karasumori Block has become, in some sense, a contemporary verticalized hanamachi.

Fig. 3-12   Urban landscape of the Karasumori Block in Shimbashi as of March 2021.

It is worth comparing these two adjacent blocks as exemplars of different urban models that emerged in postwar Japan: the spontaneous Karasumori Block, and the top-down planning of the New Shimbashi Building. Born as an initiative by the authorities to reorganize a postwar bar cluster and the surrounding public space, the New Shimbashi Building follows the fashionable models of the period: a windowless shopping-center podium, with a modernist office block on the top. Rather than the franchises one finds in the most recent redevelopments, the shopping area has a charming array of independent stores, most of them catering to niche salaryman preferences. However, the New Shimbashi Building is aging fast, and its structure is considered insufficiently reinforced against a major earthquake. Many shops are still doing brisk business, but the place is in a state of steady decay, with an increasing number of dubious massage parlors expanding from the top floors.

As with other Yamanote Line stations, redevelopment has been proposed as a solution to revamp Shimbashi's popularity and renovate its structures. However, the ownership of the New Shimbashi Building is divided among numerous owners, and thus achieving full consensus around redevelopment has taken many years. A landowners' association has finally been established,[67] and construction may begin as early as 2021.[68] The full redesign plans are not public yet, but we know that the building and much of its adjacent land, including the SL Plaza, will be consolidated as one site to allow for two 30-floor towers.[69] One can only hope that the plaza, one of the most successful and symbolic of its kind in Tokyo, will be at least preserved as open space.

The Karasumori Block represents a different way of responding to a changing Tokyo. By avoiding the merging of properties and keeping the scale small, the block's landowners can renovate and update their zakkyo buildings to the latest seismic standards with relatively small capital investments. The district's many zakkyo buildings have helped it preserve its street-level vitality even as the Karasumori Block is now being surrounded by soaring commercial redevelopment. Even vestiges from the Edo period, like the Karasumori Shrine and the block's old alleyways, have been able to survive. The Karasumori Block

Fig. 3-13   The evolution of Karasumori Block in Shimbashi (1:5,000).

0   60m

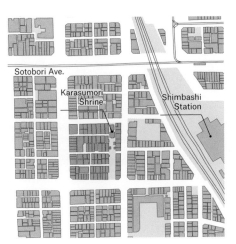

1932   The west side of Shimbashi Station was a well-known geisha district. Karasumori Shrine already had an urban context similar to its present-day incarnation, encircled by buildings with its sacred approach path integrated into the surrounding street network.

Source: *Kasaihoken Tokushuchizu* (Toshiseizusha, 1932).

1957   Shinsei Market, a postwar market built to relocate black marketeers, has appeared in front of the station, together with the plaza known as SL Plaza (SL *Hiroba*). Around the Karasumori Shrine, *ryōtei* restaurants appear after the prohibition of the geisha's *machiai*.

Source: *Tōkyō-to Zenjūtaku Annaizuchō* (Jūtaku Kyōkai, 1957).

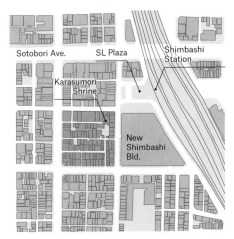

1973   The area immediately surrounding both sides of the station have been largely redeveloped. The New Shimbashi Building was completed in 1972, together with an expansion of the SL Plaza. Many buildings along the Karasumori Block edge are now mid-rise, but the land plots themselves have remained almost unchanged in size.

Source: *Jūtakuchizu* (Zenrin, 1973).

2017   The whole perimeter has been consolidated as a ring of zakkyo buildings, approaching the maximum allowed height of eight floors. Several of these buildings stand on land merged together from previous smaller plots. Behind this ring, the tiny scale of the alleyways survives.

Source: Jūtakuchizu (Zenrin, 2017).

serves as a case study of how a city can choose to evolve by adding layers over its existing cityscape, without resorting to cataclysmic changes that inevitably entail bigger developments and more controlled environments at the expense of human-scale living and spontaneity.

3.7 Learning from zakkyo buildings

The three cases above allow us to illustrate a set of emergent characteristics common to nearly all zakkyo clusters. If street spaces such as yokochō or laneways can be thought of as horizontal emergent ecosystems, zakkyo buildings succeed in verticalizing the concept, bringing the synergistic effects of street spaces into the vertical dimension.

3.7.1 Build verticalized public spaces that connect with their surroundings

The creation of multi-level urban public space has been a recurring vision among modern architects. Yet the division of public space into separate vertical levels in cities across the world has usually ended up creating residual, under-used spaces, such as disused underpasses under bridges and elevated roads. In zakkyo clusters, however, a multiplicity of slender buildings smoothly absorbs large flows of the public into vertical spaces. Shopping malls have a similar verticalizing effect, but they do it by routing pedestrian flows internally in ways that decrease the pedestrian density of their surrounding environs and walling themselves off from the public view. Zakkyo buildings are different because they achieve their vertical density by opening directly to the street, and when they cluster together they not only preserve pedestrian laneways but strengthen their central, connective role in public life.

3.7.2 Create an active edge

Zakkyo buildings stand separately from one another, without any horizontal connections above street level. Due to their deep and narrow proportions, they offer stairs and elevators facing the streets. This creates an active edge along their adjacent sidewalks. The buildings' establishments—usually one per floor, but sometimes as many as a half dozen per floor—can be quickly accessed via the elevator or stairs and are thus directly connected with the street, without intermediate halls and lobbies. This characteristic is most vividly expressed in the second generation of zakkyo buildings, where circulation is primarily outdoors and a street full of zakkyo buildings will often be lined with entrances, stairs, and elevator lobbies. Zakkyo buildings successfully exploit their full height for public use, offering the populace a wider variety of reasons to come to a given area and increasing the pedestrian density of the street.

3.7.3 Embrace the clustered possibilities of dynamic façades

Each individual zakkyo building follows relatively loose architectural regulations regarding volume and shape as well as outdoor advertisement ordinances. But when they combine together, zakkyo clusters produce a remarkable and distinctive visual cityscape, particularly at night—a cityscape which has not only become an iconic image of urban Japan, but also finds a home in Asian cities such as Hong Kong that have fostered similar architecture. Establishments inside zakkyo buildings may change frequently, but as with their horizontal yokochō counterparts the image of the whole endures over the years. As in cases of historical cities and villages, where a certain construction technique or material has given a visual consistency to the integrated whole through time, zakkyo clusters constitute a distinct form of contemporary vernacular architecture.

On Yasukuni Avenue, where the entire height of each building's façade is covered with billboards and signage, façades have become spatialized information displays. The array of signboards creates a three-dimensional information environment, where the newest offers, sales, campaigns, and businesses are taken in simultaneously. Regulating façades is always a challenge for urban planners, since it requires striking a difficult balance between preserving the existing urban character and encouraging an area's dynamism. In cities with a beloved architectural heritage, regulations often allow for near-total demolition of the interior of longstanding buildings so long as the façades are kept intact. Even external signage has been protected by ordinances and designated a tourist attraction, as in the case of New York's Times Square. Zakkyo building façades, by contrast, are always changing as businesses enter and exit—yet they maintain their overall character. The individual signs and billboards change, but you'll always recognize Yasukuni Avenue.

3.7.4   **Foster vertical economies of agglomeration**

Gathering together a range of diverse but often related establishments produces an economy of agglomeration, which fosters desirable cooperative competition between small business. As in yokochō, similar establishments within a given cluster of zakkyo buildings are in competition with each other for customers, but at the same time benefit from their mutual closeness, since it generates a sense of place that brings in more customers overall. As a result, zakkyo buildings offer a prime urban location for relatively small establishments. Although the most expensive areas of Tokyo are often dominated by franchises and chains, even zakkyo buildings in fairly central locations are full of independent and smaller businesses, allowing would-be entrepreneurs with only small amounts of capital to access a critical mass of the urban populace. With their surprisingly diverse array of offerings, zakkyo buildings serve as a vertical counterpart to the horizontal possibilities of the yokochō. Connecting small proprietors by little more than a small elevator down to the street, zakkyo buildings incubate idiosyncratic combinations of businesses and experiences that nurture urban diversity.

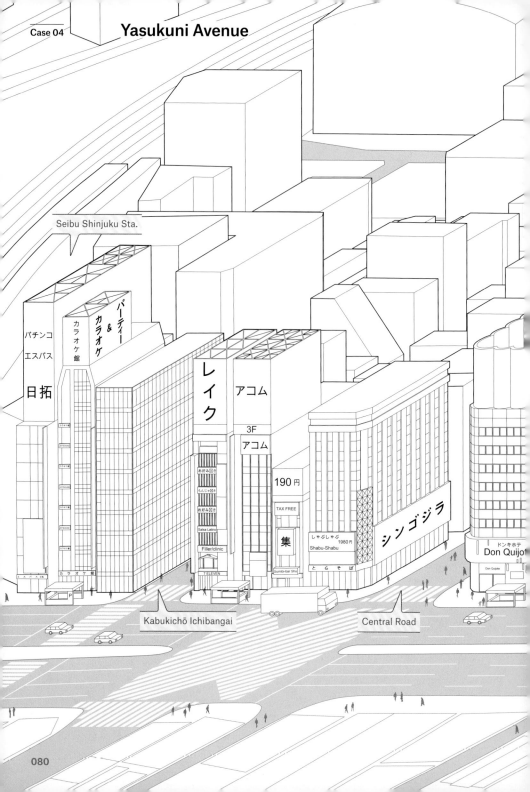

Yasukuni Avenue

Seibu Shinjuku Sta.

パチンコ
エスパス

日拓

カラオケ館

パーティー & カラオケ

レイク

アコム

3F

アコム

190 円

TAX FREE

集

シンゴジラ

しゃぶしゃぶ
1980円
Shabu-Shabu

ドンキホテ
Don Quijo

Don Quijote

お好み□
もんじゃ□
お好み□

Salsa Latino

Filler/clinic

カラオケ館

7 ELEVEN

Sumibi-bar Sho

と ら そ ば

Kabukichō Ichibangai

Central Road

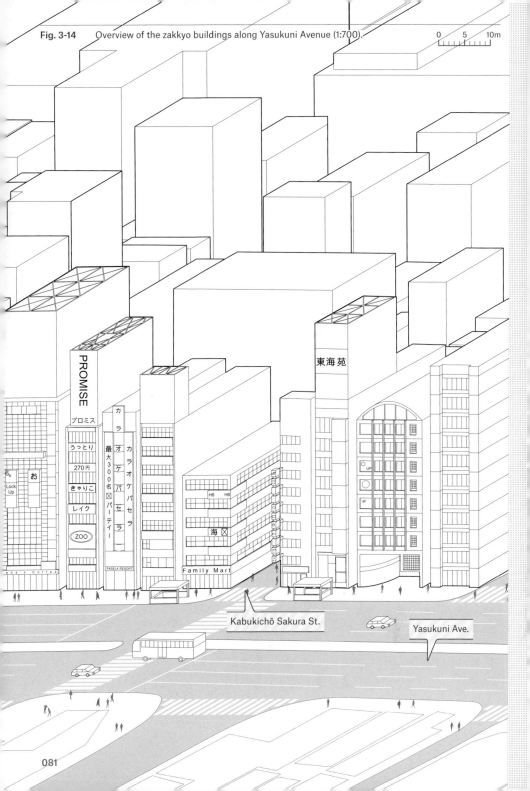

0 5 10m

PROMISE

プロミス

うっとり

270円

きゃりこ

レイク

ZOO

カラオケバセラ

カ
ラ
オ
ケ
パ
セ
ラ
ー

最
大
3
0
0
名
⊠
パ
ー
テ
イ
ー

PASELA RESORT

ZOO

お

Lock
Up

da's Coffee

HB   HB

海 ⊠

Family Mart

東海苑

UP

4F

Kabukichō Sakura St.

Yasukuni Ave.

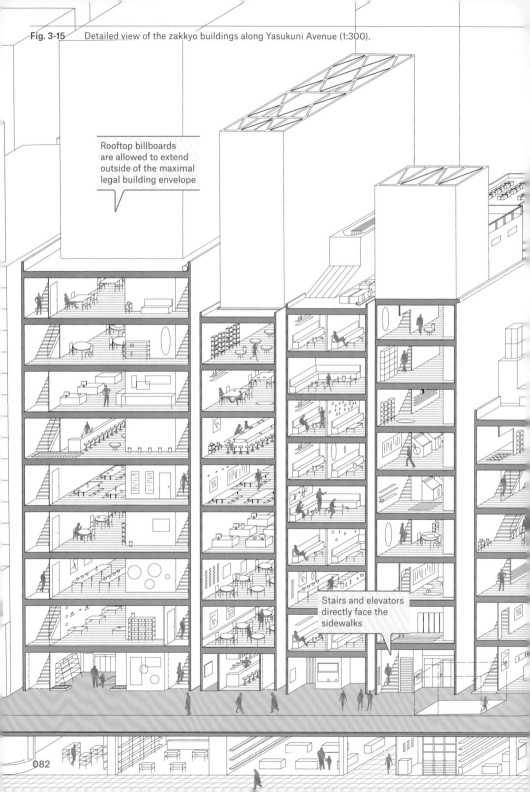

Fig. 3-15 Detailed view of the zakkyo buildings along Yasukuni Avenue (1:300).

Rooftop billboards are allowed to extend outside of the maximal legal building envelope

Stairs and elevators directly face the sidewalks

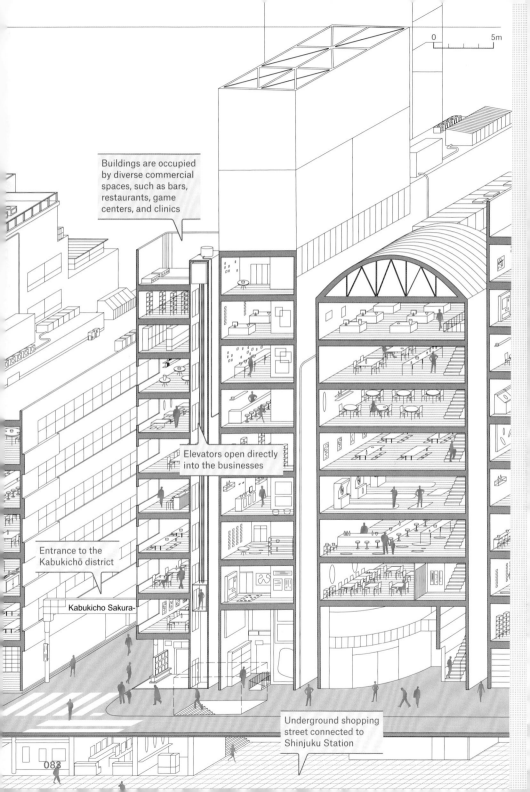

Buildings are occupied by diverse commercial spaces, such as bars, restaurants, game centers, and clinics

Elevators open directly into the businesses

Entrance to the Kabukichō district

Kabukicho Sakura-

Underground shopping street connected to Shinjuku Station

0   5m

Fig. 3-16 Analysis of the zakkyo buildings along the northern side of Yasukuni Avenue as of 2016 (1:1,500).

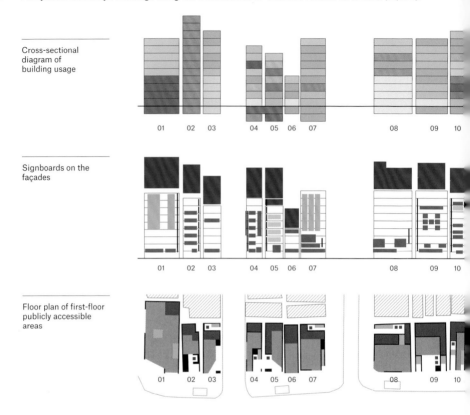

Cross-sectional diagram of building usage

Signboards on the façades

Floor plan of first-floor publicly accessible areas

Fig. 3-17 Façades of the zakkyo buildings along the northern side of Yasukuni Avenue as of August 2020.

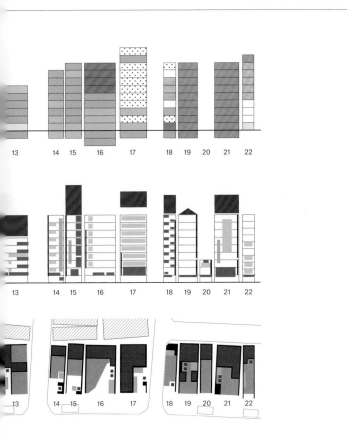

Bank
Money-lending
Other office type
Bar/Izakaya
Restaurant
Café
Retail
Clinic
Hair, nail salons, esthetician
Manga Kissa
Karaoke Box
Game center
Pachinko/mah-jong
Other
No data on store name
Non-rented, vacant space

■ Rooftop billboard
❘ Protuding billboard

Billboards on the façade:
Rigid
Hanging textile
Sticker on window

■ Elevator
▌ Stairs

Public ground floor
Private and opaque areas
Buildings not included
in the analysis

0   25m

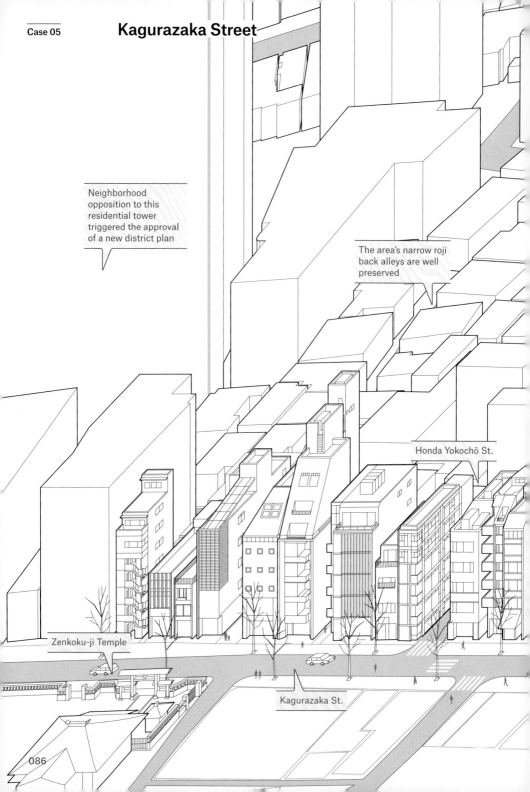

Kagurazaka Street

Neighborhood opposition to this residential tower triggered the approval of a new district plan

The area's narrow roji back alleys are well preserved

Honda Yokochō St.

Zenkoku-ji Temple

Kagurazaka St.

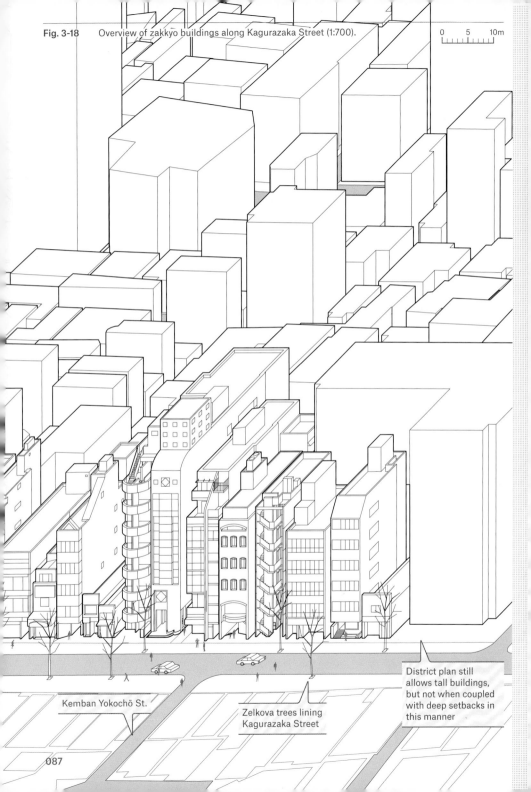

Fig. 3-18   Overview of zakkyo buildings along Kagurazaka Street (1:700).

0   5   10m

Kemban Yokochō St.

Zelkova trees lining
Kagurazaka Street

District plan still
allows tall buildings,
but not when coupled
with deep setbacks in
this manner

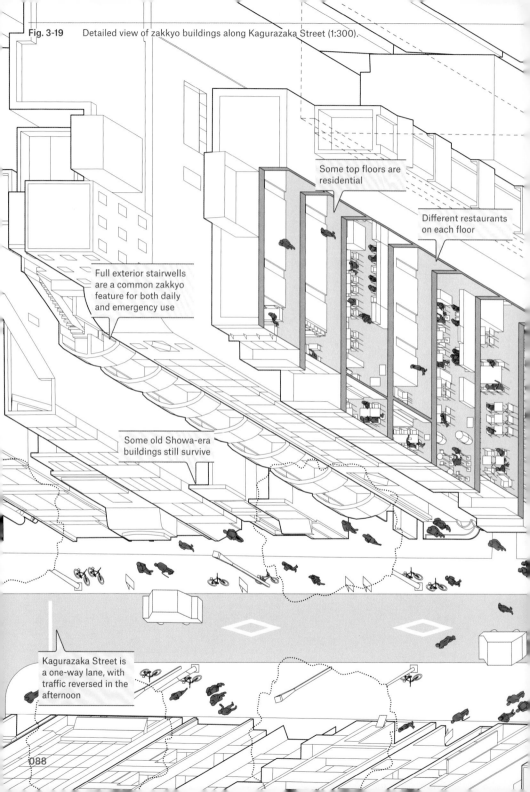

Some top floors are residential

Different restaurants on each floor

Full exterior stairwells are a common zakkyo feature for both daily and emergency use

Some old Showa-era buildings still survive

Kagurazaka Street is a one-way lane, with traffic reversed in the afternoon

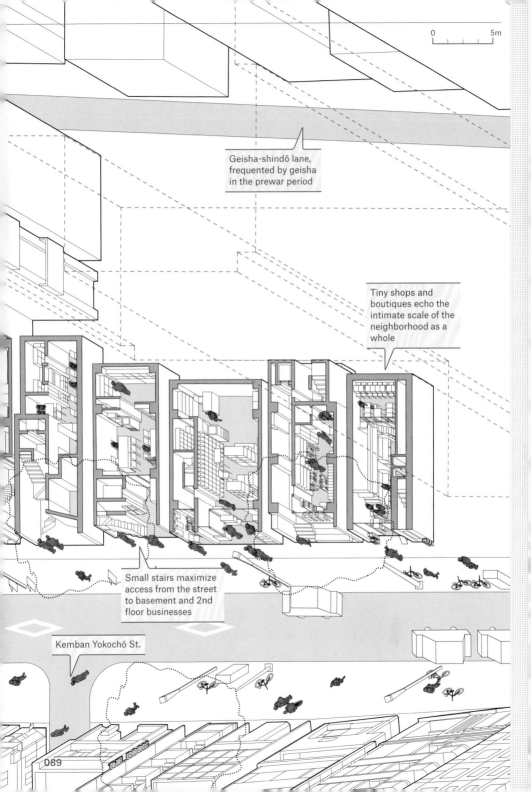

0   5m

Geisha-shindō lane, frequented by geisha in the prewar period

Tiny shops and boutiques echo the intimate scale of the neighborhood as a whole

Small stairs maximize access from the street to basement and 2nd floor businesses

Kemban Yokochō St.

Fig. 3-20   Analysis of zakkyo buildings along Kagurazaka Street as of 2020 (1:1,500).

Cross-sectional
diagram of
building usage

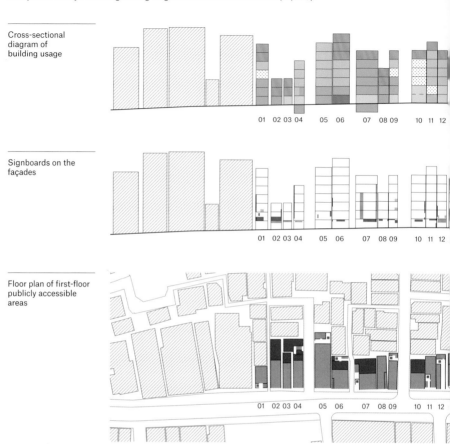

01 02 03 04   05   06   07   08 09   10   11 12

Signboards on the
façades

01 02 03 04   05   06   07   08 09   10   11 12

Floor plan of first-floor
publicly accessible
areas

01 02 03 04   05   06   07   08 09   10   11 12

Fig. 3-21   Façades of zakkyo buildings along Kagurazaka Street as of 2020.

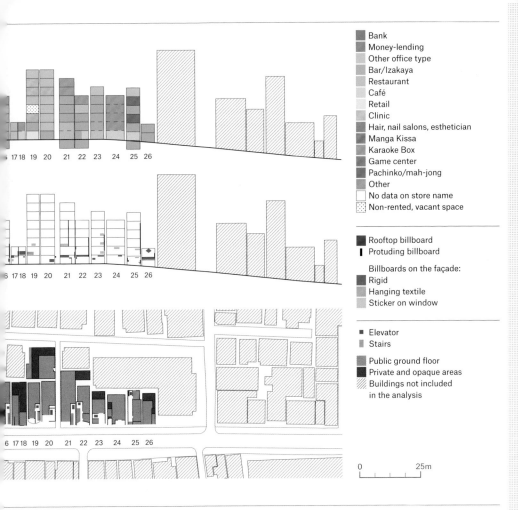

Bank
Money-lending
Other office type
Bar/Izakaya
Restaurant
Café
Retail
Clinic
Hair, nail salons, esthetician
Manga Kissa
Karaoke Box
Game center
Pachinko/mah-jong
Other
No data on store name
Non-rented, vacant space

Rooftop billboard
Protuding billboard

Billboards on the façade:
Rigid
Hanging textile
Sticker on window

Elevator
Stairs

Public ground floor
Private and opaque areas
Buildings not included
in the analysis

0 25m

17 18 19 20 21 22 23 24 25 26

Karasumori Block

Akarenga St.

Shimbashi Nakadōri St.

Karasumori St.

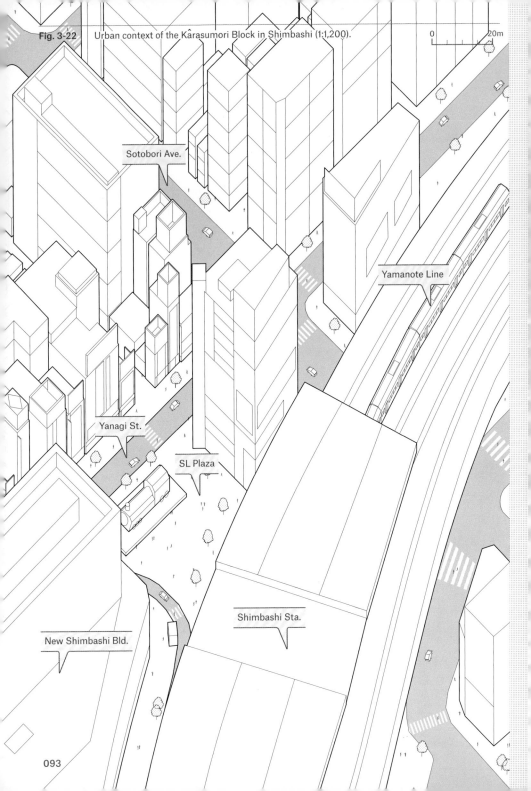

Fig. 3-22   Urban context of the Kârasumori Block in Shimbashi (1:1,200).

0   20m

Sotobori Ave.

Yamanote Line

Yanagi St.

SL Plaza

New Shimbashi Bld.

Shimbashi Sta.

Fig. 3-23   Detailed view of the Karasumori Block in Shimbashi (1:400).

Narrow alleys and low-rise buildings hide behind a perimeter of taller zakkyo buildings

Stairs and elevators accessed directly from street

Karasumori St.

Sandō pathway to the Karasumori Shrine

Karasumori Shrine: a site for the daily prayers of salarymen

Construction site

Yanagi St.

Last remaining bars of the postwar market

New Shimbashi Bld.: known as 'heaven for uncles' for its yokochō-like shops aimed at middle-aged men

0   5   10m

Fig. 3-24 Cross-sectional diagram of building usage and first-floor plan use of the Karasumori Block as of 2020 (1:1,500).

0   25m

Fig. 3-25 Floor plan of first-floor publicly accessible areas. Karasumori Block as of 2020 (1:1,500).

Fig. 3-26 Cross-sectional diagram of building usage through internal alleys. Karasumori Block as of 2020 (1:1,500).

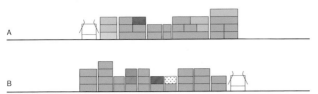

A

B

Bank
Money-lending
Other office type
Bar/Izakaya
Restaurant
Café
Retail
Clinic
Hair, nail salons, esthetician
Manga Kissa
Karaoke Box
Game center
Pachinko/mah-jong
Other
No data on store name
Non-rented, vacant space

Fig. 3-27 Façades of the Karasumori Block. Perimeter zakkyo buildings (above) and bar alleys (below) as of July 2020.

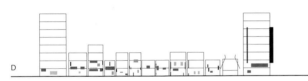

C

Rooftop billboard
Protuding billboard

Billboards on the façade:
Rigid
Hanging textile
Sticker on window

D

Elevator
Stairs

Public ground floor
Private and opaque areas
Buildings not included in the analysis

Fig. 3-28 Façades of the Karasumori Block. Perimeter zakkyo buildings (above) and bar alleys (below) as of July 2020.

C

4 UNDERTRACK INFILLS

高架下建築

Fig. 4-1 The undertrack spaces of Ameyoko as of June 2019.

4 UNDERTRACK INFILLS

4.1   What lies beneath

Tokyo has been sewn together by a dense network of rail infrastructure for over a century, with train stations serving as both gateways between areas and centers of commercial activity in their own right. The Yamanote Line, Tokyo's primary loop railway, forms the backbone of the city's urban geography. Inside the Yamanote Line, the city's train infrastructure consists mostly of subways; outside it, above-ground commuter railways stretch out radially from Yamanote Line stations toward the city's many residential suburbs. By the 1960s and 1970s, this elaborate web of railway tracks increasingly came into conflict with Japan's growing mass car culture.

Some Japanese railway operators have elevated sections of their railway track in order to avoid the dangers and traffic congestion that result when railways cross roadways at the same grade, particularly out in the suburbs. Elevated viaducts have some clear advantages over both ground-level tracks and subways; they avoid the downsides of sharing space with automobiles while at the same time generally being cheaper, faster to build, and easier to maintain than underground tracks.[70] However, elevated viaducts often have a substantial impact on the landscape and their adjacent communities, with vibrations and noise being the most common complaints.

Architecturally, such viaducts often disrupt the continuity of their cities in a different way; the spaces under their tracks become lifeless left-overs that sit largely unused. In many parts of Tokyo, however, a symbiosis has been reached between the needs of the transit network and pedestrian possibilities. The elevated tracks remain, but their undertrack spaces have been successfully developed and integrated into the existing urban fabric. Instead of a void, a journey under the tracks reveals lively restaurants, cozy shops, and even municipal services. This chapter explores the past, present, and future of these undertrack infills, uncovering the particular conditions that have allowed them to become some of the city's best magnets of human activity.

Tokyo's undertrack infills appear both in central and suburban areas. They are mostly found under railways, but can appear under highways as well. The key quality of the best undertrack infills, such as Ameyoko in Tokyo's northeast, is their permeability—they allow members of the public to easily enter and leave as they please, and are thoroughly incorporated into a broader street-level context Fig. 4-1. Unfortunately, however, many recent infill projects fail to understand—or willfully ignore—the design principles that have allowed Tokyo's most lively undertrack spaces to stand the test of time, with correspondingly lackluster results.[71]

The city's most famous undertrack infills are mainly found in Local and Mercantile Tokyo neighborhoods along the eastern stretch of the Yamanote Line, though the city's many private suburban commuter lines have undertrack spaces of their own Fig. 4-2. Their specifics vary considerably Fig. 4-3, but collectively they offer a breadth of possibilities to the public rarely seen in similar contexts outside of Japan.[72]

4.2   A century of undertrack spaces

Tokyo's oldest infill spaces originated from elevated railways built before World War II, with the earliest example being the stretch of the Yamanote loop between Hamamatsuchō and Ueno Stations built between 1910 and 1914, and the last major prewar railway elevation project concluding in the 1930s. Many of these elevated railways were occupied by black markets after the war, and some were given over to returnees from Japan's lost imperial territories as spaces to open small businesses.[73] The most famous case of this, Ameyoko, is discussed in greater detail later in this chapter. As these spaces have evolved over the decades, they have taken on an almost organic character Fig. 4-4.

After World War II, it was nearly twenty years before Tokyo's next elevated viaducts opened in the early 1960s. Japan's Golden Sixties begat a viaduct boom that lasted roughly a decade. Many of the railways connecting Tokyo to its residential suburbs were elevated, in keeping with a national policy of 'grade separation' that pushed local authorities to minimize railway road crossings by either elevating trains or moving them underground.[74] Unlike the more spontaneous and incremental colonization of pre-existing undertrack spaces in Ja-

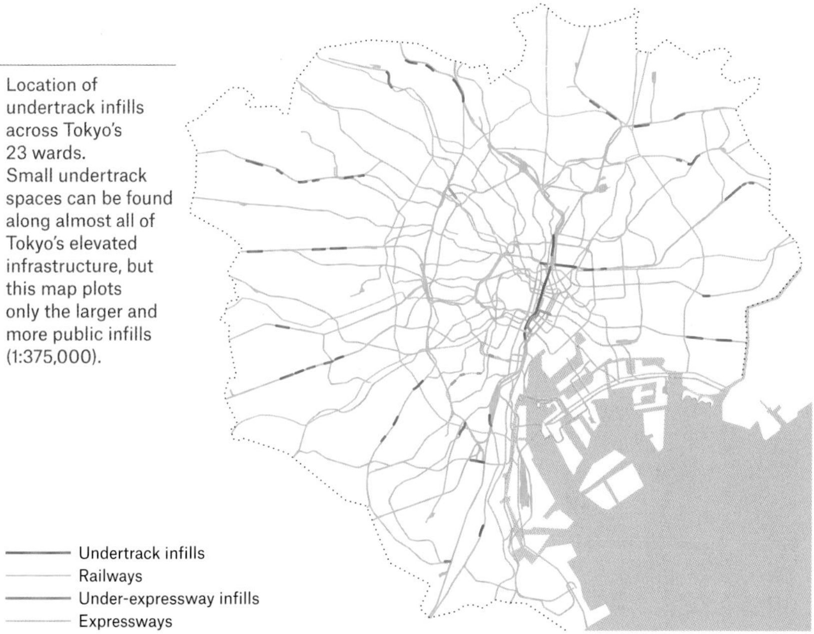

Fig. 4-2   Location of undertrack infills across Tokyo's 23 wards. Small undertrack spaces can be found along almost all of Tokyo's elevated infrastructure, but this map plots only the larger and more public infills (1:375,000).

———— Undertrack infills
———— Railways
———— Under-expressway infills
———— Expressways

Fig. 4-3   Types of undertrack spaces in Tokyo.

A   Permeable infills of prewar undertrack spaces. Example: Ameyoko in Taitō Ward. Railways built in 1883 and elevated in 1925.

Photograph: September 2018.

B   Shōtengai-style undertrack infills of the 1960s and 1970s. Example: Kōenji Station in Suginami Ward. Railways built in 1889 and elevated in 1966.

Photograph: October 2019.

C   Shopping-mall-style undertrack infills from the 1980s onward. Example: Nakamurabashi Station in Nerima Ward. Railways built in 1924 and elevated in 1997.

Photograph: January 2019.

D   Newly renovated undertrack infills since the 2010s. Example: Nakameguro Station in Meguro Ward. Built as elevated railways in 1927 and later renovated in 2016.

Photograph: June 2019.

E   Under-expressway infills. Example: Ginza Corridor in Chūō Ward. Built as part of a chain of commercial buildings under the elevated Tokyo Expressway in the 1960s.

Photograph: February 2020.

pan's postwar black market period, the newly elevated railways of the 1960s and 1970s were planned and built with the commercial use of undertrack space explicitly in mind.

Some projects of this era merely offered an identical series of generic commercial spaces with no overarching plan to give them context. However, many others were designed to fill the more communal role of the traditional Japanese neighborhood shopping streets known as *shōtengai* by offering a coherent collection of independent shops in layouts designed to welcome residents from the surrounding neighborhood. The latter strategy has stood the test of time admirably. Undertrack spaces in neighborhoods like bohemian Kōenji have become important fixtures of their communities by offering a high degree of urban permeability and fitting smoothly into the surrounding built environment Fig. 4-5.

Tokyo's infill spaces aren't limited to the city's train tracks. In the 1960 and 1970s, Tokyo hurriedly built a serpentine network of elevated expressways in preparation for the 1964 Olympics, covering over numerous existing streets, rivers, and canals in the process. There are some instances of urban infills under these expressways, although their number is dwarfed by those under railways. One such space, the Ginza Corridor Fig. 4-6, is discussed below in detail.

In subsequent decades the construction of elevated railways continued apace, but their infill commercial spaces took on dramatically different forms. From the 1980s through the early 2000s, nearly all new undertrack spaces were designed as centrally operated, windowless, and inward-looking shopping malls without easy access to their external surroundings. Several stations along the Seibu Ikebukuro Line, like Nakamurabashi Station, exemplify this trend.

In recent years Tokyo's planners and urbanists have taken a renewed interest in undertrack spaces, and a new wave of renovations emerged in the 2010s. Many still follow the shopping-mall model of blank façades and centralized management, like the sleek 2K540 Aki-Oka shopping boulevard under the northeast stretch of the Yamanote Line. But there are also infill renovation projects that consciously engage with their surroundings by featuring independent shops and facing outward toward the street, such as those built around the Nakameguro, Gakugei Daigaku, and Ōsaki-Hirokōji Stations.

4.3   Ameyoko: old-school shopping under the railways

Case 07

Ameyoko, officially known as the *Ameyoko Shōtengai* or 'Ameyoko shopping street,' is a roughly 500 m long shopping district that encompasses over 400 shops in densely packed quarters under the elevated JR lines between Ueno and Okachimachi Stations in Tokyo's northeast. Originally a black market, Ameyoko developed over time into a commercial space that brings together clothing and other shops with bars and eateries and is today a popular tourist destination. Despite the noise, vibrations, and other challenges of being located under multiple major transit lines, the numerous small establishments that call Ameyoko home have collectively built a hub of activity that draws both neighbors and visitors in large numbers Figs. 4-7, 8.

The Tokyo-Ueno railway opened in 1914 and initially ran along the ground. However, in the aftermath of the Great Kantō earthquake of 1923, concerns about the risk of fires at track crossings led the government to elevate the railway.[75] Before World War II the resulting undertrack space was initially occupied by houses. An electric transformer substation with a degree of military importance was located under the tracks as well, making the area the target of frequent air raids during the war. The Tokyo Metropolitan Government evacuated its residents as a result, leaving the spaces empty by the war's end.[76]

As with almost all of Tokyo's major train stations, black markets soon sprouted up around Ueno Station following the end of the war, including in the undertrack spaces. When the forcible removal of these street stalls began in 1949, businessman Kondō Hirokichi organized and built a market of temporary shelters in their stead. The Kondō Market was the predecessor of the current Ameyoko Center Building and consisted of 80 subdivided stalls, each occupying 1.5 *tsubo* (4.9 m²) of space. Following its example, a returnees' association received permission from the authorities to subdivide the undertrack area into equal subdivisions of 1 *ken* (180 cm) in width.[77] They set up stalls which over the years transformed into combined residence-shops with stores on the first floor and residential space for the store proprietor on the second. After minor adjustments over the intervening years, the current configuration of Ameyoko appeared in 1983 when the site of the former electric substation was redeveloped and renamed Ameyoko Plaza. Food stores are located mainly along the outer edges, with clothing stores lining the internal passages. Most stores are individually owned, but franchises, convenience stores, and supermarkets can also be found Figs. 4-9 to 11. The whole area preserves an atmosphere similar to many urban markets of Europe, with shops expanding into the streets to display their wares and restaurants setting chairs and tables outside.

In the popular telling, Ameyoko's lively atmosphere arose organically from postwar squatters and black marketeers. This certainly happened in its early days, but before long Ameyoko was also being shaped by formal urban planning. Contrary to the popular image of postwar chaos, the plans involved the collaboration of locals, the JR Corporation railway company, and the authorities. If anything, the more important factor in Ameyoko's current state has been its atomized micro-plots. The undertrack area was subdivided into equally sized lots and tenants were given their autonomy: unlike the average shopping mall, there was no centralized management, no themed interiors, no branding strategy. Despite—or perhaps because of—this laissez-faire approach, Ameyoko has maintained its commercial vitality for over half a century, a track record that would be the envy of any contemporary shopping mall operator.

4.4   Kōenji: finding the slow life in a fast city

Case 08

The undertrack infills of Kōenji Station form the core of one of Tokyo's most famously bohemian communities. Kōenji is a suburban station along Tokyo's iconic Chūō Line located less than ten minutes' ride from Shinjuku station.

Fig. 4-4 The evolution of Ameyoko (1:6,000).

0   100m

1940

Houses and an electric substation occupy much of the undertrack area that would later become Ameyoko.

Source: *Kasaihoken Tokushuchizu* (Toshisei-zusha, 1940).

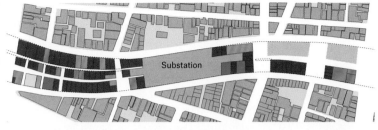

1951

The area has been reorganized as a cluster of small stores, following the Kondō Market's pioneering example.

Source: *Kasaihoken Tokushuchizu* (Toshisei-zusha, 1951).

1970

Land subdivisions have been reorganized in order to better occupy the full undertrack area.

Source: *Zenkōkū Jūtaku Chizu* (Kōkyō Shisetsu Chizu Kōkū, 1970).

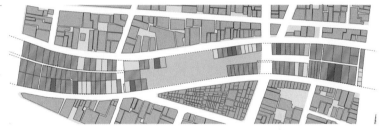

1981

The former substation has been occupied by new bars and restaurants and new pedestrian passages have been created.

Source: *Jūtakuchizu* (Zenrin, 1981).

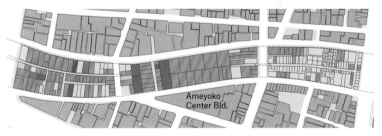

2018

With the completion of Ameyoko Plaza in 1983, Ameyoko finally reaches its current configuration.

Source: *Jūtakuchizu* (Zenrin, 2018).

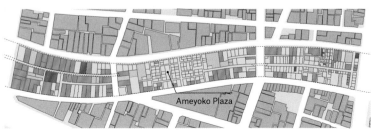

Office / public facility   Retail   Residences   Vacant store

Bar / restaurant   Service / entertainment   Substation

Despite this proximity, Kōenji developed a laid-back culture of independent stores, eateries, and live music houses that attracts Tokyoites interested in living affordably at their own pace. In Kōenji, one feels a world away from the busy office districts and high-class shopping streets of the Yamanote loop.[78]

The Kōenji area is one of many suburban developments that date to the 1920s, along with areas such as Nishi-Ogikubo and Higashi-Nakanobu which are discussed elsewhere in this book. These new communities were conceptualized around the simultaneous development of railway networks and real estate, a model created by the Hankyū Railways corporation in western Japan a decade earlier. Only a year after the opening of Kōenji Station, the Great Kantō earthquake sparked a mass movement of Tokyo's population away from the destroyed areas toward the city's western suburbs, turbo-charging the growth of communities along the Chūō Line.

In 1966 Kōenji Station was one of many stretches of suburban track elevated as part the government's grade separation policy. Unlike many other undertrack developments created in the 1960s, however, its undertrack spaces were not designed as a shopping mall. Instead, they followed the model of the shōtengai and built a commercial promenade designed to host independent stores.

The undertrack areas extend both east and west from the station exit, but it is primarily the west side that embodies Kōenji's free and open atmosphere Figs. 4-12, 13. An internal corridor of 200 m runs along the infill, accommodating 74 bars, restaurants, and stores. Both the corridor and the street are full of tables and chairs from the various restaurants and bars, creating the feeling of a single collective space Figs. 4-14 to 16. The clientele are not the hard-drinking salary-men of Shinjuku's office district, nor the classy and sophisticated denizens of Ginza. Instead of a demographic monoculture, locals and visitors of all ages and backgrounds dine in an unpretentious and undecorated space that epitomizes the district's character—a landscape of tables, chairs, people, and food among the bare concrete columns of the elevated tracks.

The future of the west undertrack space is uncertain but hopeful. Although the surrounding streets are full of businesses, some vacant spaces are starting to appear in the undertrack area; as in almost all shōtengai in Japan, business owners are aging and it is difficult to find successors. Nevertheless, Kōenji is a desirable location and before long new tenants will likely take their place. The main challenge to the undertrack area's continuity today is rising rental fees on spaces owned by the JR Corporation, a trend which threatens to push out its idiosyncratic small businesses.[79] The public's renewed interest in Tokyo's undertrack spaces has not gone unnoticed by the real estate industry. The attractive character of undertrack areas as urban dens, intimate and hidden yet centrally located, have made them a target of redevelopment. The highly subdivided land ownership of the broader Kōenji district has so far impeded large-scale redevelopment, but it remains to be seen whether its undertrack space, which is owned by a single company, will be able to resist becoming yet another shopping mall.

Fig. 4-5   The evolution of Kōenji Station's undertrack infills (1:6,000).

0   100m

1949   After the 1922 station opening, the surrounding area soon becomes a residential community.
Source: *Kasaihoken Tokushuchizu* (Toshiseizusha, 1949).

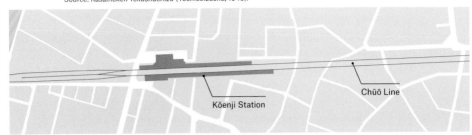

Kōenji Station

Chūō Line

1962   The area recovers from the war and densifies. In the 1950s, rotaries are created on both sides of
the station. Source: *Tokyō-to Zenjūtaku Annaizuchō* (Jūtakukyōkai 1962).

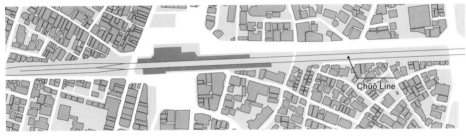

Chūō Line

1971   The rail tracks were elevated in 1966. Their undertrack space soon integrates into the local
commercial network. Source: *Zenkōkū Jūtaku Chizu* (Kōkyō Shisetsu Chizu Kōkū, 1971).

Loop Road No.7

2018   Since its completion, Kōenji's undertrack spaces have continuously expanded east and west of
the station. Source: *Jūtakuchizu* (Zenrin, 2018).

■ Office / public facility	░ Retail	▢ Vacant store
■ Bar / restaurant	■ Service / entertainment	□ Parking

Ginza Corridor: courtship under the expressway

One of Tokyo's hottest spots for finding late-night romance is under an expressway. Ginza Corridor (formally known as the Yamashita Building) is a 12 m deep and 420 m long undertrack area lining the western edge of Tokyo's luxurious Ginza district, tucked away between the Yamanote Line stations of Shimbashi to the south and Yurakuchō to the north Fig. 4-17. The corridor and its adjacent street have become, in the wonderfully euphemistic parlance of the Japanese media, a "holy land for encounters."[80] Although its fame is recent, the undertrack area has always been actively used in some form or another, transforming and adapting over the decades along with the fortunes of the neighborhood.

In 1951 a group of influential businessmen created a private company, the *Tōkyō Kōsoku Dōro*, to build a new form of hybrid architecture that would simultaneously serve as both a shopping center and an expressway.[81] Using land parallel to the Yamanote Line that was once an outer moat of old Edo the tycoons established a public-private partnership to build commercial buildings connected at the top by 2 km of elevated expressway as their shared roof.[82] To this day, rental fees from the tenants in the commercial buildings are used to finance the expressway above.

The Ginza Corridor/Yamashita Building was the first of these buildings to start construction work in 1953 and is the longest of the bunch. Its design also differs significantly from the rest. Most of the others are elongated shopping malls that route pedestrians through an internal corridor, as in so many Ginza properties. The Yamashita Building, by contrast, does not internalize circulation; its storefronts open directly onto the street. The regularly spaced pillars, high ceilings, and wide spans of the expressway's concrete structure provide a flexible framework within which interior spaces can be easily changed. Initially, most of the building's tenants were offices, but over time they were replaced by restaurants and bars and the area has naturally taken on a more social character Fig. 4-18. [83]

This dynamism and ease of evolution stands in stark contrast with other buildings of the *Tōkyō Kōsoku Dōro*. An adjacent shopping mall known as Ginza Five, for example, was built at the same time as Ginza Corridor by the very same company. As is so often the case with malls, Ginza Five felt modern when inaugurated but has failed to adapt with the times and now feels dated and run-down. Ginza Corridor, by contrast, still exudes a palpable liveliness after all these years. This is in part due to its high integration with its surroundings, a long stretch of undertrack spaces that includes both the prewar elevated Yamanote Line and vestiges of old postwar markets around Yurakuchō Station Figs. 4-19 to 21.

Although there are restaurants lining both sides of the street, most people congregate and walk along the expressway—after all, that side is where the action is. As young groups of men and women walking along the sidewalk in a search of a restaurant or a drink, the open path allows them to see and be seen by potential suitors. The dated stereotype of the typical Japanese as shy and indirect—a trope often perpetuated by many Japanese themselves—does not with-

Fig. 4-6   The evolution of Ginza Corridor (1:6,000).

0   100m

1934

The first stretch of the Yamanote Line was built here, as elevated tracks running along the old outer moat (*sotobori*) of Edo Castle.

Source: *Kasaihoken Tokushuchizu* (Toshiseizusha, 1934, 1932).

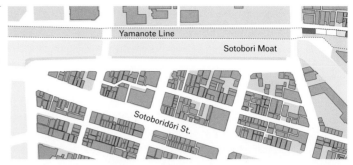

1958

The moat has disappeared, covered over by railways and the *Tōkyō Kōsoku Dōro*'s commercial buildings.

Source: *Tōkyō-to Zenjūtaku Annaizuchō* (Nihon Jūtaku Kyōkai, 1958).

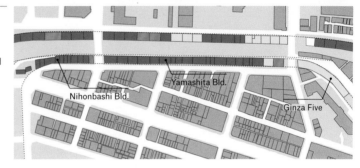

1990

Ginza Corridor's spaces have been gradually transformed from their initial use as office space into bars and eateries.

Source: *Jūtakuchizu* (Zenrin, 1990).

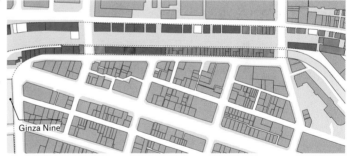

2019

Today, Ginza Corridor hosts 54 establishments under the expressway distributed across two floors and a basement. The area has become a popular dining spot, attracting redevelopment projects to surrounding undertrack spaces which hope to emulate Ginza Corridor's success.

Source: *Jūtakuchizu* (Zenrin, 2019).

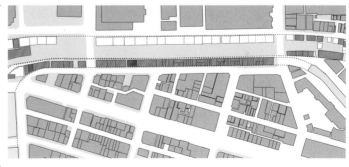

■ Office / public facility	▨ Retail □ Under construction
■ Bar / restaurant	■ Service □ Parking

stand a quick visit to Ginza Corridor. The norms of social behavior are relaxed and alcohol serves as a welcome social lubricant, with men and women brazenly engaging each other on the street for conversation, dining, drinking, and romances of various durations.

This style of social encounter along an uninterrupted street lined with eateries or cafés is a common sight elsewhere in the world but unusual in Tokyo. The traditional habit of the Sunday *paseo* in Spanish cities or the Italian evening *passeggiata* consists of strolling to explore the city's possibilities in a similar fashion, preferably along promenades lined with bars or cafés. Strolling provides a layer of healthy ambiguity, allowing for both chance encounters and the means to escape them; one can stop and talk if a stranger catches the eye, or just as easily continue walking on the pretense that they are just passing through.

Ginza Corridor's success has attracted imitators, and many of its surrounding undertrack areas are now under reconstruction.[84] In Tokyo, any approach to urban space that stands out as dynamic and successful is swiftly repackaged and commercialized by large-scale real estate operations. In doing so, however, they often lose the magic they're trying to capture; their top-down managerial styles and highly centralized decision-making culture gets imprinted onto the urban spaces they redevelop, resulting in tightly controlled and homogenized areas. To be fair, the Yamashita Building is also a centrally managed undertrack space; many of its outlets belong to nation-wide franchises that lack the idiosyncratic freshness of Ameyoko and Kōenji. Nevertheless, its architectural design has allowed it—intentionally or not—to adapt to changing surroundings, generating a bustling street space that brings economic benefits to its owners while enabling social experimentation.

4.6 Learning from undertrack infills

Undertrack infills can transform the shadowy, noisy spaces created by elevated infrastructure into something uniquely valuable. Their capacity to integrate into the surrounding city, or to perhaps even become local attractions in their own right like Ameyoko, derives from their permeability and their openness—both physical and visual—to their surroundings. For the rest of the world, there is plenty to learn from Tokyo's experience.

4.6.1 Leave room for organic growth and connect to the surrounding urban context

Undertrack infills are most vibrant when they are populated by numerous small businesses rather than operated as a centrally controlled shopping mall, as the latter tend to create closed off interior spaces with little ability to surprise or inspire. The undertrack areas of the 1980s and 1990s serve as a cautionary tale in this regard; although they make productive use of undertrack space that would otherwise be abandoned, their closed nature impedes the flow of pedestrians through their surrounding neighborhoods. The cases discussed in this chapter, by contrast, show how an idiosyncratic collection of shops that connect to their surroundings can both liven up an area and draw safety-enhancing "eyes on the street," in the famous words of Jane Jacobs.[85]

4.6.2   Concentrate, don't centralize

Undertrack infills and shopping malls both achieve a high degree of commercial density, but infills arrive at their density in a very different fashion. The best undertrack infills remain decentralized even as they become dense, with permeable access to the outside world. By preserving their connections to public space and avoiding the physical centralization of internal plazas and atriums, they feed off of the energy and social spontaneity of Tokyo's lively streets.

For real estate investors obsessed with short-term profits, undertrack infills may not be as attractive as a tightly managed shopping mall designed to keep consumers within its closed ecosystem. But from the perspective of ordinary people, they maintain all the consumer choice of a mall while offering more freedom of movement and social spontaneity. In the long term, this may actually make them more profitable—their flexibility allows them to endure through the decades by adapting to changing times and needs, outlasting generations of boom and bust by sleeker mall developments.

4.6.3   Instead of cannibalizing the local economy, build economies of agglomeration

Shopping mall-style undertrack infills aim to capture the disposable income of commuters before they even venture outside of the station. Often they are both literally and figuratively windowless, keeping the surrounding community's businesses out of sight and out of mind as thoroughly as possible. In these homogenized spaces, the spontaneity and unpredictability of small independent businesses are not welcome, and station shopping malls often directly cannibalize the customer base of surrounding local shops. Permeable undertrack infills, even those of the 1960s and 1970s, generally manage to avoid this economic vampirism and have a positive impact on their surroundings. They frequently adopt a yokochō-like configuration of small spaces with multiple independent managers. In these spaces, the general trend is toward creating economies of agglomeration, wherein businesses with a similar type, theme, or demographic target cluster together. In an economy of agglomeration, vendors compete with their neighbors in a narrow sense but also cooperate with them to attract customers, working together to build up the desirability of the location as a destination in its own right. This approach results in places with distinctive character, as seen in the exuberant food and fashion stores of Ameyoko, the relaxed izakayas of Kōenji, or the flirtatious, frisson-filled bar-hopping of Ginza Corridor.

4.6.4   Pay attention to the active edges of infill spaces

Unlike the limited entrances and exits of a shopping mall, successful undertrack infill shops tend to brush up directly against public space in a manner that allows passers-by to drop in easily. Without this connectivity, these dark and shadowy spaces tend to become abandoned and unwelcoming. Successful infills can animate otherwise dreary stretches of the street by combining human-scale commerce with a sensation of secluded urban intimacy, transforming that initial disadvantage into an attractive slice of the cityscape.

Ameyoko

To Ueno Sta.

Shinkansen tracks

Ameya Yokochō St.

Ueno Park

Chūō Ave.

Fig. 4-7 Urban context of Ameyoko (1:1,200).

0   10   20   30m

Yamanote Line

Ameyoko Plaza

Ameyoko Center Building

To Okachimachi Sta.

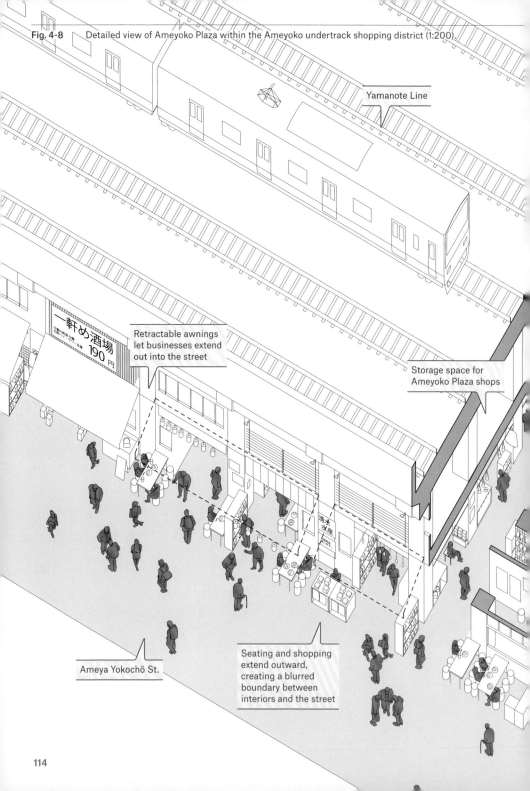

Fig. 4-8   Detailed view of Ameyoko Plaza within the Ameyoko undertrack shopping district (1:200).

Yamanote Line

一軒め酒場
190円

Retractable awnings
let businesses extend
out into the street

Storage space for
Ameyoko Plaza shops

清水水産

Ameya Yokochō St.

Seating and shopping
extend outward,
creating a blurred
boundary between
interiors and the street

Undertrack spaces seamlessly connect to the street

Okachimachi Ekimae Street

Shelves full of products serve as natural boundaries within the corridors

Ameyoko Plaza's small shops fit neatly within the structural grid supporting the train tracks above

The warrens of Ameyoko Plaza hold numerous small shops

Fig. 4-9   Ameyoko: section A (1:400).

Key plan

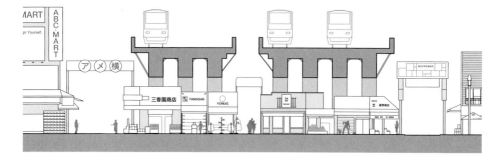

Fig. 4-11   Ameyoko: street-level use map (1:2,500). Source: Fieldwork in October 2018 and the map *Jūtakuchizu* (Zenrin, 2018).

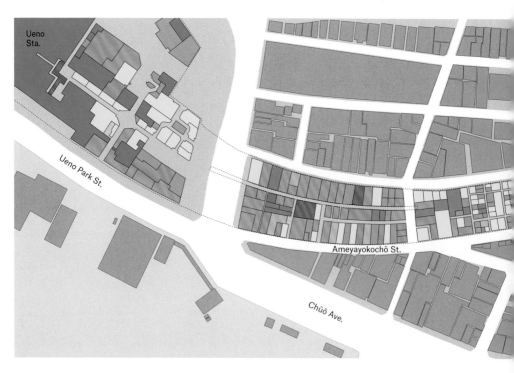

Fig. 4-10   Ameyoko: section B through the Ameyoko Plaza (1:400).

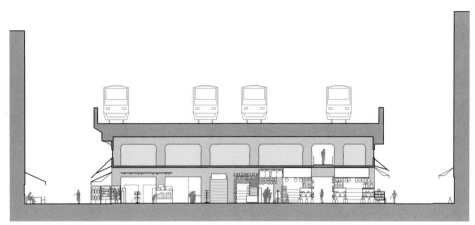

Office / station

Jewelry / accessories

Bar / restaurant

Sports store

Grocery store

Service / entertainment

Pharmacy

Vacant store

Fashion store

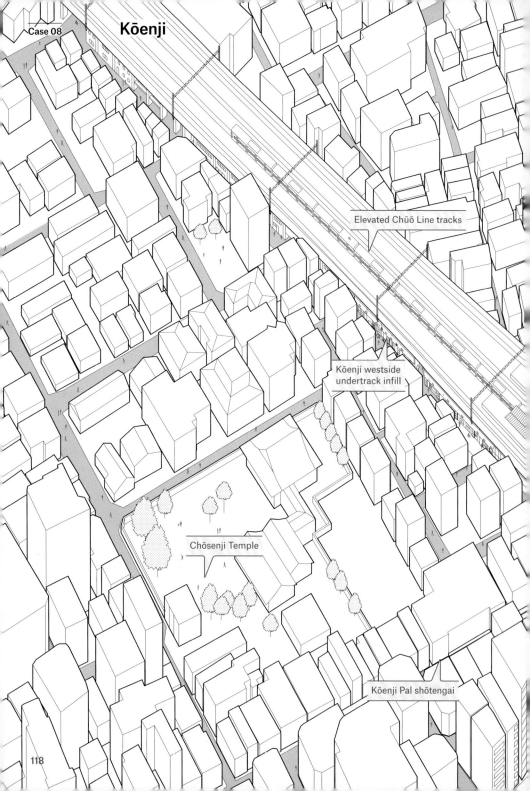

Kōenji

Elevated Chūō Line tracks

Kōenji westside undertrack infill

Chōsenji Temple

Kōenji Pal shōtengai

Fig. 4-12   Urban context of the Kōenji Station west area (1:1,200).

0   10   20   30m

Kōenji Nakadōri St.

Kōenji Sta.

Geijutsukaikan St.

Konan St.

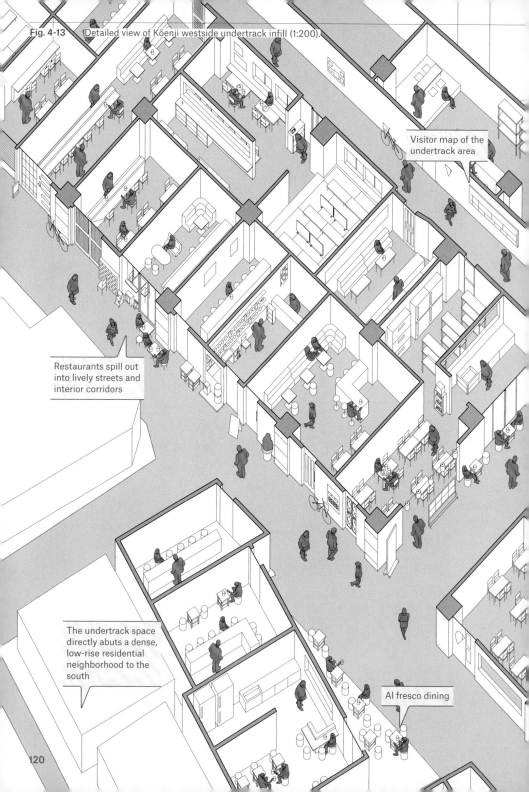

Fig. 4-13   (Detailed view of Kōenji westside undertrack infill (1:200).

Visitor map of the undertrack area

Restaurants spill out into lively streets and interior corridors

The undertrack space directly abuts a dense, low-rise residential neighborhood to the south

Al fresco dining

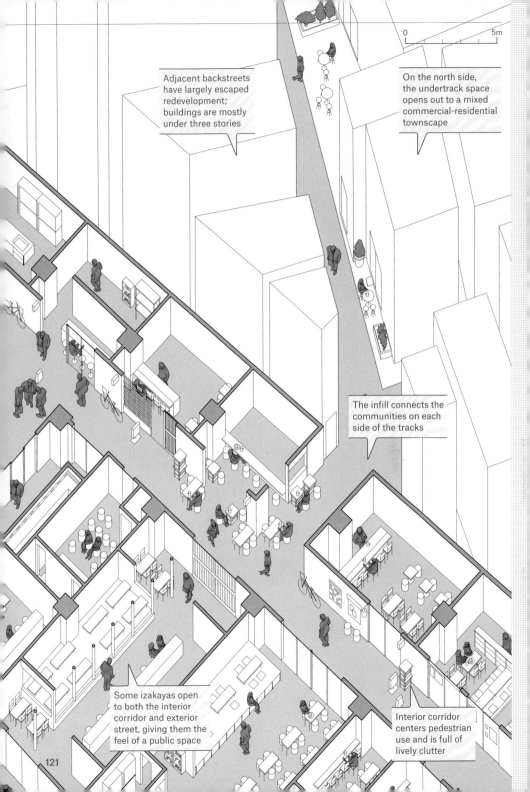

Adjacent backstreets have largely escaped redevelopment; buildings are mostly under three stories

On the north side, the undertrack space opens out to a mixed commercial-residential townscape

The infill connects the communities on each side of the tracks

Some izakayas open to both the interior corridor and exterior street, giving them the feel of a public space

Interior corridor centers pedestrian use and is full of lively clutter

0   5m

Fig. 4-14 Kōenji undertrack infills: section A (1:400).

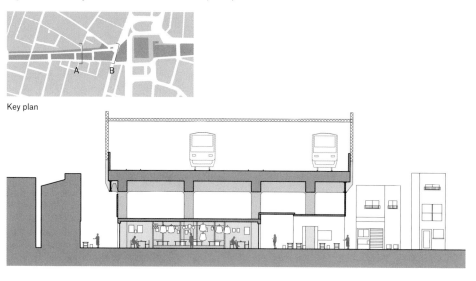

Key plan

Fig. 4-16 Kōenji undertrack infills: street-level use map (1:2,500).
Source: Fieldwork in November 2018 and the map *Jūtakuchizu* (Zenrin, 2018).

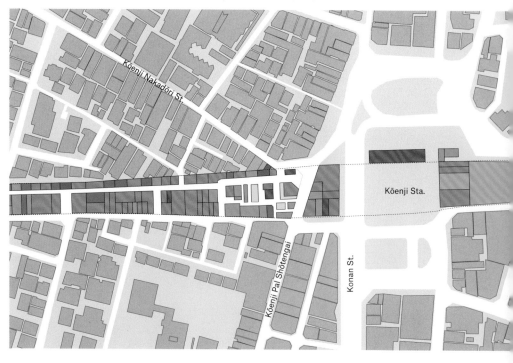

Fig. 4-15 Kōenji undertrack infills: section B (1:400).

0 5 10m

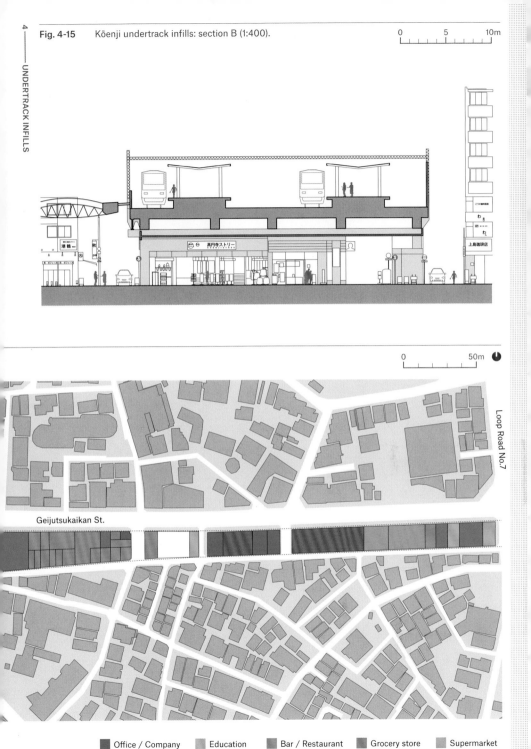

Geijutsukaikan St.

Loop Road No.7

0 50m

■ Office / Company	■ Education	■ Bar / Restaurant	■ Grocery store	■ Supermarket
■ Fashion store	■ Other retail	■ Service	■ Vacant store	☐ Parking

Ginza Corridor

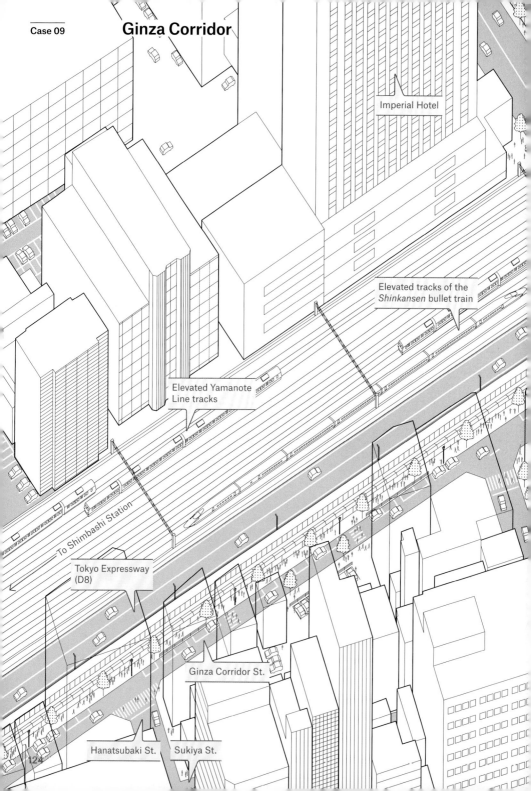

Imperial Hotel

Elevated tracks of the *Shinkansen* bullet train

Elevated Yamanote Line tracks

To Shimbashi Station

Tokyo Expressway (D8)

Ginza Corridor St.

Hanatsubaki St.

Sukiya St.

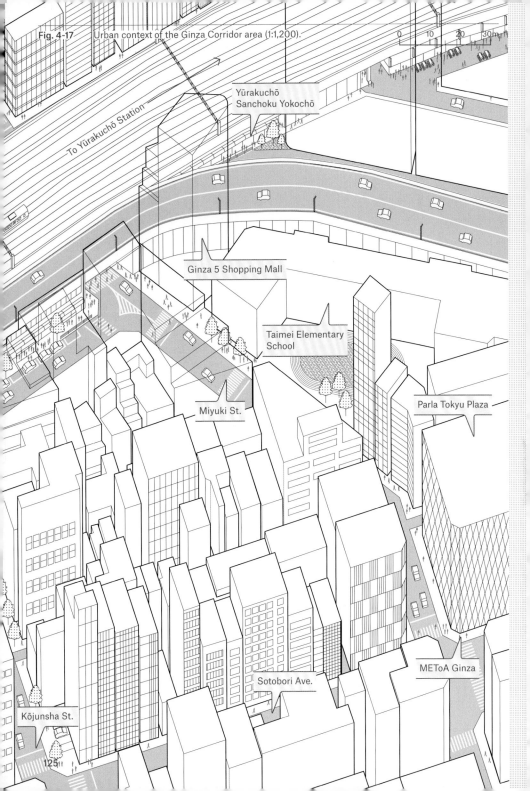

Fig. 4-17 Urban context of the Ginza Corridor area (1:1,200).

To Yūrakuchō Station

Yūrakuchō Sanchoku Yokochō

Ginza 5 Shopping Mall

Taimei Elementary School

Miyuki St.

Parla Tokyu Plaza

Sotobori Ave.

METoA Ginza

Kōjunsha St.

0   10   20   30m

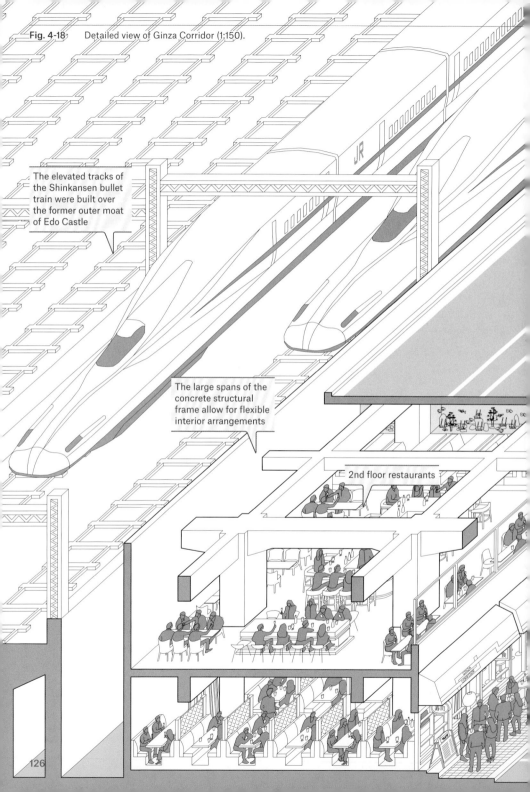

Fig. 4-18 Detailed view of Ginza Corridor (1:150).

The elevated tracks of the Shinkansen bullet train were built over the former outer moat of Edo Castle

The large spans of the concrete structural frame allow for flexible interior arrangements

2nd floor restaurants

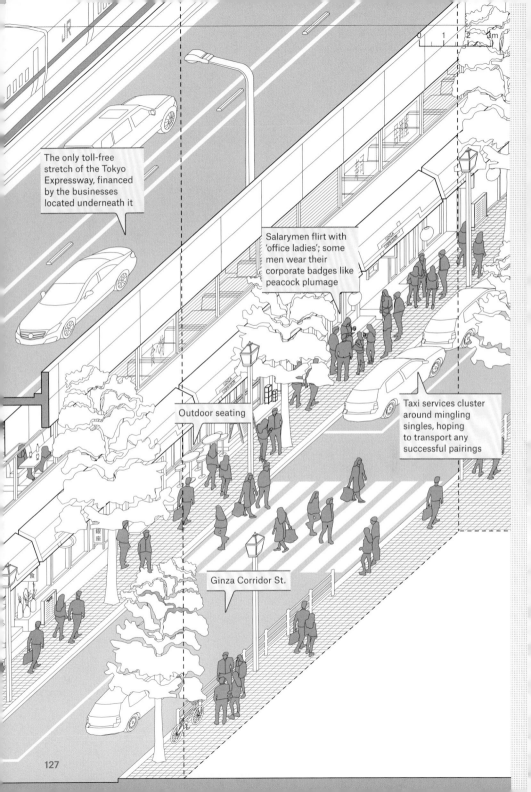

Fig. 4-19   Ginza Corridor and Yamanote Line: section A (1:400).

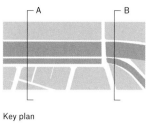

Key plan

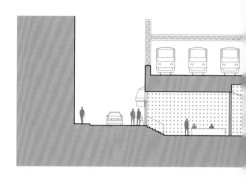

Fig. 4-20   Ginza Corridor and Yamanote Line: section B (1:400).

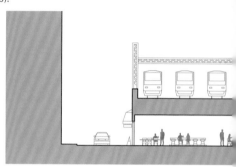

Fig. 4-21   Undertrack spaces between Shimbashi and Yūrakuchō Stations, including Ginza Corridor. Street-level use map (1:2,500) as of 2020. Source: Fieldwork in 2020, and the map *Jūtakuchizu* (Zenrin, 2019).

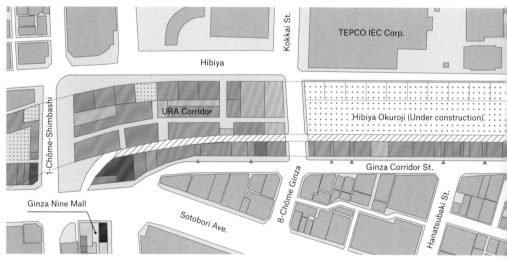

▲ Access to businesses on the second floor   ▲ Access to businesses on the basement

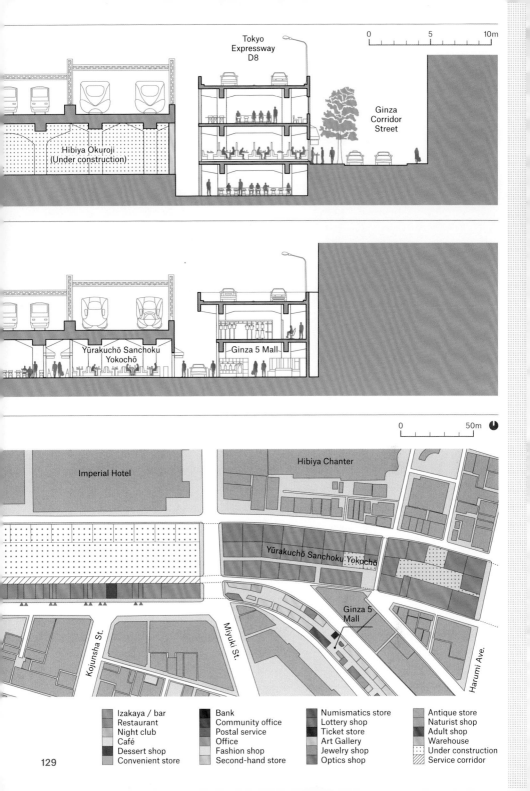

Tokyo
Expressway
D8

0   5   10m

Hibiya Okuroji
(Under construction)

Ginza
Corridor
Street

Yūrakuchō Sanchoku
Yokochō

Ginza 5 Mall

0   50m

Imperial Hotel

Hibiya Chanter

Yūrakuchō Sanchoku Yokochō

Ginza 5
Mall

Kojunsha St.

Miyuki St.

Harumi Ave.

Izakaya / bar	Bank	Numismatics store	Antique store
Restaurant	Community office	Lottery shop	Naturist shop
Night club	Postal service	Ticket store	Adult shop
Café	Office	Art Gallery	Warehouse
Dessert shop	Fashion shop	Jewelry shop	Under construction
Convenient store	Second-hand store	Optics shop	Service corridor

5 ANKYO STREETS

暗渠ストリート

Fig. 5-1   View of the Kuhombutsu Promenade in Jiyūgaoka as of September 2019.

5

ANKYO STREETS

5.1   The flowing streets of Tokyo

While Tokyo's commercial streets are known for their frantic choreography of people, signs, and sounds, its residential streets are more often marked by tranquility and community life. In both cases, however, the street is first and foremost treated as a space to move, not to linger. Authorities preempt informal street gatherings through a variety of implicit and explicit means. Even harmless pedestrian amenities, such as benches or outside seating for cafés and restaurants, are urban taboos on Tokyo's public sidewalks. Tokyo is a city full of surprises in so many respects, but the powers that be seem determined keep serendipity out of the public streets.

When the occasional street in Tokyo manages to escape these narrow expectations, it therefore becomes a cause for curiosity. Our investigations found that many of Tokyo's most interesting streets shared a common background—they are former watercourses that have been covered over and turned into paths and roads Fig. 5-1. The Japanese have a term for these watercourses-turned-streets: *ankyo*, literally meaning 'dark canal.' They are often found winding their way through Village Tokyo, though some of Mercantile Tokyo's most celebrated streets also have ankyo origins. These emergent urban spaces have surprising lessons to teach us.

In the Edo period, Tokyo was known for its dense network of rivers and canals. As the city modernized, its watercourses were gradually filled and covered, and those which remain have been fitted with deep concrete embankments. The city has lost its intimate relationship with water; what was once both essential infrastructure and a place for enjoyment has been treated for much of the last century as a natural hazard to be overcome. Fortunately, Tokyo's citizen activists and urban planners are both coming to see this state of affairs as a historic mistake, and are beginning the difficult work of recovering Tokyo's legacy as a water city.

Since the 1980s, there has been a growing interest in understanding Tokyo's origins and in particular the city's continuities with its predecessor, Edo. In a city with almost no buildings more than a century old, this historical focus manifests as a heightened interest in Tokyo's topographical history, and particularly its water legacy. Recently, there has been a wave of books, activities, and enthusiast societies all aiming to grasp Tokyo's true character through its topography. This focus is understandable, as topography has historically had a significant impact on everything from the positioning of temples and residences to the boundaries between the city's different socio-economic layers.[86] Ankyo are, in their own way, a lasting remnant of this topographical legacy and a key to understanding how Tokyo's past links to its future.

5.2   The campaign to make Japanese street life boring

Why is street life so constrained in Tokyo? As with so many elements of the city, the restricted use of streets in Japan is often explained away as being the result of Japanese culture. Street activities such as al fresco dining, terrace cafés, and street markets are portrayed as charming but ultimately foreign.[87] Somehow, an idea has taken root that the practice of staying outside in public space is simply not something that Japanese people do. However, when one peels back the layers of these hazy appeals to culture, there are concrete (and recent) public policy choices that explain this restricted use of public space.

Tokyo wasn't always this way. During the Edo period, the street was a place of both commerce and community. Old Edo wood-block prints show a spontaneous urban liveliness with bustling markets, street vendors, and children playing. This tradition continued after the end of World War II, as countless unlicensed street stalls appeared across the devastated urban landscape—Tokyo's black market era that we have discussed in previous chapters. From 1949 onward, however, the Stall Clean-up Order issued by the American occupation forces prohibited the street stalls in an effort to dismantle the black markets.[88] The new regulations have endured in various forms until the present day, causing street stalls and street markets to be relatively rare. Food-selling *yatai* carts have also increasingly been phased out of existence in response to a government perception that their informal nature facilitates organized crime.

A shifting approach to urban planning has also contributed to this hardening of norms. After the war, Japan embraced the modernist urban planning ideal of *functionalism*, which advocated for the strict separation of traffic and

Fig. 5-2   Open and covered rivers across Tokyo's 23 wards.

Sources: Yoshimura Nama, Takayama Hideo, Ankyo Maniac (Kashiwashōbō, 2015); Kurosawa Hisaki. Tōkyō burari ankyo tansaku (Yosensha, 2010).

———— Open river
———— Covered river

pedestrian flows. Its negative consequences are still visible in Tokyo today; in much of the city vehicles are given preferential treatment, while those on foot are forced to climb up high pedestrian walkways simply to cross the street. This car-centric infrastructure makes many sections of Tokyo frustrating to navigate on foot, particularly for the elderly and those with mobility difficulties.

The government's reaction to the protest culture of the 1960s also had an enduring influence. The protests drove the police to take a more direct and restrictive role in controlling public space, and pre-existing public spaces such as parks and plazas were physically subdivided to preempt large gatherings.[89] Although any given road in Tokyo belongs to either the local ward, metropolitan, or national government, any activities which might affect them are under the jurisdiction of the police and require their permission. Unlike other countries, where there is an independent municipal police force that receives funding from the city budget and is under control of the local government, Tokyo's police are under the oversight of the National Police Agency. The police tend not to allow activities that might hinder traffic, making it difficult to hold events on the streets—a policy strict enough that even requests from the municipal government are sometimes denied. Only traditional *matsuri* festivals, with their longstanding cultural support, have a relatively smooth approval process.[90]

As a consequence, the use of public space in Japan feels more restrictive than European and American cities, not to mention neighboring countries. Benches are scarce in most streets of Tokyo; even the few public spaces that do have benches, such as those in Shibuya's famous Hachiko Plaza, are intentionally designed to discourage people from lingering.[91]

5.3 Ankyo river streets in history

As a city whose watercourses once rivaled Venice, countless rivers and streams flow naturally through Tokyo's varied topography Fig. 5-2.[92] In the Edo period, these natural resources were supplemented by new canals to create a dense water network supporting everything from the population's water supply to agricultural irrigation and industrial uses. Many new canals were dug across the city, particularly around Tokyo Bay in the east, and the resulting river banks soon bustled with activity.

However, as the city modernized, Tokyo turned away from its roots as a water city. Many rivers and canals were covered in the name of progress, and rebuilding projects after the 1923 Great Kantō earthquake and World War II eliminated many of Tokyo's rivers. This process accelerated with the nation's abrupt population increase and rapid economic growth from 1954 to 1973. Many rivers and watercourses within the Yamanote Line were transformed into streets and housing plots. Others disappeared as a consequence of the drying up of spring water, which was, in turn, caused by the decrease in green tracts of land. Many of the remaining watercourses became highly polluted due to industrialization.

As a result of this degradation, in preparation for the 1964 Olympics the city carried out a number of hasty urban infrastructure works projects, one of which was sewer construction. In 1961, the Tokyo Metropolitan Government issued Report 36, initiating a policy to turn many urban rivers into covered sewers.[93] The plan took advantage of Tokyo's natural topography, offering a way to rapidly implement a functional, cost-effective sewer system as the city densified. After this period, new residential areas and urbanization projects in the suburbs followed a similar logic, and many remaining small brooks and canals were covered as a result.[94]

The case studies of this chapter focus specifically on watercourses covered hastily after the war. Many of them are narrow and difficult for vehicle traffic, and as a result they tend to be quieter and more communal. In many cases, these ankyo streets have now been entirely refurbished as greenways or promenades. To better capture this phenomenon, this chapter examines three cases, two of which feature pedestrian pathways. The Mozart-Brahms Lane, crossing secretively through the highly developed commercial district of Harajuku, offers a small-scale, intimate urban experience Figs. 5-3, 4. Another, the Yoyogi Lane, crosses an anonymous residential neighborhood and affords space for residents to expand their domestic realms Figs. 5-5, 6. The third example, the Kuhonbutsu Promenade, is an intimate boulevard with benches and trees that emerged incrementally near the suburban station of Jiyūgaoka Figs. 5-7, 8.

5.4 Mozart-Brahms Lane: Harajuku's linear oasis

Case 10

A stone's throw from Harajuku's noisy, crowded Takeshita Street—world-famous as a mecca of colorful and girly *kawaii* ('cute') fashion—there is a tranquil lane that runs parallel to it. The lane hides a completely different world of small cafés, elegant shops, and small-scale greenery that unfolds as one walks along the path. In an attempt to relate this alley to classical music, the Western stretch of the lane has a plate naming it Brahms Lane, while the Eastern part is Mozart Street. The 275 m of this curvy Mozart-Brahms Lane connect Meiji Avenue with Takeshita Street. The path itself is 1.8 m wide, but the separation between buildings along the path varies, from 3 m to a few plaza-like spaces where buildings are 12 m apart. Since the street is on a lower level than its surroundings, no car traffic is possible. Most of the buildings along the lane remain low-rise, averaging about three floors in height. Perhaps the biggest surprise of this narrow hidden lane is that it has survived at all in one of Tokyo's hottest real estate areas Fig. 5-9.

Mozart-Brahms Lane traces the path of a former stream that has its source in the Meiji Jingū precinct and flows into the Shibuya River.[95] As late as 1930, when the adjacent stretch of Meiji Avenue was completed, this brook was still irrigating the surrounding rice paddies and serving as a play space for neighborhood children.[96] After the war, the brook became increasingly polluted by drain water, and it was covered in the mid-1960s in preparation for the Olympics.

At the time, Takeshita Street was cultivating an image of fashion and youthful self-expression. Foreigners were a common sight due to its location close to Washington Heights, the United States Forces housing complex. The Olympics brought even more diversity, as Washington Heights was converted in-

Fig. 5-3 Mozart-Brahms Lane as of June 2020.

to athlete housing. Mozart-Brahms Lane acquired a commercial character, albeit with a more tranquil flavor. The cafés and antique shops that line both sides of the ankyo create a stark contrast with the Takeshita Street.

In ankyo streets like this one, river topography and height level differences create contrasts with neighboring streets. Since their narrowness and level changes are often inhospitable to cars, they often naturally become pedestrian over time. Among the 31 buildings facing Mozart-Brahms Lane, most of them have direct car access from other back streets, rather than from the lane itself. As in many quieter areas of Tokyo, a redundant web of back streets provides car access when necessary, though often in ways that are unintuitive. This spatial complexity encourages cross-town drivers to stick to major roadways rather than cut through unknown neighborhoods, allowing back streets like Mozart-Brahms Lane to preserve their pedestrian character even without a formally enforced separation between spaces for cars and spaces for pedestrians Fig. 5-10.

Over the decades, the lane has generated a delightfully idiosyncratic urban milieu. As if in a continuous cinematic sequence, the unfolding spaces along its path show an imaginative cornucopia of greenery, overhangs, stairs, objects overflowing into their outside surroundings, and level differences Figs. 5-11, 12. Its complex character, topographic diversity, narrowness, and multiple points of accessibility combine to produce an unexpected oasis of tranquility.

5.5 Yoyogi Lane: portrait of a communal backstreet

Case 11

Just one station north of Harajuku lies an ankyo street that, like most of Tokyo's backstreets, has no formal name; for this discussion, we will refer to it as Yoyogi Lane. It runs about 500 m from the elevated Shinjuku Route of the Metropolitan Expressway to the south, up to its intersection with the Odakyū Line to the north. The surrounding buildings vary from 2 to 8 floors, in a mixture of single-family houses and housing blocks. Some stretches have been widened to the minimum 4 m demanded by the law (as discussed in the next chapter) while others remain so narrow that cars cannot enter. As a result, the lane is a de-facto pedestrian street Fig. 5-13.

Fig. 5-4 The evolution of Mozart-Brahms Lane (1:5,000).

0   50m

1930
A brook flows from the Meiji Jingū Shrine compound down to Meiji Avenue. The area is still predominantly residential.

Source: *Tōkyō-fu Toyotamagun Sendagaya-chō Zenzu* (Senryūdō, 1930).

///// Cluster of buildings

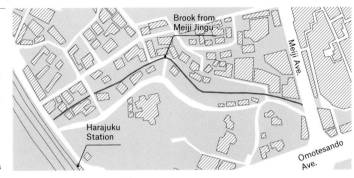

1958
The brook has already been partially covered and adjacent houses increasingly transform into apartment buildings.

Source: Shimizu Yasuo (editor), *Meiji zenki, Shōwa zenki Tōkyō Toshichizu 1958* (Kashiwashōbō, 1996).

///// Cluster of buildings

1980
After the opening of a new station exit at its entrance, Harajuku's now-famed Takeshita Street becomes fully commercial. The whole area densifies further. In the shadow of these developments, the adjacent ankyo street acquires a relaxed and intimate character.

Source: *Jūtakuchizu* (Zenrin, 1980).

2019
The district's densification and commercialization continues, but the ankyo street remains a hidden oasis.

Source: *Jūtakuchizu* (Zenrin, 2019).

Yoyogi Lane began its life as a tiny canal built in the Edo period as part of a broader irrigation system. Most of these irrigation canals were turned into streets in 1932; only Yoyogi Lane remained, until it too was covered in the 1960s Olympics craze. These days, Yoyogi Lane is in a hybrid state. Some stretches have been widened for cars; others are narrower and pedestrian-oriented. A variety of buildings face the ankyo, from large condominiums to small single-family houses. And since the majority of buildings along the lane have car access from adjacent parallel streets, the lane functions like a back-alley communal space where neighbors expand their domestic space, take walks, and bicycle while protected from cars Fig. 5-14. While condominiums tend to turn their backs to the lane, the small houses interact with the lane in a variety of ways: doors, windows, makeshift verandas, laundry poles, flower pots, bicycles, etc. This accumulation, which also appears in the narrow *roji* alleys of the dense low-rise neighborhoods discussed in the next chapter, creates an active edge along the street Figs. 5-15, 16.

Yoyogi Lane's destiny has yet to be written. The blind application of regulations such as road widening could ultimately destroy its unique qualities, so a more site-specific vision will be necessary to preserve its current status as a pedestrian-oriented residential back lane. Backstreets such as Yoyogi Lane are often unfairly derided as wasted space, with a tendency to accumulate litter and attract crime. Today, however, many cities are rediscovering their potential. They provide human-scale pedestrian-oriented community spaces where children and adults can congregate safely and enjoy physical activities. They create a transitional space from the domestic realm to the broader streets. The small-scale greenery that lines so many of their homes can collectively make them green corridors in a city where traditional parks are scarce. All of these advantages are visible in Yoyogi Lane. Today, as the city presses forward with the mega-scale redevelopment of many inner districts, preserving and nurturing the neglected urban qualities that Yoyogi Lane encapsulates is a more urgent task than ever.

Fig. 5-5   Yoyogi Lane as of February 2020.

Fig. 5-6 The evolution of Yoyogi Lane (1:5,000).

0 ⌞_ _ _ _⌟ 50m 🌓

1941

As in much of West Tokyo, this residential area's streets have inherited pre-existing agricultural land patterns. The roads and paths grew out of the former irrigation system for rice paddies; only one stream is still uncovered.

Source: *Shibuya-ku Zenzu* (Uchiyama Mokei Seizusha, 1941).

▨▨▨ Cluster of buildings

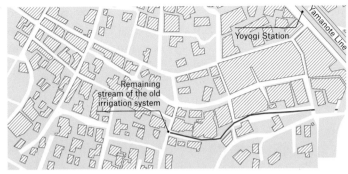

1969

After the war, the area rapidly densifies with apartment buildings and commercial businesses. Newly built roads, planned after the war, cut through the dense low-rise maze of houses.

Source: *Shōkōjūtaku Meikanhokubu* (Toto Chizusha, 1969).

▨▨▨ Cluster of buildings

1980

Large concrete buildings line the wider main streets. The stream has been completely covered and surrounded by low-rise single-family houses, acquiring the character of a back lane.

Source: *Jūtakuchizu* (Zenrin, 1980).

2019

Yoyogi Lane is still an intimate back lane. An increasing number of apartment buildings have been built with their backs toward the ankyo.

Source: *Jūtakuchizu* (Zenrin, 2019).

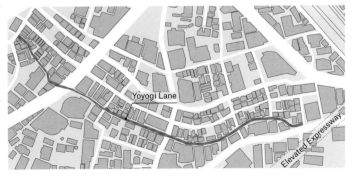

5.6 The inclusive Kuhombutsu Promenade

Case 12

The first thing that strikes visitors to suburban Jiyūgaoka's Kuhombutsu Promenade is its wealth of benches in a city famously averse to public seating. What's more, none of the benches are designed to deter the homeless, as has become sadly common in cities across the globe. In a city seemingly designed to keep pedestrians moving along, Kuhombutsu Promenade invites everyone to sit and relax.

The benches are just one marker of the degree of freedom that the promenade has achieved. Nearly everything about this promenade has undergone dramatic changes over the decades as it has transitioned from a polluted river to a vibrant public space. The state of Kuhombutsu Promenade today is not the product of a single top-down vision, but rather the end result of its many disparate actors leveraging the street's legal idiosyncrasies for their own interests. Together they carved out a unique identity for the promenade in the process, even if that was never their specific intention. In this sense, the promenade is a microcosm of everything that makes ankyo streets so interesting.

The 11 m wide promenade has a central pedestrian strip corresponding to the width of the former river, with cherry trees and benches alongside it. In practice, however, the whole promenade is pedestrian. The low buildings along the promenade—four to five stories—allow natural sunlight, and the trees provide shade in Tokyo's unforgiving summers. There are more than 200 benches in the 300 m stretch along the main commercial stretch of the ankyo Fig. 5-17.

The promenade follows the Kuhonbutsu River, and its historical evolution is similar to that of many other ankyo streets. The surrounding territory was once a wetland being used for rice paddies. It was not until 1927, with the construction of the railway by the Tōkyū Corporation, that the scattered houses of the preexisting Fusumamura Village began to densify. As with most of Tokyo's suburbs, development accelerated after the Great Kantō earthquake as new policies allowed for the change of agricultural land into residential tracts, a response

Fig. 5-7   Kuhombutsu Promenade as of July 2019.

Fig. 5-8 The evolution of the Kuhonbutsu Promenade (1:5,000).

0   50m

1937
When two suburban railroads crossing at Jiyūgaoka open, a commercial district starts to coalesce on the north side of the station, while the areas along the river remain agricultural fields.

Source: Shimizu Yasuo (editor), Meiji zenki, Shōwa zenki Tōkyō. Toshichizu 1937 (Kashiwashōbō, 1996).

///// Cluster of buildings

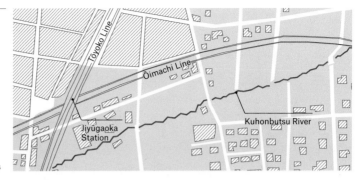

1972
The commercial area is revived after the war and the whole area urbanizes, with the commercial area extending up to the river's north side.

Source: *Meguro-ku Zenjūtaku Annaichizuchō* (Kōkyō Shisetsu Chizu Kōkū, 1972).

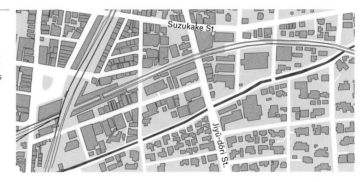

1990
The river was channelled underground in 1974, and a new greenway was built on top of it. Houses along the greenway are gradually transformed into commercial buildings.

Source: *Jūtakuchizu* (Zenrin, 1990).

2019
The promenade has continued to expand, with its design integrating into the local district plan. It has become a pedestrian-friendly space where people can gather and relax in the street.

Source: *Jūtakuchizu* (Zenrin, 2019).

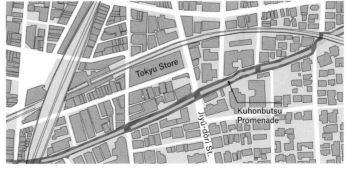

to the shortage of houses after the disaster. The 1945 air raids destroyed many of the area's commercial streets, but with high postwar economic growth they soon revived and prospered.

Unlike the ankyo streets of central Tokyo, many of which were hastily covered in the years leading up to the 1964 Olympics, the Kuhonbutsu River was channeled underground only in 1974. As with many other rivers, development was the result of pressure from the increasing population, and nearby industry had already heavily polluted its waters. Planning authorities officially labeled the new covered surface as a 'green area' or *ryokuchi*, a designation with major implications for public use. Streets (including sidewalks) are normally legally classified as roads, and thus fall under the nationalized jurisdiction of the police. Green areas, however, are managed by municipal authorities.

At first, the newly covered river wasn't much of a public space. The pavement on each side of the covered river was a different height, and the central green area was fenced. But in 1992, as Jiyūgaoka's commercial area continued expanding, the authorities implemented an improvement plan to remove the fences and unify the height levels of the pavement on both sides of the street—an unusually complex task, since the center of the street is the dividing line between two ward governments. However, the paved surface was soon occupied as an unofficial bicycle parking lot by the area's many shoppers and commuters, even after authorities forbade the practice.

The local *shōtenkai* merchants association wanted a promenade, not a parking lot.[97] A seasonal festival inspired the solution to their dilemma: they realized that the chairs they had put down as festival seating also incidentally prevented illegal parking. Before long, the association was eagerly negotiating with local authorities for the right to place benches along the promenade. The local government was happy to have the illicit bicycle parking issue handled, and the association members' offer to purchase and install the benches themselves didn't hurt.[98] The end result is the promenade that we see today Figs. 5-18, 19.

In this newly born green promenade, street life was not deterministically designed; it has emerged organically from individual choices. The shops along the promenade offer terrace spaces that are attractive to families, and so it is common to see children playing among the trees in the daytime Fig. 5-20. As night falls, they are gradually taken over by dating couples and friends sharing drinks. Here as elsewhere, the nebulous status of an ankyo street has allowed unique (for Tokyo, at least) flexibilities and transformations that were first actively promoted by local merchants and then eventually accepted by ward planning authorities, ultimately resulting in a vibrant and and inclusive public space.

5.7 Learning from ankyo streets

Ankyo streets disrupt their surrounding urban fabric in a positive way, creating ambiguous spaces open to flexible interventions. Although their individual circumstances vary, when looked at as a category they display a number of distinct emergent properties.

5.7.1 Use ambiguous spaces to allow the creation of active edges

The in-between status of many ankyo streets has enabled the residents who live among them to actively appropriate them for their own purposes. People expand their domestic realms into the small alleys (a practice sometimes referred to as *afuredashi*), much as one sees in the back alleys or roji of Tokyo's dense, low-rise neighborhoods. In ankyo streets, irregularities create opportunities for further spatial personalization. Plots that already had a primary entrance before the rivers were covered gain a second back entrance through the newly covered watercourse. These spaces become a new realm for everyday life, filling up over time with little greenery, bicycles, laundry, toys, and the like—but also eaves, windows, entrances, canopies, makeshift verandas. These custom-made modifications collectively generate an open façade that feels alive and facilitates social encounters.

5.7.2 Augment the city's walkability with emergent greenways

Often pedestrian in nature and converted into linear micro-parks, many covered watercourses have legally or de-facto been exempted from the constraining rules that govern most Japanese streets. In a city still dominated by cars, ankyo streets offer an alternative typology of walkable greenways. They stand out as visible examples of the city's latent potential, and could serve as a model for the future if Tokyo's powers that be one day come to recognize the need for better public space.

5.7.3 Foster emergent character through disruptions to the cityscape

Ankyo streets represent disruptions of the standard city grid, which imbues them with a seed of creative potential. They are anomalies both in form and in function, non-rational, enigmatic spaces that offer a sense of discovery to the curious. There is an almost archaeological pleasure to be had in understanding the urban transformation of Tokyo through the traces of its rivers. In many of these flowing streets, hints of their past life as watercourses can be seen, such as moss fed by underground moisture, or fragments of balustrades from bridges that no longer exist. Ankyo have even given rise to a whole subculture of 'ankyo-logists' who find pleasure in discovering and analyzing their multiple layers.

5.7.4 Build in redundancy to nurture the freedom to experiment

Most of Tokyo's postwar ankyo streets are, strictly speaking, unnecessary. They do not function as major roadways, and some even lie neglected and abandoned. However, many have evolved into community back lanes and public promenades. Mozart-Brahms Lane, for example, was reinvented as a linear oasis in the middle of Harajuku's crowded chaos, while Yoyogi Lane emerged as a safe residential back lane, and Jiyūgaoka's Kuhombutsu Promenade has come to resemble an open-air intergenerational living room. The redundancy of ankyo spaces has freed them to be unusually experimental; when they are not required to be one specific thing, they can become anything.

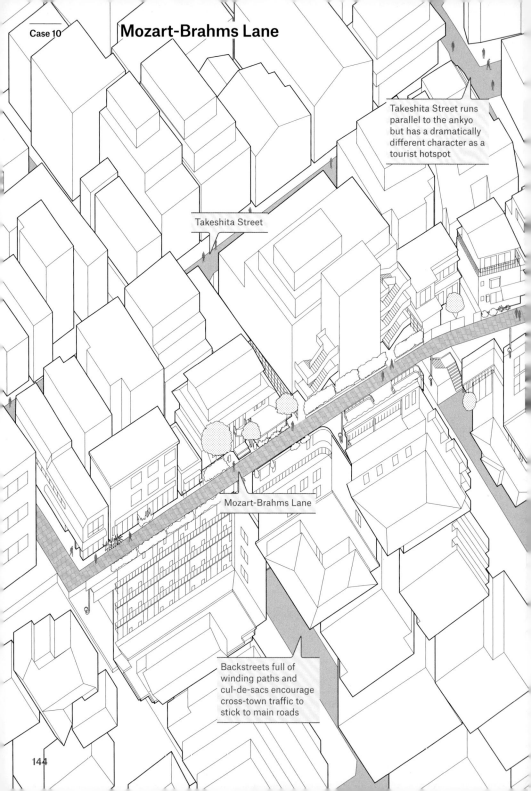

Mozart-Brahms Lane

Takeshita Street runs parallel to the ankyo but has a dramatically different character as a tourist hotspot

Takeshita Street

Mozart-Brahms Lane

Backstreets full of winding paths and cul-de-sacs encourage cross-town traffic to stick to main roads

Fig. 5-9   Overview of Mozart-Brahms Lane (1:600).

0   10   20m

Most buildings facing
the ankyo have rear
car access via the
backstreets

Stairs connect
footpaths at different
heights throughout the
ankyo street

Fig. 5-10   Street level analysis and visual sequence of Mozart-Brahms Lane as for February 2020 (1:1,500).

Fig. 5-11   The Mozart-Brahms Lane: perspective section A (1:80).

Key plan

Terrace seating

Interiors extend
outward into the lane

Micro gardens

Fig. 5-12   The Mozart-Brahms Lane: perspective section B (1:80).

0   1   2   3m

Stairs provide easy access to upper-floor businesses above the lane

Shop entrances are found at every level

Narrow lanes hinder cars from entering, creating a pedestrian-centric space

Yoyogi Lane

Small houses tend to expand outward into the lane

Condominiums tend to turn their backs to the lane

Yoyogi Lane

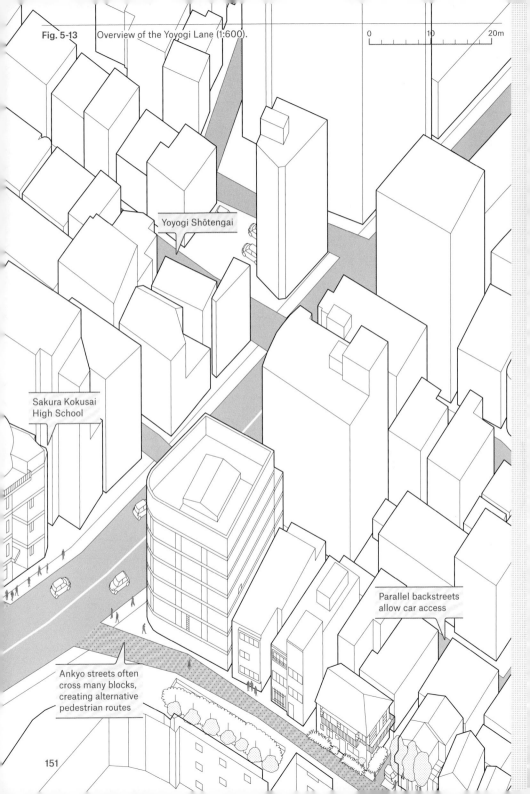

Fig. 5-13 Overview of the Yoyogi Lane (1:600).

0   10   20m

Yoyogi Shōtengai

Sakura Kokusai
High School

Parallel backstreets
allow car access

Ankyo streets often
cross many blocks,
creating alternative
pedestrian routes

Fig. 5-14   Street level analysis and visual sequence of Yoyogi Lane as for February 2020 (1:1,500).

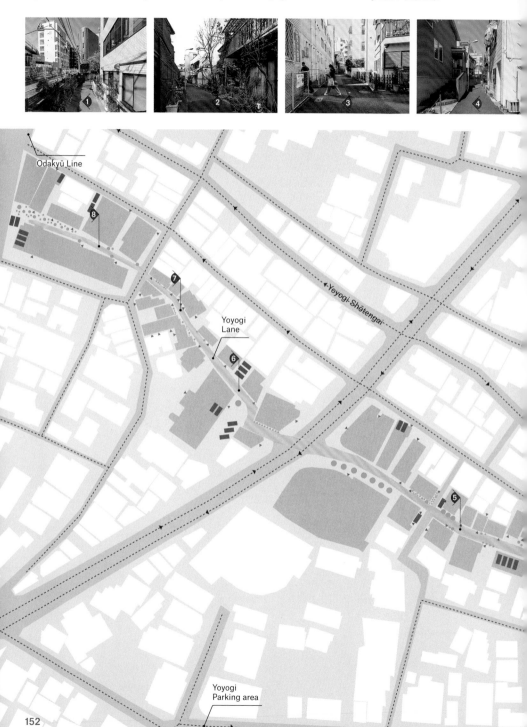

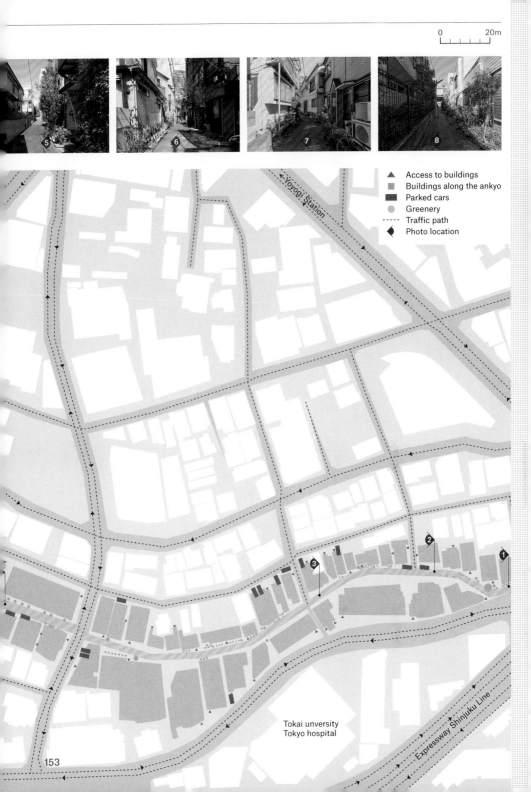

0   20m

▲	Access to buildings
▪	Buildings along the ankyo
▪	Parked cars
●	Greenery
----	Traffic path
◆	Photo location

Yoyogi Station →

Tokai unversity
Tokyo hospital

Expressway Shinjuku Line

Fig. 5-15   Yoyogi Lane: perspective section A (1:40).

0   1m

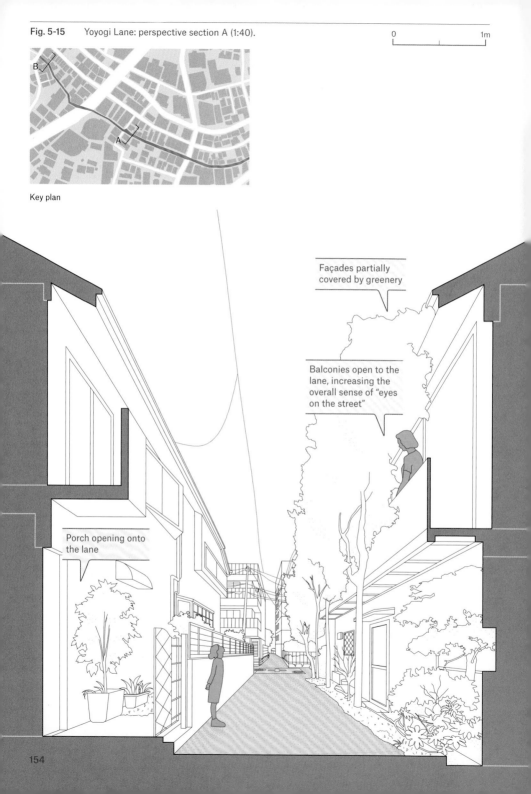

Key plan

Façades partially
covered by greenery

Balconies open to the
lane, increasing the
overall sense of "eyes
on the street"

Porch opening onto
the lane

Fig. 5-16   Yoyogi Lane: perspective section B (1:40).

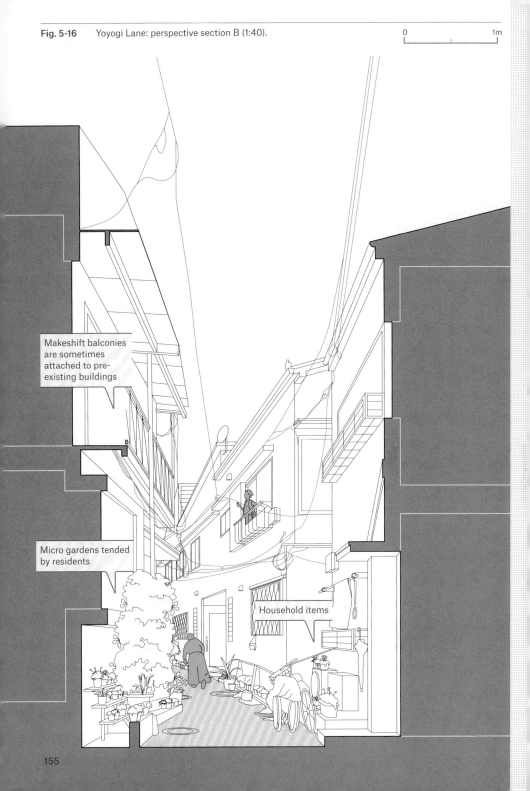

Makeshift balconies are sometimes attached to pre-existing buildings

Micro gardens tended by residents

Household items

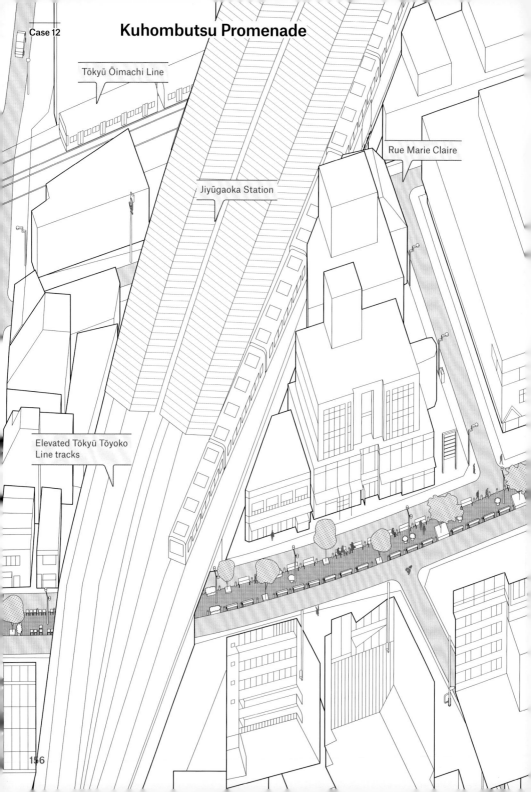

Kuhombutsu Promenade

Tōkyū Ōimachi Line

Rue Marie Claire

Jiyūgaoka Station

Elevated Tōkyū Tōyoko
Line tracks

Fig. 5-17 Overview of Kuhombutsu Promenade (1:600).

0   10   20m

Kurinoki St.

Kuhombutsu
Promenade

Jiyūdōri Street

Fig. 5-18 Street level analysis of Kuhombutsu Promenade as for June 2020 (1:1,500).

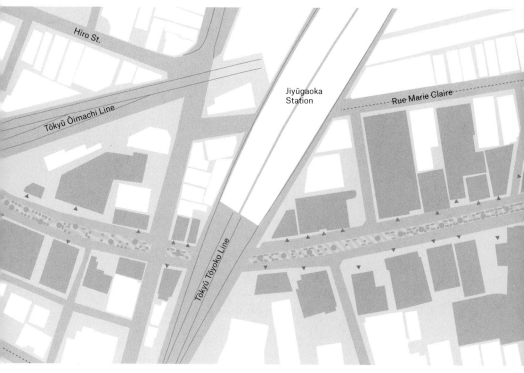

Fig. 5-19 Visual sequence of Kuhombutsu Promenade (1:6,000).

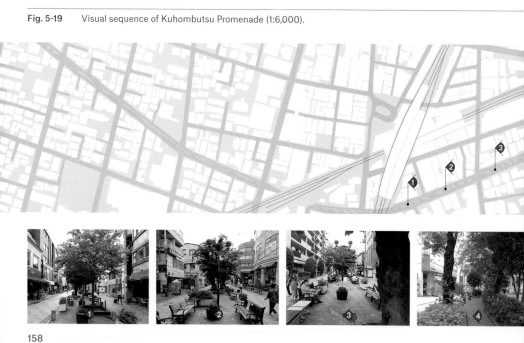

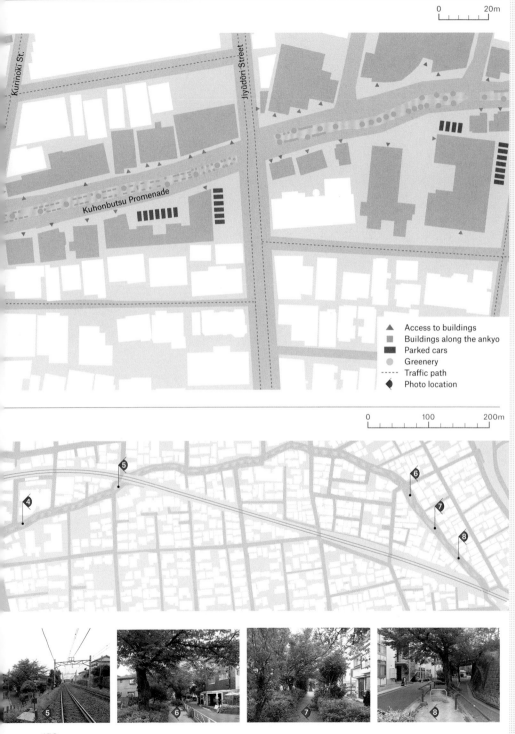

0   20m

Kurinoki St.

Jiyūdōri Street

Kuhonbutsu Promenade

▲ Access to buildings
◼ Buildings along the ankyo
◼ Parked cars
● Greenery
----- Traffic path
◆ Photo location

0   100   200m

Fig. 5-20 Kuhombutsu Promenade: perspective section (1:80).

Key plan

The district plan aims to preserve the promenade's character by specifying building heights and setbacks

Sakura trees; their cherry blossom blooms create a festival-like atmosphere along the lane each spring

Plentiful window shopping

MELSA

FLIPPER'S

Numerous benches

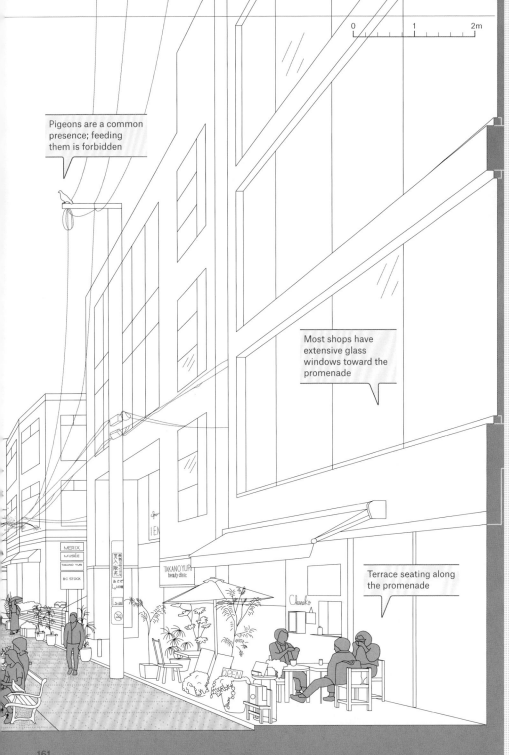

Pigeons are a common presence; feeding them is forbidden

Most shops have extensive glass windows toward the promenade

Terrace seating along the promenade

6 DENSE LOW-RISE NEIGHBORHOODS

低層密集地域

Fig. 6-1 Dense low-rise neighborhoods extend behind the high-rise buildings along the Daini Keihin Highway in Shinagawa Ward. On the right: Higashi-Nakanobu. On the left: Togoshi. September 2020.

6 DENSE LOW-RISE NEIGHBORHOODS

6.1   An ocean of houses

The stereotypical image of Tokyo in the global imagination—extremely high population density, ultra-modern buildings, neon-clad streets—does not reflect the actual urban landscape of the city. In fact, when life-long Tokyoites are asked which parts of the city feel most Tokyo-esque to them, their answers usually point in the opposite direction: they speak of the city's intimate, highly communal residential neighborhoods. Narrow streets and small single-family houses are common in Tokyo neighborhoods, at times resulting in an atmosphere more reminiscent of a quiet village than a bustling metropolis. And in the areas of Tokyo that are relatively dense, that density is achieved through a tightly knit, fine-grained, low-rise urban fabric of houses with high plot coverage Fig. 6-1. What this means in a practical sense is that the layout of these neighborhoods resembles a frantic Tetris game rather than a neat and spacious suburban grid, earning them comparisons in some respects to the so-called slums of the developing world. But what looks at first glance like disorder is in fact the natural result of organic, bottom-up growth—the same quality that makes these neighborhoods so livable.

The role of these *dense low-rise neighborhoods* in making Tokyo's urban fabric possible has not been given much attention by architects and urbanists, but recent academic studies have begun to explore their positive aspects, especially the role that their distinctive layouts—full of narrow alleys and residual gaps between houses—play in everyday life.[99] By looking at these spatial and material relationships, we can get a better sense of how they shape the unique rhythm of Tokyo's urban life.[100]

6.2   How dense, how low? A working definition

What exactly do we mean when we talk about a dense, low-rise neighborhood? Waxing poetic about these quintessential Tokyo communities is easy enough, but it's difficult to draw hard and fast rules about which areas of the city qualify. Real-world urban phenomena aren't always easy to categorize into clear-cut typologies; the best we can do is to lay out general boundaries that fit a broad archetype, giving us a sense of the phenomenon's contours and scale. These neighborhoods are typically found in areas of Village, Local, and Pocket Tokyo that fit three main criteria: *high population density, low-rise, and residential in nature*. If one defines *dense* as areas with population densities of 20,000 persons per km^2 or more and *low-rise* as buildings of up to three stories, a clear pattern emerges when we map the residential sections of the city that fit these criteria Fig. 6-2.[101]

These dense low-rise neighborhoods ring the outside of the Yamanote Line, with a clear concentration in the western part of the city. Inside the Yamanote loop they tend toward the northern inner wards, although there are still some pockets to the south as well. They largely overlap with what the Tokyo Metropolitan Government terms 'densely built-up wooden construction areas,'[102] districts that authorities consider especially vulnerable to fires, earthquakes, and other natural disasters. As Tokyo looks toward the future, these village-like neighborhoods confront two urgent problems: their *narrow streets* make vehicle access difficult, and their *weak and flammable building stock* increases the risk that natural disasters will do serious damage.

The two problems are likely to intertwine in a disaster scenario. These areas contain numerous narrow old alleys and laneways (known collectively in Japanese as *roji*), most of which are narrower than the 4 m minimum width mandated by Japan's current Building Standards Law. As Tokyo's neighborhoods have grown organically and spontaneously over the decades, many have developed into urban labyrinths full of dead-end streets and unusually shaped plots. In daily life such idiosyncrasies lend these neighborhoods a certain charm, but the challenge they pose for disaster management is very real.

The sheer amount and density of old buildings is a problem in its own right, since many are either made of wood, and thus highly flammable, or fail to meet the latest seismic standards. Wood construction is Japan's cheapest and most common type of housing, owing to the country's extensive forests and long tradition of carpentry.[103] To the outside observer these houses don't look wooden in the traditional sense; they are generally clad in mortar, metal sheets, or most commonly today, prefabricated ceramic panels that imitate the appearance

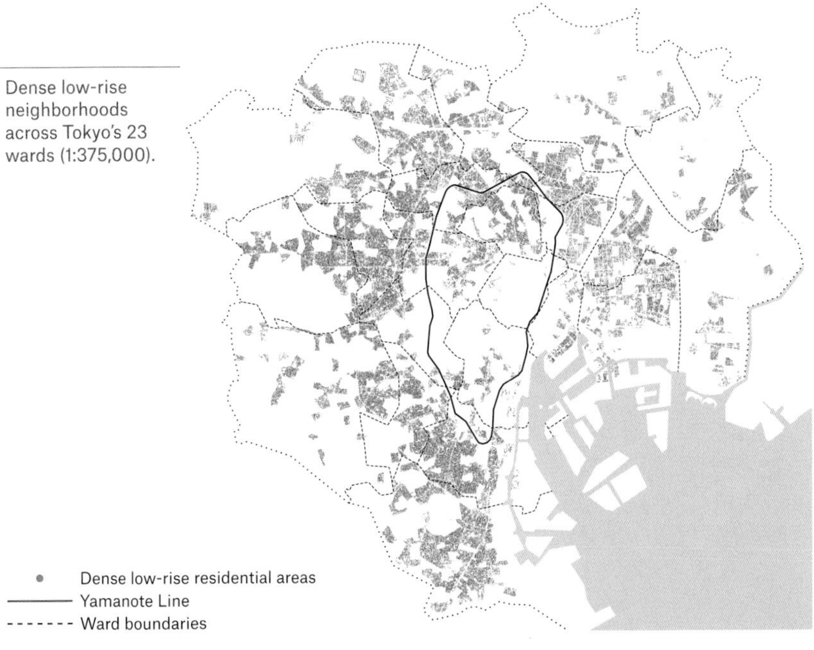

Fig. 6-2   Dense low-rise
            neighborhoods
            across Tokyo's 23
            wards (1:375,000).

• Dense low-rise residential areas
—— Yamanote Line
------ Ward boundaries

of bricks and stones. This cladding offers some protection, but the underlying wooden structures still pose fire risks, especially in very dense urban settings.

As dense as these neighborhoods are today, they were once crammed even closer together. In traditional Japanese streets, like the remaining *machiya* (traditional townhouses) of Kyoto or Kanazawa, these wooden buildings were directly attached to one another, forming continuous street frontages like row houses do in Western cities. In contemporary Japan, however, as a general rule all buildings must be detached. The 1919 Building Law established some required separation between buildings to prevent fires leaping from house to house, and the 1950 Building Standards Law expanded the rule to forbid buildings from touching each other in most cases.[104] The shift resulted in the creation of countless tiny gap spaces between buildings across Tokyo's urban landscape.[105]

Why have these problems persisted for decades, even as Tokyo increasingly becomes dominated by sleek glass towers and corporate development? It's not for lack of trying. The Japanese government attempted to solve the road narrowness issue through the 1950 Building Standards Law, which is still in effect today. The law establishes setback obligations, requiring landowners who want to rebuild a house along a narrow alley to build their new walls at least 2 m from the center of the lane. The hope was that over time, all landowners along alleys would set back their houses 2 m on each side, resulting in a 4 m wide street. Even a full 70 years after the law was established, however, countless alleys remain unchanged. Landowners are generally uninterested in living in a smaller house in the name of the public good, and they frequently use a variety of legal tactics and loopholes to resist the setback obligation and preserve their precious square meters.

On a practical level, one of the most popular ways of getting around these rules is to "renovate" an old house rather than officially "rebuild" it. The loose definition of renovation under Japanese law allows major transformations as long as at least a few structural elements from the original building are kept. Like the famed ship of Theseus in Greek philosophy, a renovated house often keeps virtually nothing from the original construction, creating a thoroughly modern interior while legally remaining the same building.

The largely failed setback obligation policy brought a perverse effect: by incentivizing renovations instead of rebuilding, many more buildings retain their wooden structural elements and thus remain flammable. Furthermore, when landowners avoid rebuilding, their properties are not updated to the latest anti-seismic standards, which generally require improvements to a building's foundation that are difficult and costly to make during the renovation process. The result in many neighborhoods is a maze of narrow alleys lined with flammable and vulnerable structures. In the event of a major earthquake, many of these areas could become death traps.

In the landowners' defense, such resistance is not always driven by narrow self-interest; these narrow alleys play an important role in neighborhood communal life. Many citizen groups are trying to preserve them in the hopes that the necessary disaster resilience can be achieved by other means without throwing the baby out with the bathwater. The challenge facing Tokyo is to address these neighborhoods' vulnerabilities while also preserving their local community and atmosphere, which often developed through decades and even centuries of evolution.

These neighborhood qualities are not necessarily found in each individual road or house, but rather in how they fit together collectively. If we're being blunt, most of the houses in these areas are architectural mediocrities at best. While Japan is rightly famous for its traditional wooden architecture, such houses are increasingly scarce even in more traditional urban areas, and most of the housing stock in question here consists of decades-old prefabricated imitations of suburban Western houses. Their interiors aren't particularly comfortable in Tokyo's punishing summers and chilly winters, since Japan's weak building regulations do not require contractors to include thermal insulation or double glazing. However, the overall layout of these neighborhoods allows them to become more than the sum of their parts.

6.3   The joys of dense, low-rise neighborhoods

If our goal is to learn from these neighborhoods, we must dissect *why* they are so beneficial in greater detail. For this discussion, we can divide their benefits into three categories: they offer an *adaptable urban fabric, transit convenience*, and *vibrant community life*.

The flexibility of these neighborhoods is unmatched, both in terms of accommodating individuality and allowing organic change over time. Their housing is all detached, unlike with similarly high-density low-rise alternatives such as row houses. That openness to every side breeds flexibility, allowing for an endless variety of home and street layouts. And since the average age of these houses is a mere 30 years, it is common to rebuild them during an owner's lifetime and thereby adapt the plot's use to new circumstances in the family. What's more, these neighborhoods tend not to be purely residential thanks to Japan's inclusive zoning rules, which give homeowners very broad leeway to do as they like with their own property. Even quiet residential lanes are sprinkled with idiosyncratic mom-and-pop businesses with homeowners living above them.

These neighborhoods are not isolated, car-dependent suburbs. The population of these areas can easily access central Tokyo via convenient suburban railway connections. The suburban tranquility of dense low-rise areas comes coupled with commutes under an hour to the urban core's hubs of activity and opportunity. Commercial centers around each station offer services ranging from hospitals and clinics to schools and *shōtengai* commercial promenades, allowing locals to smoothly handle their needs along their daily commute. This arrangement is usually the result of intentional planning by suburban railway operators, who hold substantial real estate interests in the communities their lines serve. In recent years, Western urbanists and transit scholars have come to appreciate the strengths of this integrated model. They now refer to it as Transit-oriented Development (TOD) and promote it as if it were a novel concept. In Japan, however, it has been the norm for roughly a century.

Finally, the human dimension of these communities is a key part of their appeal. The public-spiritedness of a community adds to its livability, drawing brand-new residents into urban Japan's centuries-old participatory neighborhood life. Over the years, these areas have developed a strong sense of community and civic pride. Although public greenery is scarce, residents frequently adorn the streets with planters and pots, creating an ad-hoc green fabric. The streets are kept extremely clean through personal effort rather than government services, and neighbors know and rely on each other. Elderly volunteers do much of this work. However, seasonal events and physically strenuous traditions (such as carrying the neighborhood's portable mikoshi shrine in festivals) can provide an impetus for younger residents to begin participating in neighborhood life.

6.4   The origins of a delicate balance

Although dense low-rise neighborhoods were common in Tokyo even during the Edo period, most of the city's equivalent areas today are relatively new, a result of the explosive growth of Tokyo's railway suburbs in the 1920s and 1930s that dramatically expanded the city to the south and west. Many of these suburban railway developments were inspired (at least on paper) by the British garden city model of spacious detached houses in a low-density setting with ample streets and parklands. After a hundred years of evolution, however, they came to differ greatly from this imported model. Their development accelerated after the war, especially during Japan's period of rapid economic growth in the 1960s and 1970s. Land values increased rapidly across much of Tokyo during this time, and within a few years an incredible quantity of land had been hastily developed. [106] Many areas caught up in this rapid-fire process lacked any consistent overall street plan, so development followed pre-existing organic patterns. Although these neighborhoods differ in their locations and particular histories, over the decades they've all been shaped by the same macro-level trends in Tokyo's evolution. The typical end result is a village-like, small-scale community enclosed by major arterial roads with larger buildings, an urban configuration sometimes referred to as a superblock.

These superblocks began as a byproduct of Japan's postwar reconstruction effort. After the war, the Tokyo Metropolitan Government planned for the city to eventually construct a web-like network of ring and radial arterial roads over the coming decades, most of which was eventually completed. With four to six lanes, the wide roads stood in stark contrast with the city's pre-existing network of smaller streets, alleys, and laneways, many of which remain stubbornly narrow despite the government's efforts to widen them. The superblock configuration was further encouraged from 1981 onwards by government measures designed to promote the creation of 'anti-fire blockade belts.'[107] Under this concept, the city's older, more flammable neighborhoods within interior blocks are ringed by sturdier modern buildings on their periphery, which in turn open out onto wide main roads. By law these modern buildings follow strict fireproofing regulations, creating what are effectively fire walls between districts. These measures further accelerated a decade-long trend toward taller buildings being placed along the perimeters of Tokyo's superblocks.

The current state of Tokyo's dense low-rise neighborhoods is not the result of a top-down design vision, but rather the combined effect of numerous disparate influences. Shrinking lot sizes and an increase in car ownership have caused many of the spaces once reserved for a home's frontal garden to vanish or be adapted to other purposes. At the same time, changes to the Building Standards Law over the years have made it permissible to build residences with ever-higher floor area ratios (FAR), enabling more intense land use.

During Japan's high growth period from 1954 to 1973, the trend of dividing up land in dense low-rise neighborhoods accelerated rapidly. Lower-income populations increasingly moved to areas of Tokyo once owned by the middle and upper classes, right as Japan's central government implemented a major inheritance tax.[108] Inherited land was subjected to a tax rate that, depending on circumstances, could be as high as 50% of its value and frequently required payment in a single lump sum. This led many families to subdivide their land upon the death of a patriarch, either in order to distribute it among relatives or to sell part of it in order to pay the inheritance taxes on the remainder. Smaller land plots led to smaller houses. To this day, Tokyo's wards have only experimented in a minimal way with the concept of lot size minimums, and the Japanese Building Standards Law does not contain limitations or guidelines concerning plot subdivision. Currently, the only regulation one must follow when subdividing plots is that each lot must have an access space of at least 2 m in width to provide entry from a front road.

One downside of these trends is that many neighborhoods are increasingly losing their greenery. In Japan's exclusively residential areas, the maximum plot coverage—that is, the most space that buildings on a plot are allowed to take up—ranges between 30% to 60%, but due to the small scale of Tokyo's plots and the requirement to leave some space between adjacent buildings, the remaining unbuilt space is mostly taken up with residual gap spaces rather than proper gardens. In addition to the plots' shrinking sizes, the space in front of one's home that was traditionally used for gardens now increasingly serves as a parking space, and streets that were once beautifully lined with frontal gardens have been invaded by cars and asphalt.

As seen on the map Fig. 6-2, dense low-rise areas extend across almost all of Tokyo's 23 wards. They are among the city's most ordinary landscapes and offer a high level of livability. But since their success as places to live is not the direct result of any overall design vision for the city, Tokyo's officialdom gives little thought to how to preserve them. As wooden houses are rapidly replaced by concrete condominiums, their green frontages have disappeared, with parking spaces too often arising in their place. Streets are widened for understandable safety reasons, but often the intimate atmosphere of narrow alleyways which gave the neighborhood a sense of community disappears as a result.

The following three cases illustrate both the remarkable qualities of these neighborhoods and the considerable challenges they face. Our focus is not on pure cases, but rather on areas that combine a critical mass of low-rise housing with taller buildings as well. We hope not only to identify the key qualities of the city's dense low-rise neighborhoods but also to explore how they interact with taller adjacent buildings. These case studies include the suburban neighborhood of Higashi-Nakanobu $\overline{\text{Figs. 6-3, 4}}$, the historic planned district of Tsukishima $\overline{\text{Figs. 6-5, 6}}$, and the north end of Shirokane where low-, mid-, and high-rises are closely mixed $\overline{\text{Figs. 6-7, 8}}$.

Fig. 6-3 Higashi-Nakanobu as of July 2019. Most of its streets are quiet residential lanes sprinkled with planters and pots (A, B). Cars do not dominate the wider streets, but instead share space with pedestrians and cyclists (C). Commercial activity is concentrated along the covered shōtengai (D).

Fig. 6-4 The evolution of Higashi-Nakanobu (1:10,000).

0　100m

1909　On Tokyo's rural outskirts, a few houses stand scattered in a bamboo forest.

Source: *Tokyo Seihokubu, 1909 survey* (Dai Nippon Teikoku Rikuchi Sokuryōbu, 1929).

Bamboo forest

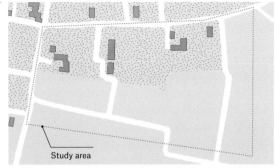

Study area

1929　With the opening in 1927 of the Nakanobu and Ebara-Nakanobu Stations the area rapidly urbanizes, although large tracts are still unoccupied. A grid of new roads is laid out throughout the new Western suburbs in preparation for new construction, mostly by absorbing preexisting paths.

Source: *Tokyo Seihokubu* (Dai Nippon Teikoku Rikuchi Sokuryōbu, 1929).

Cluster of buildings

Nakanobu Sta.

Ōimachi Line

1970　The area has become much more accessible. Nakanobu Station was elevated in 1957 to alleviate traffic on the Daini Keihin Highway. In 1968 the Asakusa Line begins alighting at Nakanobu Station. The area continues densifying, with houses occupying their blocks' whole depth and new alleyways providing access to them.

Source: *Jūtakuchizu* (Zenrin, 1970).

Skip Road Shōtengai

Asakusa Line
Nakanobu Station

Daini keihin Highway

2019　The buildings along the highway have become apartments and office high-rises. Skip Road, the local shōtengai, is still thriving with a mixture of franchises and independent stores. Many of the residences' front gardens disappeared as the area continued densifying.

Source: *Jūtakuchizu* (Zenrin, 2019).

6.5 Higashi-Nakanobu: ordinary in the best sense

Case 13

It is difficult to select a particular neighborhood to serve as a case study of suburban dense low-rise housing, since the form is the default setting of Tokyo's everyday life and an ordinary landscape for the bulk of the city's inhabitants. Indeed, almost any neighborhood meeting the basic criteria of the term could serve as a representative case. Nevertheless, the district called Higashi-Nakanobu 2nd chōme in Shinagawa Ward makes a fine example.[109] The area's population density (26,633 persons/km^2 [110]) is typical of the densities one sees in these suburban neighborhoods—a level of density that enables local commerce, usually concentrated along a commercial shōtengai promenade, and provides sufficient ridership for public transport. In keeping with this formula Higashi-Nakanobu is an area adjacent to both an arterial road and an elevated station, with a lively shōtengai to boot Figs. 6-9, 10. Due to its older construction, narrow alleyways, and dense layout, the area has been classified by the Tokyo Metropolitan Government as being especially dangerous in case of disaster.

At the beginning of the 20th century, Higashi-Nakanobu was mostly a patch of farmland smattered with occasional houses. Its urbanization accelerated after 1927, when the construction of the Tōkyū Ōimachi and Ikegami train lines allowed for easier access to the area. After the war, the adjacent *Daini Keihin* Highway was widened, creating a stark contrast between the neighborhood's nearest major roadway and its inner alleys. In the 1960s, as the area's housing density began to increase, buildings along the highway still had the same dimensions as those along the smaller alleys. From the 1970s onward, however, outer buildings along the highway were replaced with much taller structures while the inner neighborhoods simply increased in density.

Many of these neighborhoods were originally planned as garden cities by private railway companies. However, over time many such areas have increasingly deviated from this original vision, and Higashi-Nakanobu is no exception. While Tokyo's most famous 1920s garden city development, the neighborhood of Den-en Chōfu, has been able to keep its spacious plots and greenery to the present day because of its status as one of the most exclusive enclaves of Tokyo's upper class, in less rarefied neighborhoods such as Higashi-Nakanobu there is stronger pressure to build right up to a lot's maximum coverage area. As a result, densification has turned the spaces between buildings into mere gaps rather than proper open spaces.

Higashi-Nakanobu illustrates a historical irony of Tokyo's dense low-rise suburban neighborhoods. After the Great Kantō Earthquake saw deadly fires consume huge swathes of the city's dense wooden neighborhoods, spacious suburban communities became all the rage among Tokyoites with money. As they escaped en masse to the suburbs, the well-to-do hoped that these new, less crowded neigbhorhoods would be safer in the event of a disaster. Before long, however, Tokyo's continuous postwar growth caught up to the suburbs and rendered them nearly as dense and congested as the city's inner neighborhoods.

Local planning authorities are doing their best to balance Higashi-Nakanobu's land usage, such as by developing pocket parks that can also serve as evacuation areas. Recent initiatives include offering financial help to rebuild houses and set them further back from plot boundaries to enable street widening and subsidies for those willing to merge plots so that concrete fireproof condominiums can be built in place of single family housing. These measures help mitigate the vulnerability of the area to disasters, but as a result new and larger buildings tend to appear randomly, disrupting the delicate balance of any given corner of the neighborhood.

Higashi-Nakanobu could do better than this scattershot approach; looking across other similar areas of Tokyo, a more strategic approach that respects an area's unique qualities is clearly possible. Tsukishima, a district where one of Tokyo's most intense battles between small- and large-scale urban development is taking place, is a prime example of how a neighborhood can successfully preserve its small-scale urban fabric with holistic reforms.

6.6
Case 14

Tsukishima: spontaneity in the grid

Tsukishima, in Chūō Ward, is an artificial island located on the mouth of the Sumida River. The neighborhood occupies a privileged position on Tokyo's contemporary map due to its close proximity to the ritzy Ginza district, but it wasn't always so. Until recently, Tsukishima was an unassuming working-class neighborhood occupying land reclaimed for industrial use during the Meiji period. The area is famous for its narrow roji alleys, which offer its residents everyday opportunities for informal, intimate encounters and give the area a strong sense of community. However, a looming juggernaut threatens this traditional idyll—a number of newly-constructed super-high-rise condominium towers Figs. 6-11, 12.

After Tsukishima's land reclamation was completed in 1892, the area was laid out in a grid, with warehouses and factories along the surrounding canals and housing in the inner blocks. Even before the war, the district was fully urbanized. Tsukishima's good fortune during the war set it apart architecturally from the bulk of eastern Tokyo's inner neighborhoods—many of its wooden *nagaya* row houses, the backbone of Tsukishima's working class, survived the air raids. From the 1960s onward, the area further densified with more and smaller houses as it struggled to absorb a sudden population increase during Japan's period of rapid economic growth. Tsukishima's 1st and 3rd chōme are excellent examples of the district's progressive transformation. Despite abutting the north side of Kiyosumi Avenue, the broad avenue that bisects the island from east to west, they still retain Tsukishima's characteristic urban blocks which echo the urban forms and proportions of the Edo period.[111]

Tsukishima's broader streets accommodate commercial buildings, particularly Nishi-Naka Street, which is known for restaurants serving the local specialty *monjayaki*. The roji alleys, meanwhile, accommodate single-family houses and nagaya. Since violent crime in proverbial dark alleys is nearly non-existent in Tokyo, roji are often used almost as an extension of the domestic space. As in so many Tokyo neighborhoods, in Tsukishima one sees subtle transitions along the spectrum of public to private space rather than a hard division between the two.

A

B

C

D

Unlike the spontaneous and labyrinthine alleys that have arisen over time in most parts of Tokyo, Tsukishima's roji were intentionally planned by the government over a century ago. Nevertheless, concerns abound that the area's narrow alleys will be fire hazards in a disaster, and they were retroactively deemed inappropriate when national legislation established a minimum width of 4 m for all streets in 1938.

As with so many other areas, Tsukishima has suffered the perverse effects of setback obligations. Instead of rebuilding their homes, landowners kept renovating to maintain their building's size, which protected the roji alleys from

Fig. 6-6   The evolution of Tsukishima (1:7,000).

0 ⌞⌞⌞⌞⌞⌞⌟ 100m 🧭

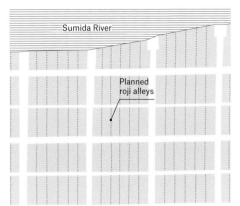

1895   Tsukishima is an artificial island constructed in 1892 at the mouth of the Sumida River. It was urbanized in accordance with a strict grid plan featuring diverse street widths, including roji alleys.

Source: *Tōkyōkubunzu* (Yūbindenshin Kyoku,1895).

1932   The area was gradually converted into industrial and residential land. Wooden tenement row houses (or nagaya) were built along the roji alleys, while industrial development took place along the river.

Source: *Kasaihoken Tokushuchizu* (Toshiseizusha, 1932).

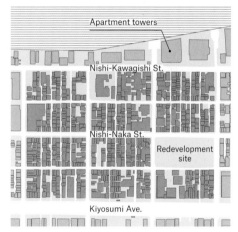

1980   The area's industrial presence has grown, but the low-rise nagaya remain almost totally intact.

Source: *Jūtakuchizu* (Zenrin, 1980).

2019   Tsukishima is now much more accessible to the public thanks to two new stations—the Yūrakuchō Line in 1988 and the Ōedo Line in 2000. The surroundings are rapidly transforming into apartment towers, with new developments planned inside this area as well.

Source: *Jūtakuchizu* (Zenrin, 2019).

widening but also preempted building improvements that would boost disaster preparedness. As a result, when the first tower development projects began in the surrounding areas in the 1980s, Tsukishima was still left mostly untouched.

Since then, however, tower development pressure has only increased. Many landowners have given up their properties in exchange for the rights to a new apartment in one of the many towers under construction. Others are keen to preserve their roji lifestyle, and have even garnered some support from the authorities for their effort. From the 1990s onward, Tsukishima's ward government pioneered regulations to incentivize rebuilding by accepting new construction along even alleys as narrow as 2.7 m—the narrowest possible legal width, rarely accepted by authorities[112]—and relaxing volume restrictions to allow new houses of up to three floors if the alley width can be increased to 3.3 m, a straightforward trade of space outward for space upward.[113] These regulations successfully spurred more small-scale rebuilding and increased the district's overall fire resistance.

Today, however, even this slice of Tsukishima is home to three planned redevelopments which will add a total of 141 floors of residential capacity. The projects are in keeping with the eagerness of Chūō Ward to increase its population and thus its tax base, a prioritization which has led them to offer public subsidies for large-scale redevelopment. This situation has sparked resistance from local citizens, who criticize the consequences of over-development: increased traffic, large shadows, ground winds and gusts created by high-rise buildings, and perhaps most importantly the loss of the area's character and community life. These community opposition groups claim that required procedures for development such as community consultations have not been followed, and argue that the positive goals of redevelopment (such as improved safety against disasters) can be met via low-rise alternatives.[114] Such approaches could be implemented incrementally by building off of the area's pioneering regulatory reforms from the 1990s. This battle is just one of many across the city, an example of the intense controversies that surround large-scale redevelopment and the ways in which current urban legislation is often biased toward the interests of development corporations. In theory, citizens have the right to be informed about redevelopment plans and to make their opinions known to planning authorities. In practice, the secrecy and speed of many decisions leaves almost no time or resources for citizens to react. Ward governments, whose financial interests frequently align with the development corporations, will often use the levers of state at their disposal to subtly influence the process away from transparency and community input.

Tsukishima's long-standing success as an intimate, Tokyo-esque neighborhood has broader implications. After all, Tsukishima is more than just another neighborhood—it is, in itself, a massive urban redevelopment, a whole artificial island. By its very existence, it illustrates that a district's feeling of organic community does not necessarily require centuries of natural historical accumulation or fancy, complicated urban designs. All Tsukishima needed was a street grid that enabled different gradients of publicness, allowing its inhabitants to organically and spontaneously shape its spaces into a community. This is a feat that urban planners could potentially replicate not only elsewhere in Tokyo, but in cities around the world.

North Shirokane: the beauty of urban diversity

The northern part of Tokyo's Shirokane district between Ebisu Street[115] and the Furukawa River is a predominantly low-rise neighborhood that has surprisingly managed to survive redevelopment despite being located in the very heart of posh central Minato Ward Figs. 6-13, 14.[116] The area contains a mixture of building scales, dominated by low-rise and mid-rise buildings with some high-rises on the periphery. Most of the buildings (about 70%) are residential, split evenly between single-family detached houses and condominiums. In addition to the neighborhood's shōtengai commercial street, the area is home to numerous *machikōba*, small artisanal 'town factories' located in the first floors of houses and tucked into small residential blocks.[117]

This area, which we refer to as 'North Shirokane,' is an example of how land intensification need not degrade the quality of a streetscape. The neighborhood's single-family detached houses tend to appear along narrower streets, with mid-rises along wider streets. In both scales, machikōba artisan workshops and other hallmarks of neighborhood life can be found at the ground level. The area's high-rises lurk on the periphery of the area along Ebisu Street, creating an organic gradation of privacy and scale.

Until the beginnings of the Meiji period the area consisted largely of paddy fields, but industrialization soon brought small factories and houses. Before the war, Ebisu Street was built to facilitate access and accelerate the area's development. From the 1960s, two divergent phenomena have shaped North Shirokane. On the one hand, landowners began combining their plots in order to construct larger condominiums. At the same time, however, inheritance taxes were pushing landowners to subdivide their land, producing ever-smaller plots and houses. The two trends were not happening on the same lots; consolidation appeared at the periphery of the area, where regulations allow higher buildings thanks to wider roads. In the inner blocks, however, subdivision was the dominant trend, although some smaller condominiums can also be found.

The area's planned redevelopment may soon upend this delicate balance. In recent years, with the opening of the new Namboku Line and the Shirokane Takanawa Station, super-high-rise buildings have appeared in the area for the first time. Plans have been made to demolish entire urban blocks, including their internal alleys, and construct towers over 40 floors high.[118] As in so many other neighborhoods, disaster readiness is being used as a pretext to push development. Unlike Tsukishima, however, fire disasters are not considered the main threat, since the district already has a high percentage of fireproof construction; brochures promoting the redevelopment instead reference the risk of flooding from the adjacent river.

This insistence that residential super-high-rises (popularly called 'tower mansions') represent the ultimate in building safety conflicts with Japan's recent

Fig. 6-7 North Shirokane as of January 2020. The neighborhood contains buildings of different scales, ages, and uses (A), including houses along tiny alleys (B) and houses with artisan factories on their first floors (C, D). The local shopping promenade is a lively, pedestrian-friendly space (E).

real-world disaster experiences, including the major floods of 2019 and the earthquake of March 2011. These disasters revealed the vulnerability of many towers' mechanical systems, as their supply lines for gas, water, and especially electricity were heavily affected. With heights reaching 50 floors and close to 1,000 households each, dwellers on upper floors of high-rises found themselves unable to access their apartments due to inoperable elevators, becoming *kōsō-nanmin* or 'high-rise refugees' camped out in tower lobbies or evacuation facilities.

Large-scale redevelopments are encouraged by an official government philosophy touting the benefits of a 'return to the city' or *toshin kaiki*, a densi-

Fig. 6-8   The evolution of North Shirokane (1:8,000).

0   100m

1887   The area along the Furukawa River, which we refer to here as North Shirokane, was mostly farmland with few dwellings.

Source: *Tōkyō Jissokuzu* (Naimushō 1887).

 Forest   Grassland   Fruit orchards

1936   New roads were laid out, mainly overlapping with old pre-existing agricultural paths. Road connectivity accelerated the district's urbanization as an industrial and residential area.

Source: *Kasaihoken Tokushuchizu* (Toshiseizusha,1936).

1991   Plots along the wider street have been merged to accommodate larger buildings, while the smaller plots along the alleys have begun to be subdivided for smaller houses.

Source: *Jūtakuchizu* (Zenrin, 1991).

2018   North Shirokane shows an intricate mix of building scales, with pockets full of low-rises and alleys interspersed throughout. Despite this being one of the last remaining low-rise sections of central Tokyo, several blocks are targeted for demolition and redevelopment into tower complexes.

Source: *Jūtakuchizu* (Zenrin, 2018).

fication of the central districts that promises to reduce commutes and ease the provision of city services. As it resists wholesale redevelopment, North Shirokane shows an alternative densification model. Shirokane 3rd chōme, the one sector of North Shirokane without any tower mansions, nevertheless achieves a density of 35,309 persons/km², a density similar to what is found in European cities that are held up as models of sustainable compact urbanism.[119] North Shirokane's dense mixture of buildings and street sizes creates compact urban diversity and allows the streets to serve as a true public space, offering an alternative blueprint for other densifying low-rise areas around the world.

6.8   Learning from dense low-rise neighborhoods

The surprising livability of dense low-rise neighborhoods defies an outside observer's first impression of them as merely cluttered and crowded. Higashi-Nakanobu, Tsukishima, and North Shirokane showcase many of the qualities that create this livability—and also the significant threats these neighborhoods face. In addition to the general characteristics mentioned earlier—adaptability, transit convenience, and community—there are also less obvious but more designable principles that contribute to these neighborhoods' livability. These principles cannot be singlehandedly attributed to any single social or physical dimension; they arise from synergistic combinations of multiple elements. When they combine, they produce physical patterns that can be observed, quantified, and even mapped out. Many of these patterns offer lessons for neighborhoods around the world, as shown visually below Figs. 6-10, 12, 14.

6.8.1   Use gap spaces to offer visual permeability and adaptability

These neighborhoods' high plot coverage and heavily subdivided land have created numerous gap spaces between houses. At first glance, these gaps could be dismissed as mere wasted space, a necessary evil in service of fire prevention. However, gap spaces serve a unique role in Tokyo; they compensate for the average neighborhood's lack of open public spaces by creating a sense of continuous visual permeability throughout the area. At the same time, they offer opportunities for gardens and other small activities. Personal items such as bicycles, laundry, and children's toys are often found scattered in these gaps, mixed in with potted plants and trees. This phenomenon is common in low-rise, high-density residential areas and is referred to as *afuredashi* or 'overflow.'

6.8.2   Encourage dispersed small greenery

In Tokyo neighborhoods, dispersed greenery has been a tradition in various forms since the Edo period: trees and bushes, plantation hedges, and potted plants can all be placed around a plot by its inhabitants, its landlord, or even a local association. Since neighborhoods usually lack centrally administered greenery such as gardens, parks, or tree-lined streets, this bottom-up tradition of placing one's own greenery serves as a partial yet meaningful substitute.

6.8.3   Structure shared spaces to naturally prioritize pedestrians and bicycles

Even with the narrowness of many streets in these neighborhoods, cars do have full access to most houses. What's more, sidewalks and other forms of pedestrian protection are virtually nonexistent. However, cars do not feel invasive, and the antagonistic dynamic between motorists and pedestrians common to so many urban neighborhoods around the world is largely absent. The difference lies in the layout of the neighborhood. Motorists cutting across town have every incentive to stick to the major arterial roads, as they gain nothing by getting lost in a labyrinth of alleys. The few cars seen in the neighborhood's interior are generally local residents, who naturally take greater care with their own community than a stranger would. The end result is a pedestrian-friendly experience even when cars and people mix freely in the street.

6.8.4   **Use diverse street types to create gradations from public to private space**

The distinctive spatial configuration of these districts has long caught the eye of both urban researchers and foreign visitors. When a neighborhood is surrounded by wide streets and arterial roads but features narrow, rambling inner alleys, the stark contrast between the two naturally creates a distinct superblock configuration, protecting the interior from traffic and lending it an air of calmness and intimacy. This diversity of street types, from the smallest roji to large arterial roads, creates different social atmospheres. The difference is reflected in residents' individual choices; on narrower streets, there are more personal belongings left about and house façades tend to be more open. On wider streets, houses tend to be more closed off and there are fewer reminders of human activity. Environments shape actions and actions shape environments in a continuous, self-reinforcing cycle.

6.8.5   **Foster a sense of collective safety via street-side doors and windows**

The urbanist Jane Jacobs once famously declared that the layout of houses and businesses in an urban space can contribute to safety by providing "eyes on the streets." In Tokyo's dense low-rise areas, the "eyes on the street" may not always be obvious; windows are often covered over, and depending on the time of day one can go long stretches without seeing another person. However, the urban scale and layout, the numerous windows and doors along streets, and the intimacy of the community all act as a deterrent, as any suspicious behavior by outsiders might be easily noticed.

6.8.6   **Allow varied building types and uses even in the most residential areas**

These neighborhoods are predominantly residential, but they easily integrate other uses. Many feature a shōtengai shopping promenade, and the first floors of houses often contain small shops, restaurants, or even light industry such as the machikōba workshops of North Shirokane. The mingling of buildings of different sizes and ages offers flexible options for both residents and businesses. Small, cheap wooden structures may pose disaster safety concerns, but on the plus side they can be easily adapted, expanded, reused, and transformed. Keeping a stock of inexpensive, transformable, and adaptable architecture in the neighborhood enhances social and economic diversity.

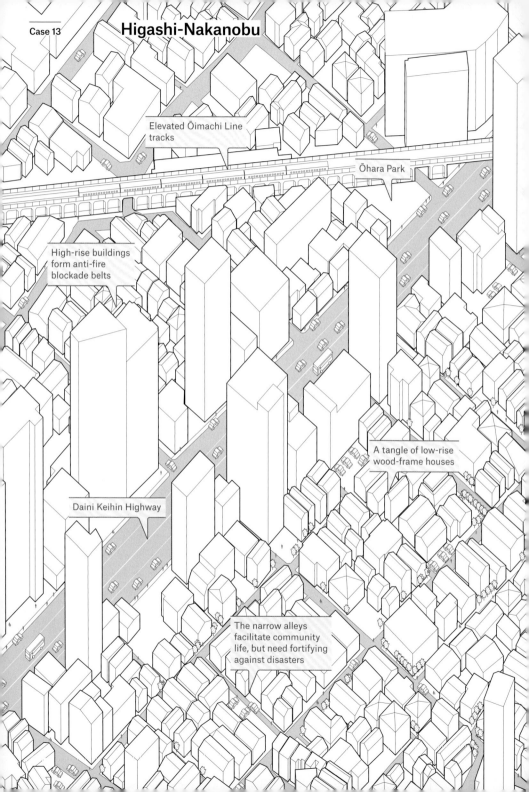

Higashi-Nakanobu

Elevated Ōimachi Line tracks

Ōhara Park

High-rise buildings form anti-fire blockade belts

A tangle of low-rise wood-frame houses

Daini Keihin Highway

The narrow alleys facilitate community life, but need fortifying against disasters

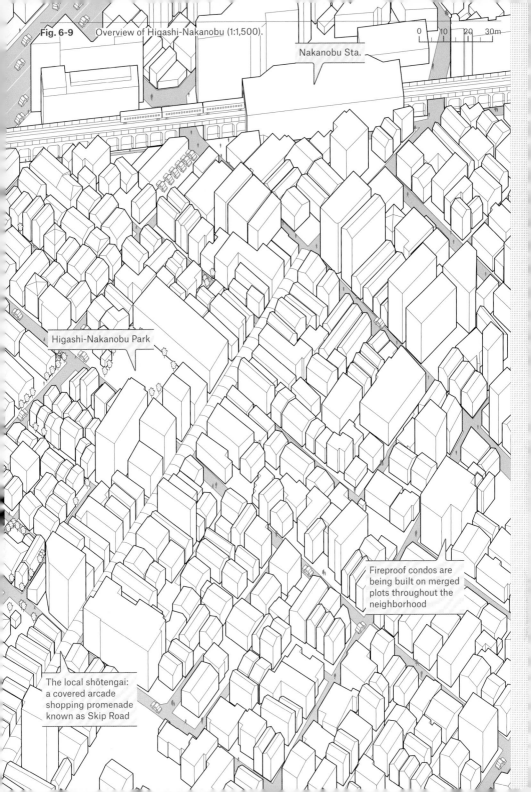

Fig. 6-9 Overview of Higashi-Nakanobu (1:1,500).

0 10 20 30m

Nakanobu Sta.

Higashi-Nakanobu Park

Fireproof condos are being built on merged plots throughout the neighborhood

The local shōtengai: a covered arcade shopping promenade known as Skip Road

Gap space

☐ Gap spaces within
building plots

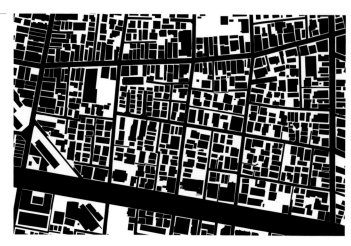

Street types by width

■ Width < 2.7 m
■ Width ≥ 2.7 m and < 4 m
■ Width ≥ 4.0 m and < 8 m
■ Width ≥ 8.0 m and < 12 m
   Width ≥ 12.0 m

Building uses

■ Residence + factory/workshop
■ Factory/workshop
■ Commercial building
■ Residence + commercial
■ Single-family house
■ Office building
☐ Apartment building
☐ Other

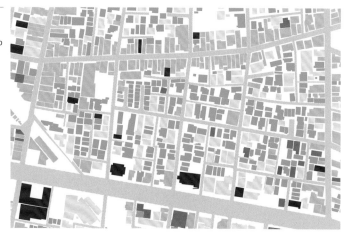

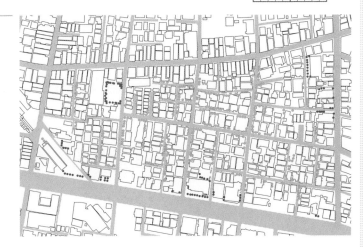

0   50   100m

Greenery

Potted plants
Trees in private gardens
Trees on public or
collective housing land

Building entrances

▲ Building entrance

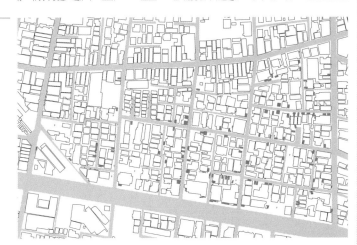

Parking pattern

Parked cars
Parked bicycles and
motorcycles

185

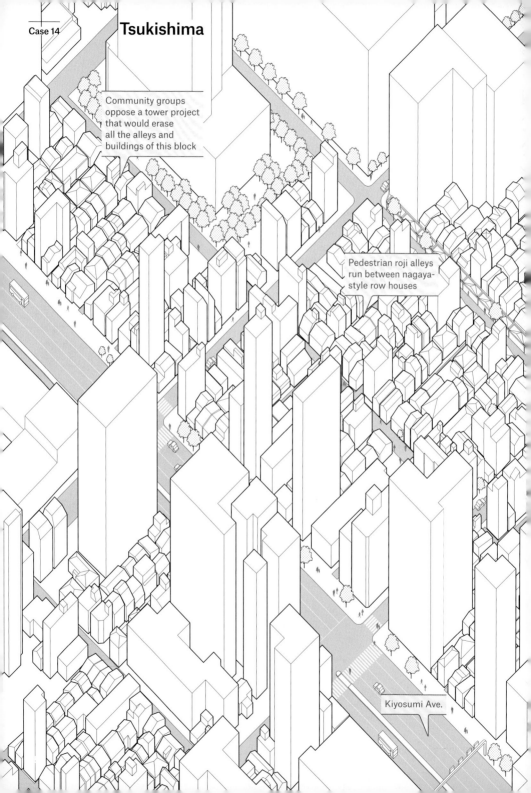

Case 14

Tsukishima

Community groups
oppose a tower project
that would erase
all the alleys and
buildings of this block

Pedestrian roji alleys
run between nagaya-
style row houses

Kiyosumi Ave.

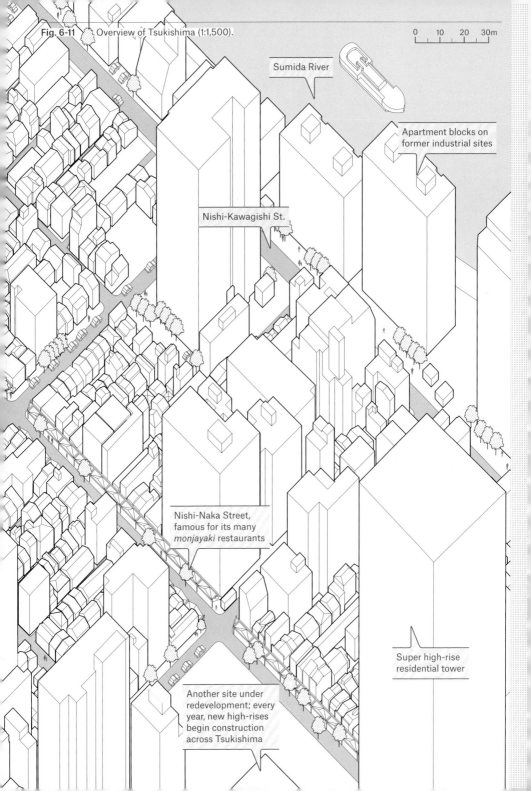

Fig. 6-11　Overview of Tsukishima (1:1,500).

0　10　20　30m

Sumida River

Apartment blocks on former industrial sites

Nishi-Kawagishi St.

Nishi-Naka Street, famous for its many *monjayaki* restaurants

Super high-rise residential tower

Another site under redevelopment; every year, new high-rises begin construction across Tsukishima

Fig. 6-12   Street level mapping of Tsukishima as of March 2020 (1:5000).

Gap space

☐ Gap spaces within
    building plots

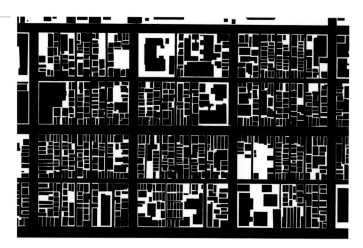

Street types by width

■ Width < 2.7 m
■ Width ≥ 2.7 m and < 4 m
▦ Width ≥ 4.0 m and < 8 m
▨ Width ≥ 8.0 m and < 12 m
  Width ≥ 12.0 m

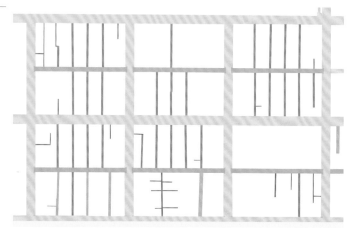

Building uses

■ Residence + factory/workshop
▦ Factory/workshop
■ Commercial building
▦ Residence + commercial
▦ Single-family house
■ Office building
▨ Apartment building
☐ Other

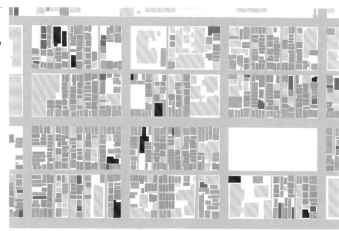

0   50   100m

Greenery

- Potted plants
- Trees in private gardens
- Trees on public or collective housing land

Building entrances

▲ Building entrance

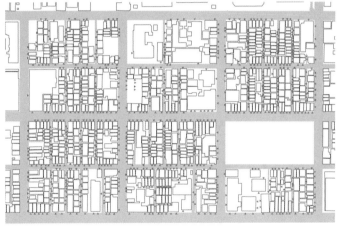

Parking pattern

- Parked cars
- Parked bicycles and motorcycles

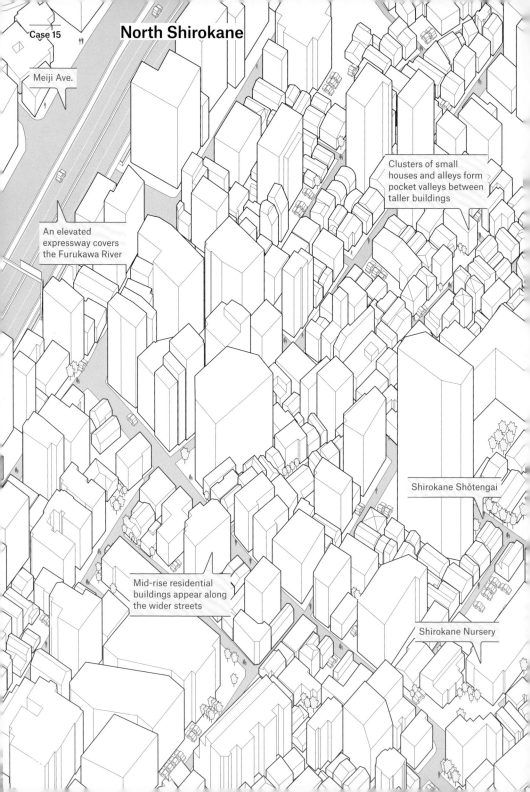

Case 15

North Shirokane

Meiji Ave.

An elevated expressway covers the Furukawa River

Clusters of small houses and alleys form pocket valleys between taller buildings

Shirokane Shōtengai

Mid-rise residential buildings appear along the wider streets

Shirokane Nursery

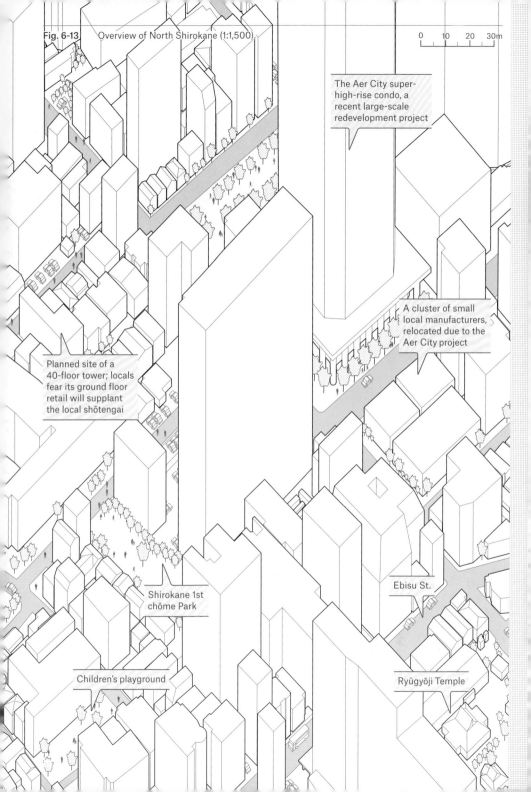

Fig. 6-13   Overview of North Shirokane (1:1,500).

0   10   20   30m

The Aer City super-
high-rise condo, a
recent large-scale
redevelopment project

A cluster of small
local manufacturers,
relocated due to the
Aer City project

Planned site of a
40-floor tower; locals
fear its ground floor
retail will supplant
the local shōtengai

Shirokane 1st
chōme Park

Ebisu St.

Children's playground

Ryūgyōji Temple

Gap space

☐ Gap spaces within
   building plots

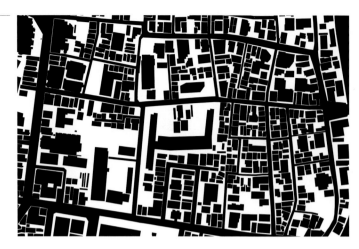

Street types by width

■ Width < 2.7 m
■ Width ≥ 2.7 m and < 4 m
■ Width ≥ 4.0 m and < 8 m
▨ Width ≥ 8.0 m and < 12 m
   Width ≥ 12.0 m

Building uses

■ Residence + factory/workshop
■ Factory/workshop
■ Commercial building
■ Residence + commercial
■ Single-family house
■ Office building
▨ Apartment building
☐ Other

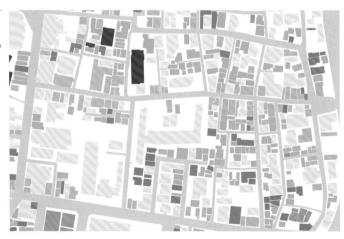

Greenery

- Potted plants
- Trees in private gardens
- Trees on public or collective housing land

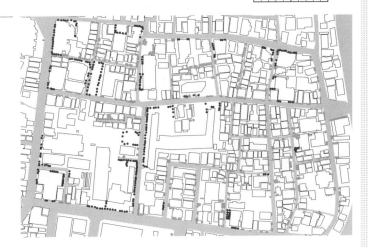

Building entrances

- ▲ Building entrance

Parking pattern

- Parked cars
- Parked bicycles and motorcycles

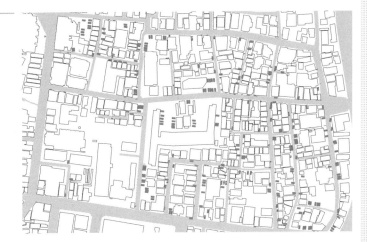

7 TOKYOLOGY

7.1 A chronology of thinking about Tokyo

Much like New York, Paris, or Rome, Tokyo is an object of intense fascination among architects and urban designers and a constant topic of their discussions and investigations. This body of studies on Tokyo—referred to here as *Tokyology*—has evolved and mutated over the decades, reflecting both changing ideas about the role of architecture and broader transformations in society.

This existing body of knowledge has laid the conceptual groundwork for our book, and we owe a debt to all who have studied and loved this captivating metropolis. At the same time, the popular discourse around these works often erases their nuances and context, giving way to unfounded assumptions and stereotyped narratives that miss the reality of the city. Part of our aim with this book is to expose these common tropes and clichés. At best they are incomplete and at worse outright falsehoods—particularly those which reduce Tokyo's complexity down to a just-so story about the city's ineffable Japaneseness. This is a challenge, since both journalists and academics writing on Tokyo so frequently repeat these clichés without inquiring too deeply into their accuracy.

In order to hash out the origins of these common tropes, we need to first examine how the study of Tokyo has evolved over time. The timeline below charts some of the most important writings on Tokyo over the past sixty years, including books in both English and Japanese.[120] In order to enable a comparison between the evolution of ideas in Japan and abroad, we have paired it with a chronology of globally influential writings on urbanism and architecture, as well as major historical events in Japan.[121] The timeline has been divided into six sections corresponding to the main theoretical approaches seen in Tokyo studies, including:

7.1.1 Omnibus works

The books in this category are compilations of heterogeneous essays and thoughts on Tokyo, mostly in English. Many also reference the latest theories by Japanese authors at the time of publication, but some are travelogues and personal memoirs, including foreigners describing their first encounters with the city. The omnibus books plotted in the timeline contain careful and insightful accounts of life in Tokyo, especially some decades-old works that have now withstood the test of time.

Due to the sheer lack of books about Tokyo in English, these compilations have become one of the main ways that Tokyo is interpreted and understood by English-language readers. Although only some portion of these are scholarly writings, the enduring influence of these books and their tropes can be seen in how Tokyo is portrayed in English today across both mass media and academia.

Even beyond their information about Tokyo itself, many of these books have a separate value as a record of the foreign gaze in different periods—that is, a chronicle of what role Tokyo played in the foreign imagination of the time. Roland Barthes's *Empire of Signs* is perhaps the most influential example of the suggestive power of the foreign gaze, despite his book's disclaimer that his descriptions of Japan are those of a "fictive nation" and a "novelistic object." The book records the complex relationship between the imagined Orient and the real Japan, one that many foreigners can relate to when recalling their own first encounters with Japanese cities. If we look beyond Tokyology into more popular writings, we see that many subsequent writers copied Barthes's tropes wholesale, including his descriptions of Tokyo as an exotic city with "an empty center" or a place "where streets have no names," but discarded his literary intentions, resulting in blatantly orientalist clichés being repeated ad nauseam.

7.1.2   **Comparisons and reappraisals**

After Japan's defeat in World War II, a widespread atmosphere of societal self-criticism took hold in the 1950s. In architecture and urban planning, however, this pessimism co-existed with enthusiasm for the opportunity to plan Tokyo anew on the perfect *tabula rasa* created by the war's scorched-earth bombings. Many architects began exploring modernist and rationalist possibilities for Tokyo's reconstruction rather than looking back to Edo or Japanese vernacular spaces, leading to a new literature directly comparing Tokyo to Western cities. As the Japanese economy recovered and the nation regained its collective vigor, however, many authors started to research Japan's rich history of vernacular urban space and architecture, and architects expressed this increasing confidence in their cultural roots through their designs.

The authors in this discursive lineage generally acknowledge that Tokyo is not as visually straightforward as Western cities. Nevertheless, they have come to appreciate the distinct character of modern Japanese cities, and even celebrate their most fluid and fragmentary aspects. Beginning in the 1980s, many embraced chaos theory as a means of understanding and vindicating Tokyo. Spurred on by the dizzying energy of Japan's economic bubble, they extolled the virtues of Tokyo's 'chaos' and argued that it was particularly suited to the new 'postmodern condition' of city life. Fragmentation, dislocation, and ad-hoc development were recast as positive urban qualities that architects could strive to channel through their buildings.[122]

7.1.3   **Edo-Tokyo analyses**

These books seek to understand the Tokyo of today by tracing the city back to its roots. With the Meiji Restoration, Edo changed its name to Tokyo, and massive reform projects were enacted to modernize the city. Soon after, however, the largely wooden city was immolated twice over—in 1923 by the fires of the Great Kantō Earthquake, and during World War II by Allied firebombing. As a result, there are few buildings still standing from the Edo-era past. When Japan later recovered and became an economic superpower in the 1970s and 1980s, growing cultural self-confidence spawned a boom in works emphasizing

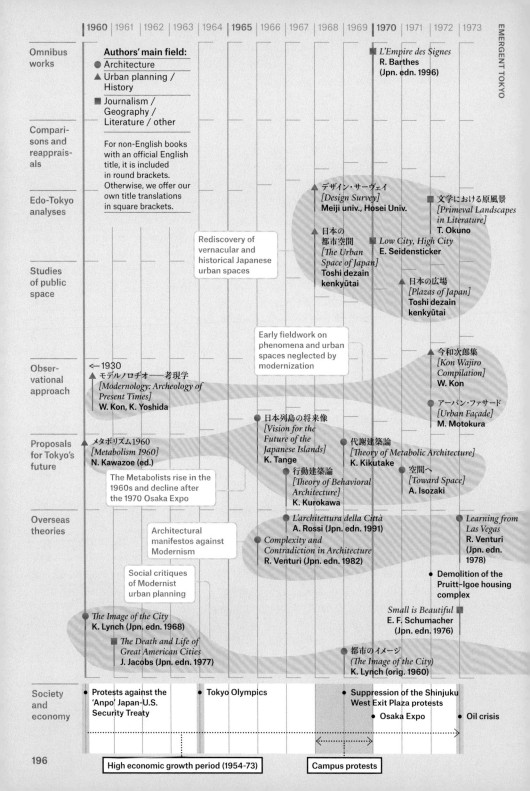

| 1960 | 1961 | 1962 | 1963 | 1964 | **1965** | 1966 | 1967 | 1968 | 1969 | **1970** | 1971 | 1972 | 1973 |

Omnibus works

Authors' main field:
● Architecture
▲ Urban planning / History
■ Journalism / Geography / Literature / other

For non-English books with an official English title, it is included in round brackets. Otherwise, we offer our own title translations in square brackets.

■ *L'Empire des Signes*
R. Barthes
(Jpn. edn. 1996)

Comparisons and reappraisals

Edo-Tokyo analyses

▲ デザイン・サーヴェイ
[*Design Survey*]
Meiji univ., Hosei Univ.

■ 文学における原風景
[*Primeval Landscapes in Literature*]
T. Okuno

Studies of public space

Rediscovery of vernacular and historical Japanese urban spaces

▲ 日本の都市空間
[*The Urban Space of Japan*]
Toshi dezain kenkyūtai

■ *Low City, High City*
E. Seidensticker

▲ 日本の広場
[*Plazas of Japan*]
Toshi dezain kenkyūtai

Observational approach

Early fieldwork on phenomena and urban spaces neglected by modernization

←—1930
▲ モデルノロヂオ――考現学
[*Modernology: Archeology of Present Times*]
W. Kon, K. Yoshida

▲ 今和次郎集
[*Kon Wajiro Compilation*]
W. Kon

● アーバン・ファサード
[*Urban Façade*]
M. Motokura

Proposals for Tokyo's future

▲ メタボリズム1960
[*Metabolism 1960*]
N. Kawazoe (ed.)

The Metabolists rise in the 1960s and decline after the 1970 Osaka Expo

● 日本列島の将来像
[*Vision for the Future of the Japanese Islands*]
K. Tange

● 行動建築論
[*Theory of Behavioral Architecture*]
K. Kurokawa

● 代謝建築論
[*Theory of Metabolic Architecture*]
K. Kikutake

● 空間へ
[*Toward Space*]
A. Isozaki

Overseas theories

Architectural manifestos against Modernism

Social critiques of Modernist urban planning

● *L'architettura della Città*
A. Rossi (Jpn. edn. 1991)

● *Complexity and Contradiction in Architecture*
R. Venturi (Jpn. edn. 1982)

● *Learning from Las Vegas*
R. Venturi (Jpn. edn. 1978)

● Demolition of the Pruitt-Igoe housing complex

● *The Image of the City*
K. Lynch (Jpn. edn. 1968)

■ *The Death and Life of Great American Cities*
J. Jacobs (Jpn. edn. 1977)

Small is Beautiful
E. F. Schumacher
(Jpn. edn. 1976) ■

● 都市のイメージ
(*The Image of the City*)
K. Lynch (orig. 1960)

Society and economy

● Protests against the 'Anpo' Japan-U.S. Security Treaty

● Tokyo Olympics

● Suppression of the Shinjuku West Exit Plaza protests

● Osaka Expo

● Oil crisis

High economic growth period (1954-73)

Campus protests

196

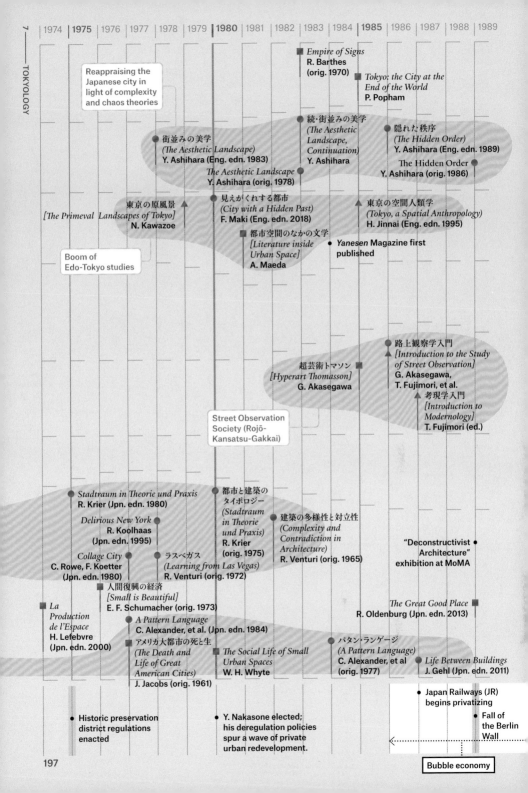

1974 | **1975** | 1976 | 1977 | 1978 | 1979 | **1980** | 1981 | 1982 | 1983 | 1984 | **1985** | 1986 | 1987 | 1988 | 1989

Reappraising the Japanese city in light of complexity and chaos theories

■ *Empire of Signs*
R. Barthes (orig. 1970)

■ *Tokyo: the City at the End of the World*
P. Popham

● 続・街並みの美学
(The Aesthetic Landscape, Continuation)
Y. Ashihara

● 隠れた秩序
(The Hidden Order)
Y. Ashihara (Eng. edn. 1989)

● 街並みの美学
(The Aesthetic Landscape)
Y. Ashihara (Eng. edn. 1983)

The Aesthetic Landscape
Y. Ashihara (orig. 1978) ●

The Hidden Order ●
Y. Ashihara (orig. 1986)

東京の原風景
[The Primeval Landscapes of Tokyo]
N. Kawazoe ▲

● 見えがくれする都市
(City with a Hidden Past)
F. Maki (Eng. edn. 2018)

▲ 東京の空間人類学
(Tokyo, a Spatial Anthropology)
H. Jinnai (Eng. edn. 1995)

■ 都市空間のなかの文学
[Literature inside Urban Space]
A. Maeda

● *Yanesen* Magazine first published

Boom of Edo-Tokyo studies

● 路上観察学入門
▲ *[Introduction to the Study of Street Observation]*
G. Akasegawa, T. Fujimori, et al.

超芸術トマソン
[Hyperart Thomasson]
G. Akasegawa ●

▲ 考現学入門
[Introduction to Modernology]
T. Fujimori (ed.)

Street Observation Society (Rojō-Kansatsu-Gakkai)

● *Stadtraum in Theorie und Praxis*
R. Krier (Jpn. edn. 1980)

● 都市と建築の タイポロジー
(Stadtraum in Theorie und Praxis)
R. Krier (orig. 1975)

Delirious New York
R. Koolhaas (Jpn. edn. 1995) ●

● 建築の多様性と対立性
(Complexity and Contradiction in Architecture)
R. Venturi (orig. 1965)

● "Deconstructivist Architecture" exhibition at MoMA

Collage City
C. Rowe, F. Koetter (Jpn. edn. 1980) ●

● ラスベガス
(Learning from Las Vegas)
R. Venturi (orig. 1972)

■ 人間復興の経済
[Small is Beautiful]
E. F. Schumacher (orig. 1973)

The Great Good Place ■
R. Oldenburg (Jpn. edn. 2013)

■ *La Production de l'Espace*
H. Lefebvre (Jpn. edn. 2000)

● *A Pattern Language*
C. Alexander, et al. (Jpn. edn. 1984)

▲ アメリカ大都市の死と生
(The Death and Life of Great American Cities)
J. Jacobs (orig. 1961)

■ *The Social Life of Small Urban Spaces*
W. H. Whyte

● パタン・ランゲージ
(A Pattern Language)
C. Alexander, et al (orig. 1977)

■ *Life Between Buildings*
J. Gehl (Jpn. edn. 2011)

● Japan Railways (JR) begins privatizing

● Fall of the Berlin Wall

● Historic preservation district regulations enacted

● Y. Nakasone elected; his deregulation policies spur a wave of private urban redevelopment.

Bubble economy

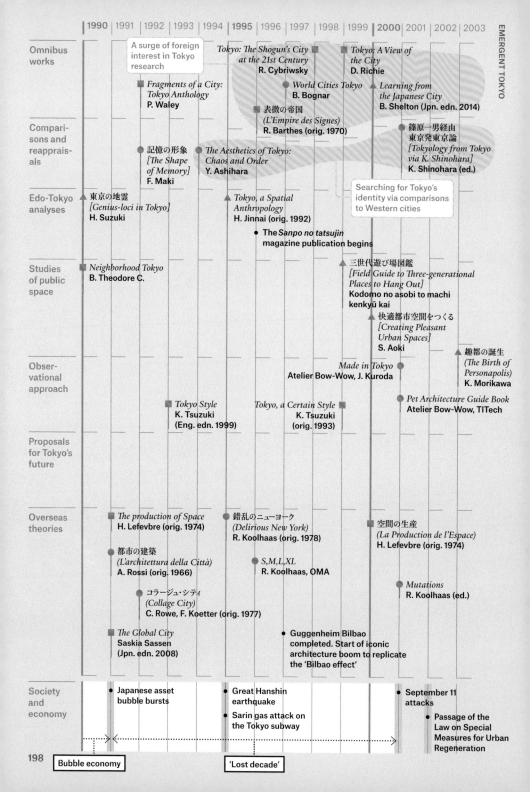

	1990	1991	1992	1993	1994	1995	1996	1997	1998	1999	2000	2001	2002	2003

Omnibus works

A surge of foreign interest in Tokyo research

Tokyo: The Shogun's City at the 21st Century
R. Cybriwsky

■ *Tokyo: A View of the City*
D. Richie

■ *Fragments of a City: Tokyo Anthology*
P. Waley

● *World Cities Tokyo*
B. Bognar

● *Learning from the Japanese City*
B. Shelton (Jpn. edn. 2014)

Comparisons and reappraisals

■ 表徴の帝国
(L'Empire des Signes)
R. Barthes (orig. 1970)

● 篠原一男経由
東京発東京論
[Tokyology from Tokyo via K. Shinohara]
K. Shinohara (ed.)

● 記憶の形象
[The Shape of Memory]
F. Maki

● *The Aesthetics of Tokyo: Chaos and Order*
Y. Ashihara

Edo-Tokyo analyses

▲ 東京の地霊
[Genius-loci in Tokyo]
H. Suzuki

▲ *Tokyo, a Spatial Anthropology*
H. Jinnai (orig. 1992)

Searching for Tokyo's identity via comparisons to Western cities

● The *Sanpo no tatsujin* magazine publication begins

Studies of public space

■ *Neighborhood Tokyo*
B. Theodore C.

▲ 三世代遊び場図鑑
[Field Guide to Three-generational Places to Hang Out]
Kodomo no asobi to machi kenkyū kai

▲ 快適都市空間をつくる
[Creating Pleasant Urban Spaces]
S. Aoki

Observational approach

Made in Tokyo
Atelier Bow-Wow, J. Kuroda

▲ 趣都の誕生
(The Birth of Personapolis)
K. Morikawa

■ *Tokyo Style*
K. Tsuzuki
(Eng. edn. 1999)

Tokyo, a Certain Style
K. Tsuzuki
(orig. 1993)

● *Pet Architecture Guide Book*
Atelier Bow-Wow, TITech

Proposals for Tokyo's future

Overseas theories

■ *The production of Space*
H. Lefevbre (orig. 1974)

錯乱のニューヨーク
(Delirious New York)
R. Koolhaas (orig. 1978)

■ 空間の生産
(La Production de l'Espace)
H. Lefevbre (orig. 1974)

● 都市の建築
(L'architettura della Città)
A. Rossi (orig. 1966)

S,M,L,XL
R. Koolhaas, OMA

● コラージュ・シティ
(Collage City)
C. Rowe, F. Koetter (orig. 1977)

● *Mutations*
R. Koolhaas (ed.)

■ *The Global City*
Saskia Sassen
(Jpn. edn. 2008)

● Guggenheim Bilbao completed. Start of iconic architecture boom to replicate the 'Bilbao effect'

Society and economy

● Japanese asset bubble bursts

● Great Hanshin earthquake

● Sarin gas attack on the Tokyo subway

● September 11 attacks

● Passage of the Law on Special Measures for Urban Regeneration

Bubble economy

'Lost decade'

| 2004 | **2005** | 2006 | 2007 | 2008 | 2009 | **2010** | 2011 | 2012 | 2013 | 2014 | **2015** | 2016 | 2017 | 2018 | 2019 |

Small Tokyo
D. Radović,
D. Boontham
(eds.)

日本の都市から学ぶこと
(*Learning from the Japanese City*)
B. Shelton (orig. 1999)

> Architects spotlight Tokyo's dense low-rise neighborhoods

Tokyo: Portraits and Fictions
M. Tardits

Tokyo Totem
MONNIK ed.

> Exploring links between Tokyo's topography and urban development

Tokyo Metabolizing
K. Kitayama, Y. Tsukamoto,
R. Nishizawa

都市のエージェントはだれなのか
[*Who is the Agent of the City?*]
K. Kitayama

アースダイバー
[*Earth Diver*]
S. Nakazawa

中央線がなかったら
見えてくる東京の古層
[*Tokyo's Historical Layers Hidden by the Chūō Line*]
H. Jinnai

アースダイバー
東京の聖地
[*Tokyo's Sacred Places*]
S. Nakazawa

• The TV show
Buratamori
begins broadcasting
on NHK

東京「スリバチ」地形散歩
[*Strolling Tokyo's 'Suribachi' Topography*]
N. Minagawa

City with a Hidden Past
F. Maki, et al.
(Orig. 1980)

Roppongi Crossing
R. Cybriwsky

Tokyo Vernacular
J. Sand

Tokyo Void: Possibilities in Absence
M. Jonas, H. Rahmann

Tokyo Roji
H. Imai

路地からのまちづくり
[*Community Design from the Roji Alley*]
Y. Nishimura

都市の自由空間
[*Free Urban Space*]
K. Narumi

路地研究
[*Roji Research*]
A. Ueda, O. Tabata

権力の空間/空間の権力
[*Space of Power/ Power of Space*]
R. Yamamoto

アナザー
ユートピア
[*Another Utopia*]
F. Maki
(ed.)

江戸東京の路地
[*The Roji Alleys of Edo-Tokyo*]
S. Okamoto

まち路地再生のデザイン
[*Design for the Regeneration of Roji Alleys*]
K. Okamoto, S. Aoki, et al.

広場(*Hiroba*: All About 'Public Space' in Japan)
K. Kuma, H. Jinnai (ed.)

> Calls for the regeneration of street spaces and *roji* alleys

環境ノイズを読み、
風景をつくる
[*Making Landscapes by Reading Environmental 'Noise'*]
K. Miyamoto

> Renewed interest in public spaces by Japanese architects

コモナリティーズ
(*Commonalities*)
Atelier Bow-Wow

ひとり空間の都市論
[*Urban Theory of One-person Spaces*]
Y. Nango

東京R計画
Remapping Tokyo
CET

Hyper den-City
H. Yatsuka

地域社会圏
主義
[*Local Community Area Principles*]
R. Yamamoto,
et al.

都市をたたむ
[*Folding Up the City*]
S. Aiba

Fibercity
H. Ohno

> Proposals for local regeneration and planned urban shrinkage

エリアリノベーション
[*Area Renovation*]
M. Baba, Open A

Rebel Cities
D. Harvey (Jpn. edn. 2013)

反乱する都市
(*Rebel Cities*)
D. Harvey (orig. 2012)

エコロジカル・
デモクラシー
(*Design for Ecological Democracy*)
R. T. Hester
(orig. 2010)

Design for Ecological Democracy
R. T. Hester
(Jpn. edn. 2018)

建物のあいだのアクティビティ
(*Life Between Buildings*)
J. Gehl (orig. 1987)

Mapping Urbanities
K. Dovey, et al.

Project Japan
R. Koolhaas

サードプレイス
(*The Great Good Place*)
R. Oldenburg (orig. 1989)

グローバル・シティ
(*The Global City*)
Saskia Sassen
(Jpn. edn. 2008)

The Possibility of an Absolute Architecture
P. V. Aureli

Tactical Urbanism
M. Lydon, A. Garcia

• Global financial crisis (known in Japan as the 'Lehman shock')

• Tohoku earthquake and tsunami, culminating with the Fukushima nuclear disaster

Japan quadruples its inbound foreign tourism in five years, primarily from China

• Japan's population begins to decline

Era of rising international tourism

the long-neglected continuity between Edo and Tokyo, with authors condemning the rash imitation of the West that drove Tokyo's early postwar development and rediscovering the qualities of traditional Japanese cities.

Jinnai Hidenobu's *Tokyo: A Spatial Anthropology*, published in Japanese in 1985 and translated into English a decade later, is the most influential book within this vein of analysis in either language. The book's enduring insight is that although individual buildings from the Edo era are largely nonexistent in today's Tokyo, many patterns of life and urban spatial structures have endured even through the 20th century's incredible upheavals—almost as if the city were a biological organism capable of regrowing a lost limb. Viewed from this angle, Tokyo offers a way of thinking about urban preservation that defies the usual focus on conserving buildings and monuments. Edo's heritage is visible all across Tokyo, embodied not by individual works of architecture but rather by the city's underlying physical and social configuration. Factors ranging from the size, shape, and layout of land plots within a neighborhood to the city's networks of sacred places all reflect deeply rooted rhythms and structures of communal life.

7.1.4	**Studies of public space**

Discussions of Tokyo's public space are another recurring vein of analysis. Much of this thinking centers on the city's evolving relationship with the concept of public plazas. Prior to the Meiji Restoration, the Japanese approach to public space usually did not include the sort of parks, wide avenues, and plazas that dot the average Western city, though the Meiji era's Western-inspired modernization saw them begin to sprout up across Japan. After the allies imposed a socio-political revolution on Japan in the postwar period, urban planners across the country responded by building town halls with open plazas intended as spatial support for the country's new postwar democracy, most notably Tange Kenzo's governmental buildings of the 1950s. By the 1960s, however, gathering spaces such as plazas became objects of controversy. Youth culture movements and mass protests by groups outside Japanese society's traditional power centers used the new plazas to coalesce in the streets; for the powers that be, curbing the gathering spaces of Tokyo became a means of defending against threats to their own control.

Japanese thinking on public space has followed an evolutionary path similar to the other threads of Tokyo discourse. As national self-confidence increased, Meiji-era imitation and postwar deference to foreign practices gave way to reappraisals and a desire to express Japanese vernacular character through public spaces. However, the question of who should create and control public spaces remains unsettled. As discussed in greater detail in the next chapter, Tokyo's urban core is currently seeing a rise in 'privately owned public spaces' tied to corporate redevelopment projects, at the expense of genuine public space.

7.1.5	**Observational approach**

Another body of work focuses on careful observations of spaces that might seem marginal or deviant at first glance. [123] Pioneered by the prewar graphical studies of urban investigator Kon Wajirō, this lineage is defined by an appreciation for the rich disorder of everyday life and serves as a critique of how modernist and bureaucratic planning methods often rely on excessively sanitized abstractions rather than grappling with messy realities. In these works, Tokyo is a metropolis exemplified by its accidents and abnormalities, a case study of how the creativity and infinite possibility of city life defies the reductive rationality of planning.

7.1.6 **Proposals for Tokyo's future**

The sixth and final theoretical approach includes publications that primarily serve as proposals for action. Since the Metabolist movement, especially Tange Kenzo's *Plan for Tokyo*, architects, urban planners, and others have laid out a succession of visions for Tokyo's future. These efforts took a backseat in the 1980s and 1990s as the city was reshaped by the bubble economy's boom and bust, which left many architects and urbanists resigned to letting market forces dictate Tokyo's development. Recently, however, there has been a major resurgence in alternative visions of what Tokyo can become. New publications are tackling the oncoming challenges of population decrease and an aging society, and stakeholders across the city are advancing new agendas in areas such as sustainability, building renovation, adaptive reuse, and recycling.

7.2 Self-orientalism: nihonjinron in Tokyology

Many works on Tokyo gravitate towards discussions of Japanese cultural identity, attempting to tie the uniqueness of the Japanese city to some broader uniqueness of Japan's people and culture. In some cases, this affirmation of Japaneseness can serve as a corrective to the predominance of Western theories in architectural and urban design, exposing how Western cultural assumptions erroneously and unthinkingly present themselves as universal. However, an over-emphasis on Japaneseness can lead to a mistaken vision of Japanese cities as being mysterious, exotic, and unknowable to outsiders. Essentializing non-Western cultures implicitly sends the message that Western cities are more rational, dynamic, flexible, and ultimately superior—a pathology that fits within the long and unfortunate tradition of Western orientalism.[124]

Foreigners aren't the only ones trafficking in orientalist tropes. Many Japanese authors leap to center Japanese uniqueness in their writings on Tokyo, even in the face of other, more prosaic explanations for differences between Japanese and Western cities, as a means of stressing national cultural identity. This self-orientalizing approach has flourished in a genre of writing called *nihonjinron* (literally 'theories or studies on the Japanese people') filled with stereotypes of Japanese character and identity.

Nihonjinron writings assume the existence of an immutable quality of Japaneseness that has always existed, is shared by all Japanese, and fundamentally differs from Western-ness. They emphasize Japan's uniqueness to argue that these unique qualities make Japanese society difficult or impossible for outsiders to analyze and understand.[125] By cherry-picking explanations rooted in ethnicity, language, psychology, and social structure, nihonjinron often tries to skirt around inconvenient historical facts that its unitary narratives cannot explain, doing a disservice to the fantastic diversity of both Japanese and Western societies.

Although some works of nihonjinron offer healthy challenges to dominant Western ideas, the genre is often the domain of political ideologues.[126] Nihonjinron arose in the 1970s as an attempt to create a national cultural consensus after the political and social upheaval of the 1960s, particularly the 1960 protests against the passage of the revised security treaty between Japan and the United States, and its primary function is to center the values of Japan's dominant elites and protect the country's status quo power hierarchies.[127] For example, despite nearly every period of Japanese history being marked by profound political struggles, nihonjinron insists on depicting the Japanese as a harmonious, group-oriented, conflict-avoidant society—an idea that Japan's elites have weaponized to discourage mass protests by declaring them to be non-Japanese.

Despite these attempts to portray the Japanese as a harmonious and homogeneous people since time immemorial, the idea of Japan as a homogeneous nation is actually a relatively recent development. Ironically, the dominant ideology in early 20th-century Japan explicitly held that Japan was a multi-cultural society originating from a melting pot of various Asian ethnicities—which, according to imperialists of the time, gave Japan the intrinsic capacity to incorporate other nations into the Japanese Empire.[128]

The assumptions of nihonjinron have deeply permeated both Japanese society and international academic circles. Many of its books are best-sellers at home and abroad, and for better or for worse its ideas clearly have staying power. Two dominant nihonjinron-influenced ideas deserve serious scrutiny: discussions around Japanese notions of *public space* and *plaza-fication*.

7.2.1 *Nihonjinron* and the history of public space in Japan

Discussions of Japanese cities often claim that in pre-modern Japan there was no notion of public space. Sometimes this idea is presented as a self-criticism, portraying Japanese cities as feudal and lacking the public sphere that enabled democracy to develop in the West. Other authors reject the very concept of public space as incompatible with Japanese society due to its Western origins.

When pressed for specifics, their arguments tend to revolve around how best to translate the word 'public' into Japanese. The character generally used for this concept (公, pronounced kō or ōyake) also refers to the imperial family and carries a historical connotation of the state and officialdom, a stark contrast with the Western equivalent's roots in notions of the common people and their interest as a collective. Some even argue that the Japanese language originally lacked a proper corresponding term, since it was only in the Meiji period that translators began using kō/ōyake to translate Western texts containing the word public. The lack of a word, they claim, demonstrates the absence of the concept itself in Japanese life.

These arguments are missing some critical historical context. The choice of a character with imperial connotations to refer to all things public fit within the Meiji government's political strategy of identifying themselves with the restored imperial family.[129] And while pre-Meiji Japanese writings might not contain the exact equivalent of public space, Japanese of earlier eras held notions that the common people shared a collective interest and used community spaces in ways similar to their contemporaries in the West.[130] It is true that open public spaces are less prevalent in contemporary Japan than in many Western cities, but linguistic determinism is a rather weak explanation for Tokyo's failings in this regard—particularly when the obvious obstacles posed by Japan's legal and administrative framework are staring us in the face. When these barriers are successfully overcome, as in the case of citizen initiatives to establish public space for street markets or other events, Tokyo's residents enjoy them just as one would see in the West.

7.2.2
Hiroba-ka: Plaza-fication

The Western *plaza* or *piazza* captured the imagination of Japanese intellectuals and architects during the 1950s and 1960s. In their writings, large open spaces were frequently idealized as embodiments of public openness and democracy. The fact that no exact spatial equivalent to the European plaza existed in Japan was seen as both a consequence of and a cause for Japan's self-perceived lack of democratic and civic traditions—a questionable conclusion when one considers that plazas have also been commonly used throughout history for authoritarian and anti-democratic assemblies.[131]

Some Japanese urbanists influenced by nihonjinron saw the topic in a different light. The authors of an influential Japanese architecture magazine published a seminal counter-narrative in 1971, arguing that although it was true that Japan had no Western-style plazas (*hiroba*), there were nevertheless "Japanese" open spaces that, for the purpose of specific activities, *temporarily became plazas*.[132] They proposed that the Japanese had a unique ability to turn a space into a plaza, a concept they termed *hiroba-ka* or 'plaza-fication.' This bled into hypothesizing about a more general Japanese propensity towards making spaces through activities, unlike the "Western" tendency toward "material expression," using examples such as Japanese civic religious practices to make their point:

> This [hiroba-ka] is fundamentally related to the world view of the Japanese, who manifest a Buddhist sense of the evanescence of life, or the Shinto-originated consciousness of reconstructing shrines. Instead of [focusing on] material expression, the Japanese came to show more interest in the process and styles of human behavior, and this relates to their attempts to make plazas through events and activities.[133]

Although their goal was to paint hiroba-ka as distinctly Japanese, the examples given can easily be found in other cultures. Buddhist temples and Shinto shrines, for example, have ready equivalents across East and Southeast Asia. Looking beyond Asia, their emphasis on informal public life and everyday practices aligns with Western contemporaries such as Jane Jacobs and Jan Gehl, who criticized the stiffness of modern Western planning and developed theories highlighting the importance of ordinary activities.[134] This misguided embrace of national exceptionalism is sadly not exclusive to Japanese urbanists. When Gehl himself tried to apply his lessons from observations of Italian public spaces to his native Denmark, he found considerable opposition. Scandinavia's culture differed markedly from that of Italy, the criticism went, so what was there to be learned from such a different place? Fortunately, Gehl ultimately managed to overcome the cultural determinists, and today Danish cities proudly boast a range of successful public spaces and projects inspired by his pioneering ideas.

The notion that everyday urban spaces can temporarily become plazas for planned events such as festivals or for spontaneous activities is not unique to Japan. Nevertheless, when Japanese cities are the topic of international discussion, the idea of hiroba-ka is often parroted verbatim without much in the way of criticism or modification.[135] Foreign commentators seem happy to confirm their orientalist preconceptions of Japan as a culture whose underpinnings are incomprehensible from a Western viewpoint, and their Japanese counterparts are frequently delighted to confirm that view for their own purposes. In hiroba-ka discourse the Japanese are said to emphasize temporality, favoring less permanent architecture marked by periodic events and temporal change, while Westerners prize physicality, building monumental structures designed to endure and serve as stable public spaces in everyday life. But urban space has never been defined by a binary choice between physicality and temporality. Just as in any other country, lively public spaces in Japan thrive by striking a balance between the two that fits both their physical setting and their societal context.

7.3 Charting a new critical approach to Tokyo

The world has much to learn from Tokyo, but the orientalist stereotypes that permeate writings on the city are an albatross around the neck of the global urbanist community. By unpacking the role that nihonjinron and other clichés play in foreign perceptions of Tokyo, we hope to redirect attention toward aspects of the city that are genuinely worthy of deeper study. Tokyo should interest anyone across the globe who dreams of building better, more livable cities, and each form of Tokyo writing has valuable stories to tell.

The *omnibus* approach is helpful in a practical sense, as it provides lively snapshots of contemporary Tokyo and its foreign lens sometimes highlights urban phenomena neglected by local Japanese researchers. But at some point, Tokyology must move beyond the enthusiastic bewilderment and surface-level descriptions one typically finds in popular writings inspired by the omnibus books and begin drawing design lessons, explaining not only the 'what' of Tokyo but also the 'why' and 'how.'

Comparisons and reappraisals offer valuable accounts of how order emerges in Tokyo in unexpected ways. Its adherents were the first to suggest chaos theories as a way of overcoming overly rigid theoretical paradigms. However, we reject the sharp dichotomy these works often draw between Japan and the West, as it represents a reductionist, unnecessarily binary way of thinking. While it is important to accept Tokyo on its own terms, there is a need to explore how it can improve and evolve by learning from other cities. In these discussions, comparisons with Western cities (and indeed any other city in the world) are a legitimate source of inspiration and not merely a foil to define Tokyo against.

Edo-Tokyo analyses reveal how the construction and reconstruction of Tokyo has been an incremental process over the centuries. However, taking Edo as a source of design inspiration and a primary reference has only limited utility when addressing contemporary situations that lack a direct historical precedent. Edo is an important reference point, but looking constantly to Tokyo's past feels insufficient for charting Tokyo's future in an increasingly globalized world—a risk not only with Edo studies but also with Japan's recent surge of Showa-era nostalgia. As Tokyo rises to the challenge of becoming a more multi-cultural city, it must find ways to creatively merge its Edo-derived cultural roots with the diverse cultural backgrounds of inhabitants arriving from every corner of the globe.

Studies of *public space* have been instrumental in understanding the true diversity of public spaces in Japan, beyond the idealized archetype of the plaza. However, these works tend to essentialize the Japanese and their cities in a fashion remarkably similar to nihonjinron, and as a result they are sometimes used to preempt positive change and defend the status quo. Discussions of public space need to move beyond debates over Japan's unique national character and toward a more practical question: are Tokyo's public spaces truly meeting the city's communal needs?

The *observational approach* to Tokyo has a strong track record of finding extraordinary or unusual layers in ordinary and neglected areas of the city. However, many articles and studies inspired by its books often rely on extreme imagery to fetishize Tokyo's most deviant corners, capturing the global imagination by portraying Tokyo as a city of radical freedom where anything is possible. This results in a funhouse mirror effect in the global conversation, where the city's visually captivating extremes crowd out the more prosaic Tokyo experienced by the vast majority of its residents. As entertaining as it can be to delve into Tokyo's odd corners, few of these studies are bold enough to go beyond that and lay out a vision of what cities around the world can learn from Tokyo's unique approach to balancing its mainstream and its margins.

Finally, the revival of *proposals for Tokyo's future* after the vacuum of the 1980s and 1990s is a positive development, reinforcing the role that the interlinked disciplines of architecture and urbanism can play in answering the new challenges of the 21st century. The best proposals offer a set of resilient design principles backed by concrete examples and case studies, moving beyond mere snapshots of the past and present to envision Tokyo as it might be.

In this book, we have tried to incorporate the varied analyses and perspectives plotted in our timeline while at the same time maintaining some critical distance from them. Our goal is to demystify Tokyo as much as possible, enabling those without a specialist's knowledge of the city to engage critically with it. Once the layers of orientalism and self-orientalism are removed, Tokyo is no longer the exotic mystery that many foreigners wish to see, nor the uniquely Japanese city that some Japanese authors are happy to sell. Instead, Tokyo emerges as a city at the crossroads of global forces, a metropolis undergoing a complex process of evolution and struggle, and a living, breathing home to tens of millions. Its urban ecosystems are unusual in a global context but entirely comprehensible with the right approach, and if properly studied they can serve as a model for cities around the world.

8 A TOKYO MODEL OF EMERGENT URBANISM

8.1 Tokyo's rising corporate-led urbanism

The patterns explored in this book—yokochō alleyways, zakkyo buildings, undertrack infills, ankyo streets, and dense low-rise neighborhoods—collectively point toward a distinct urban model: a Tokyo model of *emergent urbanism* that arose as much from the bottom up through serendipity and painful necessity as it did through intentional design.

After the devastation of World War II, enacting an all-encompassing master plan for Tokyo's reconstruction was an organizational and financial impossibility; the city focused on citizen-led, small-scale redevelopment because it had no choice. All across Tokyo, family businesses and individual residents scraped together their meager resources to erect small buildings on modest plots of urban land. The resulting dense low-rise neighborhoods had narrow streets and lacked public space, but their built environments were unusually flexible and adaptable. The black marketeers of Tokyo's postwar transit hubs were being transferred by the government into ramshackle lines of stalls, which then evolved over time into iconic yokochō. Decades later, in the run-up to the 1964 Olympics, the rush to cover unsightly small waterways birthed the ankyo streets. The combined effect of all these small-scale transformations has created a cityscape with an unparalleled degree of adaptability and spontaneity.

Of course, not all of Tokyo fits this model. More often than not, in fact, Tokyo's planners have imposed modernist universalist visions of city management and development, treating the city as if its unique character and history were of little relevance. Generations of bureaucrats have refashioned Tokyo using a toolkit largely interchangeable with their counterparts in the generic suburbias of the world, with questionable results ranging from postwar *danchi* housing blocks and sprawling 'new town' suburban developments to the artificial mallscape of Odaiba island in Tokyo Bay. Looking ahead, emergent Tokyo is but one of several possible visions for the city's future, and the competition to define the Tokyo of tomorrow will be fierce.

With private corporate interests increasingly dominating urban policy across Japan, Tokyo's bureaucratic modernist planning has begun to recede. The dominant force transforming the city in recent decades is now corporate-led urbanism, also known in academic circles as 'neoliberal urbanism.' The city's most prominent developers have launched a new wave of large-scale redevelopment projects designed to take full advantage of Japan's increasingly deregulated building process. With many of the government's old approval procedures stripped away, these corporations can entirely conceive, implement, and manage large tracts of the city in what amounts to the privatization of urban planning. To be fair, the relationship between these corporations and the government has a complex and uniquely Japanese character, and some of the longest-running firms have been involved in building Tokyo since the Meiji period. But as they have gained the ability to remake Tokyo on an unprecedented scale, the results feel interchangeable with similar developments abroad: sleek yet generic super-high-rise towers placed on top of shopping-mall-like commercial podia, all without a hint of serendipity or idiosyncrasy.

The various changes to the city's redevelopment processes all lean in one direction: to incentivize private-sector rebuilding by relaxing floor area ratio (FAR) and height limit regulations. This is not inherently a bad idea, but it runs the risk of homogenizing the city; after all, the vibrant aspects of Tokyo's cityscape explored in this book aren't easy to scale upwards. At first glance, one saving grace is that these new rules require developers to set aside open space for public use in exchange for allowing more intensive land use Fig. 8-1. Unfortunately, these spaces usually end up being a pale imitation of genuine parks and plazas. These so-called Privately Owned Public Spaces (POPS) tend to be unwelcoming, artificial patches designed more to check bureaucratic boxes than to meet human needs. The problem of POPS is not limited to Tokyo; they have sprung up in cities around the world as a result of similar horse-trading between developers and government.[136]

Tokyo's corporate redevelopments vary in size, use, and location. Some consist of plot-sized rebuilding efforts. Others are based on merging several plots, filling a whole urban block with residential and office towers. The trend toward ever-larger redevelopments first accelerated in the bubble period and declined when the bubble burst, only to resume again in 2002 when the Law on Special Measures for Urban Renaissance loosened regulations as part of a national plan to reignite the economy. The new law created special zones in central urban areas where all existing urban regulations were suspended, including FAR and zoning, allowing new rules to be negotiated with the private sector on a case-by-case basis. One byproduct of this shift is that Tokyo's recent redevelopments are far

---

Fig. 8-1

Regulations governing redevelopment generally allow for bonus building volume and Floor Area Ratio in exchange for providing Privately Owned Public Space. The diagram at the right shows one of such regulations, the Comprehensive Design System or *Sōgō-sekkei*. Adapted from Tokyo Metropolitan Government's Bureau of Urban Development.

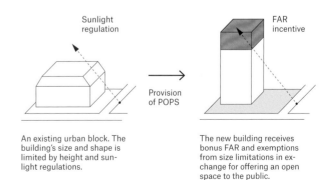

Sunlight regulation

Provision of POPS

FAR incentive

An existing urban block. The building's size and shape is limited by height and sunlight regulations.

The new building receives bonus FAR and exemptions from size limitations in exchange for offering an open space to the public.

more heavily concentrated than the dispersed projects of the 1980s, giving their developers enormous local power Fig. 8-2. Many of the larger redevelopments are adding entertainment and cultural programs to their retail and commercial spaces with the hope that they can evolve from mere skyscrapers to full-fledged urban destinations. These deeply integrated mega-complexes, which we can refer to as *corporate urban centers*, were first pioneered by the Mori Building Company's Ark Hills Roppongi project in 1986. With high-end lofts and services targeted at international diplomats and businessmen, Ark Hills combined amusement, shopping, offices, and housing—a successful formula that served as a blueprint for later projects such as Yebisu Garden Place, Roppongi Hills, and Tokyo Midtown.

These corporate urban centers were at first narrowly conceived as strategic attempts to accommodate international corporations and attract the global managerial class to Tokyo. Since the 2000s, however, authorities and developers increasingly pitched them as a panacea for all of Tokyo's ills, including the lack of open spaces, disaster vulnerability of older buildings, and dearth of centrally-located housing stock. The Mori Building Company, as the originator of this model and one of Japan's most prominent developers, openly describes their redevelopments not as isolated projects but as a part of a broader operation to transform Tokyo into a "vertical garden city."

In effect, their plan resuscitates Le Corbusier's failed and long-abandoned vision for "towers in a park" urbanism—that is, a city designed around high-rise towers scattered across a park-like landscape devoid of traditional street life. In the context of Tokyo, Mori Building's concept is fundamentally at odds with the typical intricate street pattern of Tokyo. But beyond that, it lacks even the social utopianism that animated Le Corbusier's vision. Le Corbusier aimed to use his towers to improve the living conditions of the working classes, but in Mori's "vertical garden city" the towers become vertical gated communities and the green space between them takes on the exclusionary air of a corporate campus. [137] Their most famous redevelopment, Roppongi Hills, was hailed in its inauguration in 2003 as a symbol of Japan's urban regeneration. But with its isolated towers and intimidating luxury shopping spaces, it now stands as a symbol of social segregation and the privatization of public space Fig. 8-3.

8.2   Tokyo's corporate urban centers: what fails and why

Are these large-scale redevelopments a positive road map for Tokyo's future? Developers often advertise them as solutions to the city's shortcomings—but whose problems are they intended to solve? One way to answer these questions is through the lens of *access*. For example, Tokyoites suffer long work commutes from distant suburban homes, and the building of new residential towers in the center of the city is often presented as a way to ease this pain. However, the astronomical price of a Roppongi Hills address is beyond the reach of the vast majority of the population. Without any policy to promote social diversity as a goal of redevelopment, sections of inner Tokyo are rapidly being overtaken by private enclaves with the feel of an exclusive suburb.

Fig. 8-2

Graph. The left bar indicates the number of redevelopment projects in a given time-frame; the right bar indicates how much additional area (in hectares) these projects placed under redevelopment.

Map. Since the 2000s, large-scale redevelopments have mainly been clustered in Tokyo's central wards and around major transportation hubs.

Regulations have been adjusted over time to facilitate redevelopment. Longstanding regulatory systems laid out by Japan's Urban Planning Law (*Kōdo riyō chiku, Tokuteigaiku, Saikaihatsu-tō sokushinku*) require laborious committee approvals for any changes to Floor Area Ratio limits in local urban plans. However, the FAR bonus for public spaces offered by the newer Comprehensive Design System has allowed numerous redevelopments to bypass these processes. Additionally, the 2002 Law on Special Measures for Urban Regeneration lets the central government designate Urban Regeneration Special Areas with streamlined planning approval processes that lessen local government control.

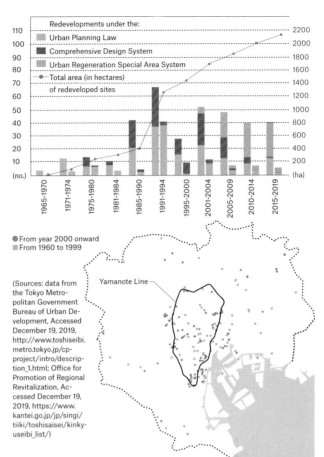

Redevelopments under the:
Urban Planning Law
Comprehensive Design System
Urban Regeneration Special Area System
— Total area (in hectares) of redeveloped sites

(no.) — (ha)

1965-1970, 1971-1974, 1975-1980, 1981-1984, 1985-1990, 1991-1994, 1995-2000, 2001-2004, 2005-2009, 2010-2014, 2015-2019

● From year 2000 onward
■ From 1960 to 1999

Yamanote Line

(Sources: data from the Tokyo Metropolitan Government Bureau of Urban Development, Accessed December 19, 2019, http://www.toshiseibi.metro.tokyo.jp/cp-project/intro/description_1.html; Office for Promotion of Regional Revitalization, Accessed December 19, 2019, https://www.kantei.go.jp/jp/singi/tiiki/toshisaisei/kinky-useibi_list/)

Fig. 8-3
Roppongi Hills, opened in 2003, epitomizes the Corporate Urban Centers' approach: office and luxury residential towers rise up from an elevated podium of shopping and entertainment spaces which are themselves separated from the street. Adapted from Google Earth 2019.

Google Earth 2019

In addition to their pricing, the newly constructed apartment towers tend to be designed as closed communities for wealthy elites thanks to their self-contained nature and array of residents-only facilities. Symbolically speaking, the spread of isolated super-high-rise towers disconnected from their surrounding low-rise neighborhoods embodies what Japanese media have begun to refer to as Japan's *kakusa-shakai* or 'disparity society'—that is, it reflects the country's increasing social stratification in recent decades and runs counter to the long-professed national ideal of an egalitarian, homogeneous, middle-class country. If left unchecked, Tokyo may experience the same sort of affordability crisis that New York, London, and Paris have undergone as the global affluent classes return en masse from the suburbs, displacing the working and middle classes in the process.

Similarly, the commercial complexes built into the base of these new tower developments do not cater to the economic diversity of the city. Although the promoters of corporate-led urbanism offer a mix of residences, offices, shopping, and entertainment, this diversity is ultimately superficial. Since they only accept commercial tenants with established reputations and proven profitability, their shops are the usual array of luxury brands and large franchises, weakening their innovative and creative potential.[138] These redevelopments concentrate the same well-to-do demographic, eschewing the broad social mix that has historically characterized the city. Tokyo's classic neighborhoods, by contrast, are models of flexibility. The ground floors of their multi-story homes often host a wide range of commercial and public endeavors ranging from bars and restaurants to artisan workshops, boutiques, or even community spaces. Without a corporate profit imperative hanging over them, inhabitants are freer to experiment with businesses that are not particularly remunerative but carry more personal meaning.

This push for redevelopment also has environmental consequences. The forest of high-rises along Tokyo Bay is often mentioned as the cause of Tokyo's increasingly punishing heat island effect, as they block the flow of wind that once mitigated Tokyo's suffocating, boiling summers.[139] For their neighbors, these skyscrapers often cast long shadows and block out sunlight. Their height creates intense ground winds and gusts that can at times make navigating the surrounding streets incredibly unpleasant. The costs for neighbors are felt not only in terms of diminished comfort but also financially since buildings shrouded in shadow face higher heating bills when they receive less sunlight.

And what of the public space they promise? The so-called POPS are in practice controlled and managed like the common spaces of a shopping mall. While technically open to the public, they are secluded, intensely surveilled spaces that either do not invite activities beyond capitalist consumption or actively prevent them. Visitors are greeted by signboards with long lists of restrictions as they enter, a reminder that POPS are defined more by what they prohibit than by what they enable. Both city bureaucrats and developers justify POPS as a way of increasing green space, but their greenery is hostile by design. Vegetation is often used as a barrier, both to separate POPS from adjacent public sidewalks and to subdivide the space in order to dissuade large gatherings of people. High-end landscaping materials are employed to match the aesthetic of a corporate campus, exuding a sense of exclusiveness that makes pedestrians hesitate to enter these spaces (a hesitation that is often heightened by Japanese social norms). Many have access restrictions set up in the manner of a construction site or a police line that are designed to appear temporary, but in fact are permanent barriers intended solely to discourage use of the space Fig. 8-4.

Fig. 8-4 What POPS looks like at eye-level. A, B: Blank, windowless façades; C: elevated platforms separating POPS from the public street level; D) greenery used to fragment open spaces, and temporary fences used to preempt gatherings and activities; E) highly manicured outdoor spaces used only for controlled events if anything; F) extensive lists of prohibitions, including eating and drinking.

(A, C: Roppongi Hills; B, F: Futako Tamagawa Rise; D: Shirokane Aer City; E: Tokyo Midtown)

These issues with POPS stem from an inherent flaw in how they are regulated. The maintenance of these pseudo-public spaces depends on their cost-conscious owners, who naturally try to decrease their own maintenance costs by reducing public access. This goes against the spirit of the regulation, which grants extra FAR or height in exchange for making a public contribution to the city through the creation of public space. Without any detailed guidelines on how to define this publicness, nor any monitoring and enforcement of whether these spaces are indeed kept open to the public, the actual consequence of such redevelopments is to accelerate the privatization of the city.[140]

In design terms, the monotony, lack of imagination, and naked commercialism seen in most of these massive redevelopments may feel surprising given the internationally acclaimed talent of Japanese architects. However, even when independent Japanese architects have won important competitions abroad, they only rarely receive commissions from the large corporations leading mega-redevelopment projects at home. In Japan, the architectural field has grown increasingly polarized into two almost completely disconnected worlds. On the one hand are the so-called *ateliers*: small-sized offices, often with connections to local academia, whose members not only work as professional architects but also promote architecture as a cultural activity and frequently win international acclaim for their efforts. On the other hand, we have the corporate world of large architectural offices, including the general contractors and developers' design departments.[141] Practically speaking, only firms from the latter group are placed in charge of these redevelopments, and design quality has suffered as a result. These corporations' hierarchical and bureaucratic decision-making processes are biased toward creating financial value from sheer size rather than from architectural or urban quality.

8.3   Safety as a pretext for homogenization

An increasing number of citizens, government officials, and even developers themselves now acknowledge the negative consequences of these large-scale redevelopments. Even despite these drawbacks, however, one argument still stands tall: the idea that they are necessary for public safety. The new towers withstand earthquakes, and their isolated plots create open spaces for evacuations. There is an economic logic as well; only profitable, spatially efficient high-rise towers, they argue, can pay for the enormous costs of gradually acquiring, demolishing, and ultimately redeveloping the tiny, convoluted properties of Tokyo's inner neighborhoods. Although some downsides of apartment life became apparent after the 2011 Great East Japan Earthquake, when electricity blackouts stopped elevators for long periods, their general sturdiness reinforced the message that 'safety necessitates redevelopment' and the construction of high-rise towers continued apace.

High-rises may indeed be safe, but they are not the only way to achieve safety. There are plenty of effective methods to make the small-scale side of Tokyo's cityscape more resilient as well, but they would require newfound political will to carry out. District plans that strategically broaden roads or incentivize disaster-proof rebuilding can make a difference when local authorities are willing to invest the necessary time and effort to realize them. What's more, small-scale Tokyo is resilient in ways that go beyond the strength of buildings. Mutual aid through social networks is a critical part of disaster response, as demonstrated by Japan's communal experiences during the 2011 Great East Japan Earthquake. In the Tohoku region, community ties and social cohesion were essential to saving lives and bolstering post-disaster solidarity. These new isolated towers, whose inhabitants are strangers to one another and to their surrounding community, cannot contribute similarly to Tokyo's future resilience. At any rate, the boom of tower redevelopments is not a uniquely Japanese phenomenon, but rather a global one; it is happening in major cities around the world, regardless of whether they are located in earthquake-prone regions.

8.4   Emergent urbanism versus corporate-led urbanism

As corporate-led urbanism spreads across Tokyo, its deficiencies when compared with emergent urbanism are becoming clear. Many Japanese architects privately voice these criticisms, but few are willing to publicly challenge the city's powerful development corporations, leaving it to geographers, activists, and social researchers to confront this renovation of Tokyo in a corporate image. [142] Many feel a sense of resignation, since the developers project an aura of inevitability—both in their construction, which is often the result of patient corporate land accumulation over the span of decades, and their eventual sterility once completed, as new corporate construction cannot reproduce the gradual, organic development of older areas that gives them such an attractive atmosphere.

Even if corporate-led urbanism feels inevitable, that doesn't mean that it actually is. Emergent urbanism gives us better options than either our present corporate-led urbanism or the blanket modernist prescriptions of the past, allowing us to thoughtfully design the necessary conditions for a lively and spontaneous city into existence. If corporate urban centers such as Roppongi Hills represent the most explicit expression of the mega-developers' approach for Tokyo's future, the five emergent patterns in this book epitomize its antithesis—a true Tokyo model of emergent urbanism.

For now, Tokyo is vast enough that these two competing paradigms manage to co-exist across the city. While they may at times appear superficially similar on paper—for example, they both center private actors in the making of the city—they differ in very fundamental ways. A traditional *shōtengai* shopping street full of owner-operated small businesses will have an entirely different character than a corporate outdoor mall devoted to chain stores, even if both can simplistically be described as open-air districts for private enterprise. Understanding the difference between these two models in practice is essential for envisioning the possible fates that await Tokyo in the future Table 1.

Table 1	Competing paradigms of Tokyo	
	Corporate-led Tokyo	**Emergent Tokyo**
Dominant power center	Single large corporation	Numerous owners and operators
Economic strategy	Succeed through economies of scale	Succeed through economies of agglomeration
Scale	Large scale, shaped by corporate capital	Small scale, shaped by the local community
Boundaries	Closed, exclusionary boundaries	Permeable, inclusive boundaries
Configuration	Hierarchical configuration	Networked, interconnected configuration
Method of creation	Substitution of preexisting urban fabric and reliance on top-down management	Evolution of preexisting urban fabric and bottom-up, incremental growth

Corporate urban centers are conceived, owned, and operated by major real estate developers (for example, Roppongi Hills by Mori Building and Tokyo Mid-town by Mitsui Fudōsan), concentrating land ownership in the hands of an oligopoly of developers. Emergent Tokyo is the result of complex interactions among numerous small landowners, community organizations, and other decision-makers. In emergent Tokyo, although there might be differences in the size and power of these actors, no single actor predominates. The benefits of land ownership are broadly distributed, and the physical diversity of the built environment spontaneously emerges over time in response to the varying human needs of the community's participants.

Corporate-led redevelopments are designed according to the logic of economies of scale and thus depend on a large volume of consumers and commerce in order to achieve profitability. Emergent Tokyo, on the other hand, thrives via *economies of agglomeration*, wherein multiple small agents compete, cooperate, and co-exist in communion with each other. These economic ecosystems display a high degree of innovation and creativity, fostering concentrated communities of small, idiosyncratic entrepreneurs driven by more than simple profit. Yokochō can be seen as a concrete example of this creative potential.

Corporate-led urbanism tends toward large-scale real-estate operations shaped by the interests and ambitions of global capital. Its primary architectural expression is the high-rise tower and the windowless shopping mall. Emergent Tokyo, meanwhile, often features areas subdivided into numerous smaller units, such as a neighborhood full of small single-family houses with ground-floor shops or the tiny bars of Tokyo's yokochō alleyways—intimate spaces which can be commercialized with small amounts of capital by a single family or even an individual. Smallness allows personalization and creates diverse urban spaces. Smallness does not mean weakness; an agglomeration of small elements creates something larger than the sum of its parts and gives a neighborhood a rich and resilient identity.

In most of Tokyo's large-scale redevelopments, entrances to and from the street are scarce in number and often lead to elevated platforms separated up from the street level. This separation is a conscious design decision aimed at subtly producing faux-public space—that is, space that is nominally public but in practice keeps out the messy spontaneity of the public sphere. Emergent Tokyo, by contrast, has porous boundaries and is accessible as part of the city's broader public space network, since its inhabitants depend on direct contact with the broader public for all aspects of daily life and commerce. As a result, these spaces tend to be socially inclusive (or at least as inclusive as public space generally is), while corporate redevelopments tend to be exclusionary.

The corporate urban centers popping up across Tokyo are more often than not configured around a centralized hierarchy of space, frequently with a plaza or atrium at their center. Emergent Tokyo tends to adopt a networked configuration, with fuzzy boundaries enabling openness and connections to its surroundings. The economic and social logic of these spaces depends on that openness and interconnection, unlike the corporate preference for isolation from the broader environment.

Corporate-led Tokyo and emergent Tokyo each have different natures and origins. Corporate-led districts exist as the result of top-down decisions that designate specific areas of Tokyo for forms of redevelopment that in practice only the oligopoly of major developers and contractors can realistically take part in. They are built all at once on large plots, either demolishing the existing urban fabric in the process or becoming isolated islands in the midst of the surrounding city. Tokyo's emergent urbanism results from collective interactions over long stretches of time—a bottom-up process of shaping the city. These neighborhoods emerge from both a fine-grained subdivision of land and the numerous little individual decisions of a wide variety of actors. Their character and identity arise naturally, not as the result of a corporate branding strategy.

These divisions are not written in stone, and some have argued that with time, corporate redevelopments can evolve to offer a higher degree of adaptability and integration with their surroundings. However, characteristics such as idiosyncrasy, permeability, and adaptability are difficult to replicate artificially by simply tossing money at the problem. If these traits are in fact necessary preconditions for unleashing emergent interactions, as our case studies suggest, then corporate redevelopments are unlikely to ever foster the sort of urban ecosystem that defines Tokyo's more livable and creative districts.

8.5   Designing the conditions of emergence

At this point, corporate-led urbanism has shown itself to be incapable of producing cities that feel like emergent Tokyo. But can emergent spaces be designed by other means? If emergence is a self-organized process, what is the role then of a designer? In practice, what does cultivating emergence actually entail? Answering these questions is a fundamental responsibility of architecture and urbanism as a publicly minded profession. But as we discussed at the outset of this book, Tokyo's architects are faced with both urban market fetishism from the business community and a non-judgmental post-critical approach from many architectural theorists. As a result, many have turned away from the task of designing the city. For emergent urbanism to thrive, we must reawaken their critical and creative capacity to challenge Japan's corporate-dominated status quo.

Corporate-led urbanism corrodes city life in part because it enables large development companies to act as oligopolists within the slices of the city that they dominate. When markets function correctly they are self-organizing, meaning that they dynamically determine prices through open competition. However, oligopolies and cartels—in this case, Japan's construction-industrial complex—seek to cement their existing profitability by coordinating with each other for their guaranteed mutual benefit, rather than competing to win the public's favor. Development oligopolies damage the capacity of cities to generate their own complexity and spontaneity; all that messiness and uncertainty, the lifeblood of emergent urbanism, is antithetical to their interests.

Of course, not all aspects of a city need to be emergent. Fundamental infrastructure such as railways and disaster preparedness planning are obvious examples where at least some degree of centralized control and management is desirable. However, over time the balance has tilted too far away from emergent urbanism as oligopolistic interests assert themselves. Their use of financial clout and power relationships to steer local politics is pushing Tokyo, neighborhood by neighborhood, toward profitable predictability and away from dynamic urbanism. This trend toward oligopolistic dominance of urban development is a global phenomenon that municipalities and even national governments have found difficult to control.

However, all is not lost; there will always be ways for architecture to foster livable, vibrant cities. A growing number of architects and urban planners are creating a diverse toolkit of strategic interventions designed to nurture a city's emergent capacity for complexity and spontaneity. In these interventions, the designer's role is not to dictate exactly what the end result of complex interactions should look like, but rather to design into being the necessary preconditions for emergence to occur. Tokyo offers a vivid blueprint of what this looks like in practice: neighborhoods filled with a multiplicity of independent owners and operators, economies of agglomeration, small-scale architecture, urban spaces that are physically and socially permeable, interconnected networks rather than top-down hierarchies, and bottom-up incremental growth rather than corporate redevelopment.

Golden Gai, Shinjuku's densely packed micro-bar district, offers a clear example of how to design organic, distinctive urban spaces. To modern observers, Golden Gai is often dismissed as a retro relic from the high-flying Showa era that would be impossible to reproduce today in a new development. Their skepticism is understandable; after all, plenty of shopping malls and mixed-use developments have tried and failed to create similarly lively small-scale districts, with results that generally feel akin to a theme park.[143] The *authenticity* of Golden Gai seems at first glance to be the result of a spontaneous historical development which we can aspire to preserve but not to reproduce.

However, compared with the centuries-long histories of so many storied urban districts, Golden Gai, which was created in the 1950s, is relatively young. And despite its image as an organic, self-organized result of informal urbanism, Golden Gai's spatial configuration was strictly planned as an equal and repetitive subdivision of row houses. The area's physical conditions of smallness, its motley crew of owners and bartenders, and its openness to the surrounding public spaces of Shinjuku are what actually produce Golden Gai's perceived authenticity. They are intentional choices, and they are choices that can be made again.

Since emergent urban patterns are ultimately the result of conditions that we can design, we need not leave the city to chance. However, many of Tokyo's emergent patterns were not the result of any clear unitary vision, and their current form is often to some extent unintended. Due to this lack of vision, these emergent patterns are often in a fragile state. There are no policies in place to preserve or enhance them, and year by year the erosion continues. Zakkyo buildings and yokochō keep disappearing under developer pressure. Many dense low-rise neighborhoods are becoming saturated by luxury housing. Tokyo has become an unintended laboratory experiment to discover how much stress emergent urban spaces can endure before they break. In the right hands, however, Tokyo could not only sustain its best aspects but also pioneer new forms of consciously designed emergent urbanism.

Will lessons from Tokyo truly be applicable in other contexts? The dominant narrative in discussions of Japanese cities is one of cultural exceptionalism, deterring both foreign and Japanese authors from exploring whether Tokyo's successes might be transferable to other national contexts. Some hesitation in making grandiose claims is certainly warranted, since the patterns explained in this book directly resulted from the specific social, economic, and cultural dynamics of postwar Japan. And it is entirely fair to stress the importance of pre-existing cultural norms, such as by tracing the acceptance of narrow alleys in current Tokyo back to the cramped labyrinths of Edo's commoner districts.

The point is not to deny these local particularities, but rather to acknowledge their influence without treating them as monolithic and immutable. Places and cultures do actually change and evolve, but essentialist views on the Japanese—if one can even agree on a definition of who constitutes 'the Japanese'—push the idea of an ethnically shared Japanese character that binds an entire nation to a list of alleged psychological traits while ignoring any evidence to the contrary. The same hazy logic is often brought to bear in discussions about the Japanese city. For example, it is common to hear that the physical and social sense of smallness and intimacy found in Tokyo ultimately constitutes something uniquely Japanese—ignoring the many similar spaces found across East Asian or even European cities. Emergent Tokyo is a product of the context in which it was born, but it is not a physical expression of Japan's collective psyche, civilizational spirit, or cultural DNA.

Tokyo as a whole is not the result of any harmonious consensus, cultural or otherwise—quite the contrary, Tokyo's past and present are both battlefields full of controversies and radically opposed forces. The city today is increasingly dichotomized between the two urban visions that Japan's laws, regulations, and economic context most consistently enable—the vast scale of the skyscraper as a triumph of economic efficiency, and the tiny scale of the dense low-rise neighborhood as a triumph of individual property rights. While corporate-led development has clawed its way to numerous victories recently by consolidating support from government authorities and economic elites, growing opposition from local town-building *machizukuri* groups and resident associations may soon cause the pendulum to swing back in the other direction. Too many authors, both Japanese and foreign, miss these pivotal controversies entirely when they embrace the myth of a monolithic Japanese society. The struggle between these opposing forces is the lifeblood of Tokyo's dynamism, and understanding their interplay is central to any attempt to bring Tokyo's lessons to the world.

Standing amid a redevelopment rush based on the monotonous repetition of skyscrapers and shopping malls, it is time for us to reconsider Tokyo's emergent urban patterns in a new light. Not out of nostalgia for Tokyo's past or the desire for an exoticized Other, but because they demonstrate a set of concrete values that we can rely on as we imagine what future cities can become. Tokyo's underlying design principles have allowed this complex and seemingly disorderly metropolis to produce lively, wildly diverse, inclusive, and innovative urban spaces. If given the chance, they could breathe new life into other cities around the world.

Endnotes

CHAPTER 1
INTRODUCTION: WHY TOKYO?

1 The emergent patterns selected in this book are among the most archetypal cases Tokyo has to offer. Reality offers few or no pure cases corresponding to theoretical conceptions, but a definition of the "ideal type" (as in Max Weber's *Idealtypus*) helps us to understand and classify urban forms according to their degree of proximity to a theoretical ideal. In this book, each pattern is not only defined but further illustrated with a real-world "epitome case" in Tokyo wherein, in the words of Roman Cybriwsky, "one can see the bigger place in compression or in miniature" (Roman Adrian Cybriwsky, *Tokyo: The Changing Profile of an Urban Giant* [Belhaven Press, 1991], 151). The descriptions of each pattern and epitome case are based on primary research, including a range of fieldwork mapping and observational studies carried out from 2005 to 2020. The contents derive in part from previous research papers published by the authors. Full methodological details and previous research reviews can be found in those papers. The results of these efforts are shown whenever possible, via detailed maps, graphs, and photographs.

2 The boundaries of chōme [丁目] often coincide with physical boundaries such as rivers, topographic changes, and wide roads. One can map our neighborhood archetypes onto the city using grid calculations or other systems, but chōme better capture Tokyo's organic socio-spatial development even if they are more idiosyncratic and less standardized than a grid.

3 Tokyo is no longer defined as a city (Tokyo-shi) but rather as a metropolis (Tokyo-to) that includes the rural and mountainous areas on its western edge as well as a string of islands stretching hundreds of kilometers to the south. However, as in most discussions, this book uses 'Tokyo' to refer to the 23 wards that comprise its urban core.

4 On a definitional note, in this book we basically follow Japan's Urban Planning Law, which defines low-rise as 1 to 2 floors, mid-rise as 3 to 5, and high-rise as 6 or more. However, we count buildings of up to 3 floors as low-rise. Since the residential low-rise zoning maximum height is 12 m, maximizing space within those boundaries often leads to compact 3-floor houses. The term 'super high-rise' is not legally defined but often refers to buildings higher than 60 m (20 floors).

5 In practice, many of these urban fabrics overlap heavily with each other. Local Tokyo, Pocket Tokyo, and Yamanote Mercantile Tokyo all offer a similar mix of residential and commercial usage shaped by west Tokyo's postwar development. Oftentimes, Tokyo neighborhoods with very different historical development paths and built environments can nevertheless end up sharing a range of commonalities: for example, Pocket Tokyo and Mercantile Tokyo have numerous differences, but both types embrace forms of mixed use that simultaneously enable residential life, commerce, and entertainment.

6 This nihonjiron approach begins in the 1970s, when Japan starts to be seen as an economic superpower, and achieves full expression in the 1980s with the bubble economy.

7 Ashihara Yoshinobu, *The Hidden Order* (Kodansha International, 1989, original Jpn. 1986), 148.

8 See for example Barrie Shelton, *Learning from the Japanese City*, 2nd ed. (Routledge, 2012), 129.

9 Jane Jacobs, *The Death and Life of Great American Cities* (Vintage, 1992, original ed. 1961); and Rem Koolhaas, *Delirious New York: A Retroactive Manifesto for Manhattan* (The Monacelly Press, 1978). Other examples include Lynch (1960) on Boston, Jersey City, and Los Angeles, and Venturi, Scott-Brown, and Izenour (1977) on Las Vegas.

10 For a discussion of post-criticality in architecture see Pier Vittorio Aureli, *The Possibility of an Absolute Architecture* (The MIT Press, 2011), 32.

11 Beyond natural and biological phenomena, the Mexican-American philosopher Manuel De Landa and Australian urban researcher Kim Dovey have drawn on the prolific 20th-century French philosopher Gilles Deleuze and complexity theory more generally to apply the concept of emergence to the study of societies and cities. They use the term "assemblage" to refer to an order that emerges from the non-hierarchical interactions of its constituent parts. See Manuel De Landa, *A New Philosophy of Society* (Continuum, 2006); Manuel De Landa, *Assemblage Theory* (Edinburgh Univ. Press, 2016); Kim Dovey, *Urban Design Thinking: A Conceptual Toolkit* (Bloomsbury, 2016).

CHAPTER 2
YOKOCHŌ ALLEYWAYS

12 For some examples see Fujiki TDC and Kawakami Buraboo, *Maboroshii Yami-ichi wo yuku, Tokyo-no Ura-roji "futokoro"* (Shoku-kikō Mirion, 2002). Also these Japanese websites: "Tokyo Deep Annai," accessed Sep. 21, 2011, http://tokyodeep.info; "Information Design Lab," accessed Oct. 5, 2011, http://asanoken.jugem.jp; "Kōji, roji-ura, yokochō," accessed Sep. 23, 2011, http://yaplog.jp/emjp; "Tōkyō no shōtengai wo arukō" accessed Sep. 23, 2011, http://tokyo-syoutengai. seesaa.net; The media have also noticed the popularity of the yokochō phenomenon among youngsters and foreigners. See Takano Tomohiro, "Wakamono, gaikokujin ni mo ninki, 'yokochō' buumu ha itsu made tsuzuku no ka," *Newsweek Japan edition*, Aug. 25, 2017, https://www.newsweekjapan.jp/nippon/season2/2017/08/198324_1.php.

13 See Ino Kenji ed., *Tokyo Yami-ichi Kōbōshi* (Sōfūsha, 1999, 1st ed. 1978); Matsudaira Makoto, *Yamiichi Maboroshi no Gaidobukku* (Chikuma Shobō, 1995); Hatsuda Kohei, "Sengo Tokyo ni okeru barakku nomiyagai no keisei to henyō: sensai fukkō-ki, kōdoseichō-ki ni okeru eki-mae saikaihatsu ni kan suru kōsatsu," *Journal of Architecture and Planning*, no. 579 (May 2004): 105–10; Hatsuda Kohei, "Sengo Tokyo no maaketto ni tsuite: Yami-ichi to senzen no ko-uri ichiba, roten to no kankei ni kan suru kōsatsu," *Journal of Architecture and Planning*, vol. 76, no. 667 (Sep. 2011): 1729–34.

14 Takahashi Toru, "Tokyo no roten shūyō kenchiku ni kan suru kenkyū," *Summaries of technical papers of Annual Meeting AIJ* (2003): 469–70.

15 This chapter derives in part from our previous research. See Jorge Almazán and Rumi Okazaki, "A morphological study on the yokochō bar alleys: Urban micro-spatiality in Tokyo," *Journal of Architecture and Planning*, vol. 78, no. 689 (2013): 1515–22; Jorge Almazán and Nakajima Yoshinori, "Urban micro-spatiality in Tokyo: Case study on six yokochō bar districts" in *Advances in Spatial Planning*, ed J. Burian (InTech, 2010).

16 Toshi Dezain Kenkyūtai, *Nihon no hiroba* (Shokokusha, 2009, 1st ed. 1971).

17 In Japanese there are two ways to write the word: 横町 and 横丁.

18 For this analysis, we do not count as yokochō the various department stores, *kaikan* buildings, and underground spaces that also originated from postwar black markets, despite the distinction between these types of spaces and the concept of yokochō sometimes being blurred in specific cases. Undertrack spaces, some of which originate from black markets, are addressed in Chapter 4 of this book.

19 Almazán and Okazaki, "A morphological study on the yokochō bar alleys: Urban micro-spatiality in Tokyo."

20 For the concept of "third place," see Ray Oldenburg, *The Great Good Place: Cafes, Coffee Shops, Bookstores, Bars, Hair Salons, and Other Hangouts at the Heart of a Community* (Da Capo Press, 1999).

21 Almazán and Nakajima, "Urban micro-spatiality in Tokyo: Case study on six yokochō bar districts."

22 Edward Seidensticker, *Tokyo Rising: The City Since the Great Earthquake* (Harvard Univ. Press 1991), 153.

23 The order is known as the *roten seiri rei* [露店整理令].

24 Golden Gai has two business associations. The *Shinjuku Sanko-chō Business Development Association*, which covers the northern part of the district, and the *Shinjuku Golden-gai Commercial Association*, for the southern part.

25 Ogawa Michiko and Kawaguchi Yuki, *Shinjuku no Goldengai-Hanazono Annai* (Daiyamondo-sha, 2008)

26 Maeda Kyōko, "Yokochō kara no kasseika wo hakaru," *Fudōsan Forum 21*, Vol. 232, Aug. 2009, 15–17.

27 In Japanese: 人世横丁.

28 *Gekkan rejaa sangyō shiryō*, "Jimoto saihakken: Chiiki seikatsusha ni

kōdō henka no kikai wo unagasu. Keesu sutadii Ebisu yokochō," Gekkan rejaa sangyō shiryō, Mar. 2009.

29 Maeda, "Yokochō kara no kasseika wo hakaru."

30 Shimoyama Moeko, Goto Haruhiko, and Baba Kiyomasa, "Shinjuku Golden Gai ni okeru shin-kyū tempo no konzai to sono kōshin no jittai ni kan suru kenkyū: tempo kōshin-ji no kyū-tenshu kara no adobaisu ni chakumoku shite," *Journal of the City Planning Institute of Japan*, vol. 52, no. 3 (Oct. 2017).

31 Before the revision, the Law on Land and Building Leases (a national government law) tended to protect the lessee. The lessor could not refuse the renewal of a contract without valid reasons. Even if the lessor managed to vacate the property, the lessor had to pay a compensation fee for the eviction. In 2000, the law was revised and fix-term lease contracts were introduced. Now the lessor could decide a lease term, and refuse to renew it once the term expired, without the need to pay compensation fees. Without the previous hurdles, a new flow of store owners came to Goldengai. Landlords could vacate their properties and lease them to a younger generation looking for opportunities to become a bar owner with little capital.

32 "Interview to Koichiro Mikuriya," Shibuya Bunka Project, Apr. 16, 2018, https://www.shibuyabunka.com/keyperson/?id=152.

33 Takahashi, "Tokyo no roten shūyō kenchiku ni kan suru kenkyū."

34 The Tokyo government signed a contract with Shibuya's association of relocated merchants (the *Shibuya Jōsetsu Shōgyō Kyōdō Kumiai* or "Shibuya Permanent Commercial Association") to sell the land of Nombei Yokochō with a five-year loan. See Ishigure Masakazu, *Sengo Tōkyō to yamiichi* (Kajima Shuppankai, 2016), 306–9.

35 From an interview to the association representative in: "Shibuya Higashi-chiku Machizukuri Council," Shibuya tōyoko mae inshokugai kyōdō kumiai Murayama Shigeru daihyō riji, accessed Feb. 20, 2020, http://www.east-shibuya.jpn.org/miyashita/article/%5Bインタビュー%5D_渋谷東横前飲食街協同組合_村山茂代表理事.

36 Atsushi Miura, *Yokochō no inryoku* (Ïsutoshinsho, 2017), 186.

37 "Mitsui Fudōsan," accessed Mar. 15,

2020, https://www.mitsuifudosan.co.jp/corporate/news/2020/0120/index.html.

38 The Nakajima Aircraft Musashino Factory, located in the neighboring Musashino city.

39 Fujiki TDC, *Tōkyō Sengo chizu yamiichi ato wo aruku* (Jitsugyō no nihonsha, 2016), 104.

40 James Farrer, "A Bangladeshi Bar Down Willow Alley," Nishiogiology, accessed Jan. 1, 2020, https://www.nishiogiology.org/miruchi-jp.

41 Farrer, "A Bangladeshi Bar Down Willow Alley."

42 The street that connects the Ome-Kaidō with the Nishi-Ogikubo Station. See "Official planning in Suginami City," accessed Mar. 14, 2020, https://www.city.suginami.tokyo.jp/guide/machi/toshikeikaku/1033914.html.

43 Several websites record and organize the activities of the groups opposed to the road widening, like "Nishiogi Annai-jō," accessed Mar. 14, 2020, https://nishiogi.in/181226hojo132_2/; and "Nishiogikubo no dōro-kakuchō wo kangaeru kai" accessed Mar. 14, 2020, https://blog.goo.ne.jp/ndk/e/ee-8a1817f8fbfd3fa8ec2126fc30e610.

44 Almazán and Nakajima, "Urban micro-spatiality in Tokyo: Case study on six yokochō bar districts."

CHAPTER 3
ZAKKYO BUILDINGS

45 Peter Popham, *Tokyo: The City at the End of the World* (Tokyo: Kodansha International, 1985), 111.

46 On the laudatory side: Barrie Shelton, *Learning from the Japanese city: West meets East in Urban Design* (E & FN Spon, 1999), 96; and Donald Richie, *Tokyo: A view on the city* (Reaktion Books, 1999). On the critical side: Ashihara Yoshinobu, *The Aesthetic Townscape* (The MIT Press 1983) Original in Japanese: *Machinami no Bigaku* (Iwanami Shoten, 1979); Alex Kerr, *Dogs and Demons: the Fall of Modern Japan* (Penguin Books, 2001).

47 Ashihara, *The Aesthetic Townscape*, 30.

48 Sanki Choe, Jorge Almazán, Katherine Bennett, "The extended home: Dividual space and liminal domesticity in Tokyo and Seoul," *Urban Design International*, 21 (2016): 298-316. https://doi.org/10.1057/

udi.2016.10.

49 See "Hōkoku Taishō Kenchi-ku-butsu no Handan [Selection Criteria for buildings to be object of report]," Tokyo-to Bōsai Kenchiku Machizukuri Center [Tokyo Metropolis Center for Disaster Prevention, Architecture and Town Development], accessed 16 Aug., 2006, http://www.tokyo-machidukuri.or.jp/index.html. For land use classification, see "Tokyo no tochi riyō: Heisei 13-nen Tokyo-to Ku-bu [Tokyo's Existing Land Use in 2001], Tokyo Metropolitan Government, 2001.

50 The relatively visible presence of these businesses across Tokyo often surprises the first-time visitor to Japan. The Prostitution Prevention Law, effective since 1958, limits the definition of prostitution to vaginal intercourse. As a result, other forms of commercial sex, known as fūzoku, are legal. Fūzoku activities are regulated by the 1948 Businesses Affecting Public Morals Regulation Law, which regulates establishments such as 'soaplands' and 'pink salons.'

51 Jorge Almazán and Tsukamoto Yoshiharu, "Tokyo Public Space Networks at the intersection of the Commercial and the Domestic Realms: Study on Dividual Space," Journal of Asian Architecture and Building Engineering, vol. 5, no. 2 (Nov. 2006): 301–8.

52 "Tokyo-to Oku-gai Kōkoku-butsu Jōrei [Tokyo Metropolis Outdoor Advertising Regulations]," The Tokyo Outdoor Advertising Association, accessed 24 Aug., 2006, http://www.toaa.or.jp/jyou/index.html.

53 The available information on the uses and number of floors in the existing maps is fragmented and sometimes inconsistent. For precise information we consulted the original building register at the Shinjuku Ward Office and the Tokyo Metropolis Government Office. Further details can be found in the following research conducted by Keio Univ. Jorge Almazán Studiolab: Nobutaka Kawai, Shinjuku eki higashi-guchi shūhen ni okeru kenchiku yōto no suichoteki hensen ni kan suru kenkyū: Yasukuni-dōri to Shinjuku-dōri wo taishō to shite. Graduation thesis, 2016.

54 Tokubetsu Toshi Keikaku Hō [特別都市計画法].

55 Tochi Kukaku Seiri Jigyō [土地区画整理事業].

56 The hanamachi reached its peak around 1937, with 140 restaurants and 180 geisha shops, with over 700 geishas. See Okamoto Satoshi, Edo→Tōkyō Naritachi no Kyōkasho (Tankōsha, 2018).

57 See Fujii Sayaka, Okata Jun'ichiro, and André Sorensen, "Inner-city redevelopment in Tokyo: conflicts over urban places, planning governance, and neighborhoods," in André Sorensen and Carolin Funck eds., Living Cities in Japan: Citizens' movements, machizukuri and local environments (Routledge, 2007), 247–66.

58 Kagurazaka's prestige became a magnet for large developments. Using new regulations that allowed higher building if buildings were set back from the street, a new 14-floor condominium was erected in 1995, flouting both the average height and the street's frontage continuity. A more severe shock came in 2000, when the community was informed of the imminent construction of a 31-floor apartment tower, this time at the back of the main street. Radically bulkier and higher than its surroundings, the project also proposed to eliminate one of the neighbors' beloved roji alleys to accommodate the tower.

59 NPO Hōjin Ikina Machizukuri Kurabu, Ikinamachi kagurazaka no idenshi (Tōyō shoten, 2013).

60 'District plan' translates the Japanese chiku keikaku [地区計画].

61 The salaryman is the stereotyped image of a life-long employee of a large corporation, devoted to hard work during the day and aggressive stress release by drinking at night.

62 Yoshida Takahiro and Jinnai Hidenobu, "Shimbashi to Yokohama no hikaku: Kōtsū no hensen ga toshi-kūkan no tenkai ni ataeta eikyō," Summaries of technical papers of Annual Meeting AIJ (Sep. 2008): 335–36.

63 Hatsuda Kosei, "Zakkyo biru kara mita sengo Tokyo no toshi saikaihatsu," Shichō No. 71, (May 2012): 17–33.

64 Yoshida and Jinnai, "Shimbashi to Yokohama no hikaku: Kōtsū no hensen ga toshikūkan no tenkai ni ataeta eikyō."

65 The 1961 Urban Remodeling Law (usually called 市街地改造法, officially named 公共施設の整備に関連する市街地の改造に関する法律). This law promoted the unified remodeling of urban areas, involving widening of public streets and plazas together with the construction of new buildings. This law, which is no longer in force, is a predecessor of the Urban Redevelopment Law that has facilitated many of the contemporary large-scale redevelopments.

66 Fujiki TDC, Tōkyō Sengo chizu yamiichi ato wo aruku, 47.

67 More than 90% of the New Shimbashi Building and neighboring landowners have joined the association, called the "Shimbashi Station West Exit Area Urban Redevelopment Preparatory Union." See "Shimbashi no daikibo saikaihatsu de SL hiroba ya Nyū Shimbashi biru ga kieru!?," Nikkan Gendai degitaru, accessed Feb. 13, 2020, https://www.nikkan-gendai.com/articles/view/life/224161.

68 Toyo keizai online, accessed 27 Mar., 2020, https://toyokeizai.net/articles/-/219053?page=3.

69 Kensetsu Shinbun, accessed 27 Mar., 2020, https://www.kentsu.co.jp/feature/kikaku/view.asp?c-d=160805000001#2shinbashi.

CHAPTER 4
UNDERTRACK INFILLS

70 That being said, as cities across the globe shift their focus from facilitating vehicular traffic to becoming more pedestrian-friendly, the 20th-century preference for constructing large-scale elevated transportation infrastructure is beginning to fall out of favor globally. In Tokyo too, stretches of elevated track have recently been put underground in densely built-up areas.

71 Including mAAch ecute Kanda Manseibashi on the Chūō Line and 2K540 Aki-Oka under the Yamanote Line between Okachimachi and Akihabara Stations.

72 Among those publicly used undertrack spaces, we deliberately selected stretches that showed continuity of purpose along a length of at least 100 m. Shorter cases also exist, but our goal here is to show how undertrack spaces have managed to become an integral part of the urban fabric. The length of 100 m is comparable to the length of an average urban block.

73 Takayuki Kishii, "Use and Area Management of Railway under-Via-

duct Spaces and Underground Spaces near Stations," *Japan Railway and Transport Review*, no. 69 (Mar. 2017): 7.

74 These projects for grade separation are known as *Renzoku Rittai Kōsa Jigyō* [連続立体交差事業].

75 Kobayashi Ichirō, *Gaado Shita no Tanjō: Tetsudō to Toshi no Kindaishi* (Shodensha Shinsho, 2012), 15.

76 Osada Akira, *Ameyoko no sengo rekishi: Kaa baito no tomoru yami-ichi kara 60 nen* (Besuto Shinsho, 2016), 14.

77 Kobayashi, *Gaado Shita no Tanjō*, 112.

78 Miura Atsushi and SML, *Kōenji: Tōkyō shin-joshi machi* (Yōsensha, 2010).

79 According to interviews with members of the *Nishi-Shōtenkai* (West Merchants' Association) conducted by the authors in Jun. 2020.

80 *Deai no seichi* [出会いの聖地].

81 Tōkyō Kōsoku Dōro Co., Accessed Mar. 12, 2020, http://www.tokyo-kousoku.co.jp/.

82 The stretch of the outer moat along Ginza Corridor was also covered by bullet train tracks in 1959. The decision to make the Tōkaidō bullet train was taken in 1958, before Tokyo was selected in 1959 for the 1964 Olympics. See "Shinkansen no Rekishi," accessed Jun. 10, 2020, https://www.nippon.com/ja/features/h00078/.

83 Even the character of current restaurants and bars seems to adapt rapidly. Fieldwork by the authors in the early 2000s shows that many of them were rather simple eateries, like yakitori izakaya, targeted at the Shimbashi's male dominated salaryman workforce. Now, they are moodier and more sophisticated, in an effort to attract women and couples on dates.

84 In 2019 a new undertrack commercial space (called Uracori, or back corridor) was opened, and on the north the old undertrack spaces of Yurakuchō were renewed and collectively branded as Yūrakuchō Sanchoku Yokochō. The biggest reconstruction is under the JR lines, on the Hibiya side under the railways. The whole stretch will be branded as Hibiya Okuroji, a commercial center with exclusive fashion stores, cafés, and restaurants. See Hibiya Okuroji, accessed May 4, 2020, https://www.jrtk.jp/hibiya-okuroji/.

85 Jane Jacobs, *The Death and Life of Great American Cities* (Vintage 1992, original 1961).

CHAPTER 5
ANKYO STREETS

86 The most famous publication is Nakazawa Shi-ichi, *Aasu Daibaa* (Kodansha, 2005).

87 Often, the contemporary Japanese vocabulary used to describe these spaces are foreign loan words. For example, even urban activists trying to create street markets in Japan usually do not use the native Japanese term (*ichiba*) but rather the *katakana* versions of the French 'marché' (*marushe*) or the English 'market' (*maaketto*).

88 Hatsuda Kosei, "Sengo Tokyo no maaketto ni tsuite: Yami-ichi to senzen no ko-uri ichiba, roten to no kankei ni kan suru kōsatsu," *Journal of Architecture and Planning*, vol. 76, no. 667 (Sep. 2011): 1729–34.

89 Nick Kapur, *Japan at the Crossroads: Conflict and Compromise after Anpo* (Harvard Univ. Press, 2018): 218.

90 To relax these conditions, in 2011 a special permit for road occupation (*dōro senyū kyoka tokurei* 道路占有許可の特例) was created to accommodate increasing public demands regarding street use. Some local governments have begun sidewalk café pilot projects under this new permit system, but they remain isolated experiments.

91 This is an observation often heard from newcomers to Tokyo. For a detailed discussion see Edan Corkill, "Standing up for the right to sit down in public," *The Japan Times*, Oct. 10, 2010, accessed Jun. 5, 2019. https://www.japantimes.co.jp/life/2010/10/10/general/ standing-up-for-the-right-to-sit-down-in-public/#.XPdialj7RPY.

92 Below is a list of Tokyo's five river basins, followed in parentheses with representative ankyo river street examples (*gawa* means river in Japanese): Shakuji-gawa (Inaduke-gawa); Kanda-gawa (Momozono-gawa, Shoan-gawa, Yabatagawa South Greenway); Shibuya-gawa (Cat street, Mozart-Brahms Lane, Udagawa promenade, Harajukumura-bunsui, Kōhone river, Shirokane-Sankocho tributary); Meguro-gawa (Kitazawa-gawa, Toriyama-gawa green-

way); Nomi-gawa (Kakinokizaka river greenway, Komazawa river greenway, Kuhonbutsugawa promenade). See full details in Yoshimura Nama and Takayama Hideo, *Ankyo Maniac* (Kashiwashobō, 2015) 6–7.

93 Report 36 (in Japanese: 36答申).

94 Kurosawa Hisaki, *Tokyo Burari Ankyo Tansaku* (Yōsensha, 2010) 49.

95 The source is the *Kiyomasa-no-ido*, one of the popular spots inside the Meiji Jingū Shrine.

96 Tate Mitsuhiko, *Yamanote 29 eki: Burari roji ura sanpō, usureyuku machi no kioku wo tazunete* (Gakkenpursu, 2011).

97 Specifically the association of the south exit area. In Jiyūgaoka there are 12 associations, coordinated since 1963 by the larger Jiyūgaoka Shopping District Promotion Association [自由が丘商店街復興組合] See Jiyūgaoka official website, accessed Apr. 29, 2020, https://www.jiyugaoka-abc.com/shopguide/service/999999.html.

98 See a detailed description of the events in Okada Kazuya and Ako Mari, *"Jiyūgaoka" Burando: Jiyūgaoka Shōtengai no chōsen-shi* (Sangyō Nōritsu Daigaku shuppanbu, 2016) 42–43.

CHAPTER 6
DENSE LOW-RISE NEIGHBORHOODS

99 There have been examinations of the socio-psychological role of *afuredashi*, the extension of one's private belongings into alley spaces (Aoki Yoshitsugu and Yuasa Yoshiharu, "Kaihōteki roji kūkan de no ryōikika to shite no afuredashi: Roji kūkan he no afuredashi chōsa kara mita keikaku gainen no kasetsu to kenshō, sono 1," *Journal of Architecture Planning and Environmental Engineering*, no. 449 (Jul., 1993): 47–55; Aoki Yoshitsugu and Yuasa Yoshiharu, "Afuredashi no shakai-shinrigakuteki kōka: Roji kūkan he no afuredashi chōsa kara mita keikaku gainen no kasetsu to kenshō, sono 2," *Journal of Architecture Planning and Environmental Engineering*, no. 457 (Mar. 1994): 125–32. There is also research on the role of gaps and alleyways as residual spaces (Kim Youngseok and Takahashi Takashi, "Misshū jūtakuchi no 'jūko gun' ni okeru roji to sukima no yakuwari ni kan suru

kenkyū," *Journal of Architecture Planning and Environmental Engineering*, 469 (1995): 87–96. Taken together, they offer the intellectual space for a reappraisal of dense low-rise housing itself.

100 This chapter derives partly from previous research from the authors in Kyōjima (Sumida Ward) and Himonya (Meguro Ward). See Jorge Almazán, Darko Radovic, and Suzuki Tomohiro, "Small urban greenery: Mapping and visual analysis in Kyōjima-sanchōme," *Archnet-IJAR, International Journal of Architectural Research*, vol. 6, issue 1 (2012); Mizuguchi Saki, Jorge Almazán, and Darko Radovic, "Urban characteristics of high-density low-rise residential areas in Tokyo: A case study," *Journal of the Faculty of Architecture, Silpakorn Univ.*, Vol. 26 (2012).

101 The density here is not only the net density of the low-rise fabric. We used official statistics on gross population density, available per chōme. Therefore this density includes open spaces like parks and streets as well as other building typologies like high-rise towers.

102 *Mokuzō misshū chiiki* [木造密集地域].

103 *Mokuzō* or 'wood construction' includes traditional Japanese-style buildings, but in a city pulverized twice in the 20th century, those are extremely rare. *Mokuzō* refers primarily to buildings with a timber structural frame; traditional wooden construction methods are rare, and almost only applied in historical preservation. Current techniques have evolved into highly engineered and completely prefabricated framing methods. In addition to these local systems, the US balloon-frame method using 2x4-inch timber is very common in the Japanese construction industry.

104 Foreign visitors often think that this is because of earthquakes, but the main reason is for fire prevention. The Building Standards Law does not state any specific setback dimension. It is the Civil Code (Article 234, clause 1) that specifies a 50 cm minimum distance from the adjacent land plot. Neighbors can agree not to follow the 50 cm rule and instead use the Building Standards Law´s Article 63 that allows buildings to touch the lateral site boundaries if the building façade is built according to the official fire-proof

structural standards (*taika kōzō*). For example, many buildings along shōtengai invoke this regulation to validate their almost continuous urban façades without gaps between buildings.

105 Amir Shojai, Nomura Rie, and Mori Suguru, "Side Setback Areas in Residential Zones in Japan: A Socio-psychological Approach Towards Studying Setbacks, Case Study of an Inner Osaka Neighborhood," *Journal of Asian Architecture and Building Engineering*, vol. 16, no. 3 (2017): 589–96.

106 Kim and Takahashi (1995): 87.

107 *Enshō shadan tai* [延焼遮断帯].

108 *Sōzokuzei* [相続税].

109 For brevity, we will refer to the area as simply Higashi-Nakanobu.

110 National Census of 2010. Summary compiled by Shinagawa Ward, accessed Mar. 3, 2020, https://www.city.shinagawa.tokyo.jp/ct/other000081500/51-5kokuchou.pdf.

111 The basic block size is a square of 60 x 60 *ken* (109 m x 109 m), subdivided into two halves, with each half split into six subdivisions. The street widths become narrower as they progress into the interior of the block. The blocks are surrounded by streets 6 ken wide (10,9 m), the streets halving them are 3 ken wide (5.4 m), and the final six subdivisions are created by tiny alleys or *roji* (2.7 m, and even 1.8 m).

112 Called *san-kō-dōro*, or third category streets. Current Building Standards Law contemplates this category, but local planning authorities very rarely deign to designate a street with this categorization. Given the nation-wide obligation of 4 m streets, under the rationale that it is necessary for safety, very few local planning authorities take the perceived risk of authorizing them.

113 See a detailed description in Nishimura Yukio, *Roji kara machizukuri* (Gakugei shuppan: 2006) 211–13.

114 Ai suru Tsukishima wo mamoru kai, accessed Apr. 6, 2020, https://lovetsukishima.jp/.

115 This is a common unofficial name for the street. Also known as Shirokane-Kitasato-dōri, the official name is Tokyo Prefectural Road 305 Shiba-Shinjuku Ōjisen.

116 Our study area corresponds to the 1st, 3rd, and 5th chōme, which we coined here as North Shirokane,

located between Ebisu Street and the Furukawa River.

117 Zoning recognizes this character, as North Shirokane is a designated "semi-industrial zone."

118 One project, currently under construction, will have 45 floors (白金一丁目東部地区市街地再開発組合. Accessed Apr. 6, 2020. https://www.shirokane-1.com/). The other project, currently at a planning phase will have 40 floors (The Daily Engineering and Construction News 日刊建設工業新聞, accessed Apr. 6, 2020, https://www.decn.co.jp/?p=96688.).

119 This is the resident "night" population, according to the 2015 National Census. See Minato Ward's website, accessed Mar. 2, 2020, https://www.city.minato.tokyo.jp/toukeichousa/kuse/toke/jinko/kokusechosa/shibaura.html. Regarding European compact city density, we can take Barcelona as a reference. Its famous Eixample, the 19th-century grid disstricts, has a density of 35,105 persons/km².

CHAPTER 7
TOKYOLOGY

120 In architecture and urban design, books remain the primary medium by which ambitious attempts at theory and synthesis are disseminated. Although peer-reviewed academic papers also contain valuable contributions, in the interest of space, we have decided to plot only books. For older books, we selected those most frequently cited in the field. For more recent works from the year 2000 onward, it is still too early to assess their long-term impact with any authority, so we have opted for incorporating books by renowned authors as well as those that express a coherent core argument or idea, rather than the many collections offering grab-bag assortments of articles and essays that the city tends to attract.

121 This categorization of texts within approaches or lines of discourse is admittedly something of a simplification. Most authors cited here would vociferously protest against being pinned down into a single category since ideas are intricately interrelated and influence other in complex ways. This timeline, however imperfect, can help as an

initial way to navigate the rich and complex body of Tokyology. In its simplified clarity, it can open the door for competing categorizations and improvements.

122 Such as Maki Fumihiko's Spiral Building (1985) and Shinohara Kazuo's Centenial Hall (1987).

123 Jordan Sand, *Tokyo Vernacular: Common Spaces, Local Histories, Found Objects* (Univ. of California Press, 2013); Kuroishi Izumi, "Urban Survey and Planning in the Twentieth-Century Japan: Wajiro Kon's 'Modernology' and Its Descendents," *Journal of Urban History*, vol. 42 (3) (2016): 557–81.

124 Edward Said, Orientalism (Pantheon Books, 1978).

125 Peter N. Dale, *The Myth of Japanese Uniqueness* (The Nissan Institute, 1986); Yoshino Kosaku, *Cultural Nationalism in Contemporary Japan: A Sociological Enquiry* (Routledge, 1992); Sugimoto Yoshio, "Making Sense of Nihonjinron," *Thesis Eleven*, No. 57, (May 1999): 81–96.

126 Dale, *The Myth of Japanese Uniqueness*.

127 Nick Kapur, *Japan at the Crossroads: Conflict and Compromise after Anpo* (Harvard Univ. Press, 2018), 267.

128 Oguma Eiji, *A Genealogy of Japanese Self-Images* (Trans Pacific Press, 2002); originally published in Japanese in 1995, as *Tan'itsu minzoku shinwa no kigen: "Nihonjin" no jigazō no keifu*, literally "The origin of the myth of the ethnic homogeneity: The genealogy of 'Japanese' self-images."

129 Dale, *The Myth of Japanese Uniqueness*.

130 Jinnai Hidenobu, *Tokyo: A Spatial Anthropology* (Univ. of California Press, 1995); Jinnai Hidenobu, "Diversity of Unique Japanese Public Spaces," in *Hiroba: All About Public Spaces in Japan*, edited by Kuma Kengo and Jinnai Hidenobu (Tankosha, 2015).

131 Sand, *Tokyo Vernacular*, 25–27.

132 Toshi Dezain Kenkyutai, *Nihon no hiroba* (Shokokusha, 2009, 1st ed. 1971).

133 Toshi dezain kenkyutai, *Nihon no hiroba*, 19 (translation by the author).

134 Jane Jacobs, *The Death and Life of Great American Cities* (Vintage; Reissue ed. 1992, original 1961); Jan Gehl, *Life between Buildings: Using Public Space* (Van Nostrand Reinhold Company Inc., 1987, original ed. 1971).

135 The extension of the *hiroba-ka* thesis into an idea of an intrinsic Japanese approach to space was further developed by Shelton into the notion of "content over form": according to Shelton, while in the West the emphasis is on the context and form of a space, in Japan it is on the content and activities that take place there. See Shelton, *Learning from the Japanese City* (Taylor & Francis, 1999): 67. Hidaka and Tanaka go beyond even that generality to affirm that "In Japan, 'public' is more a mental construct than a physical presence." See Hidaka Tanya and Tanaka Mamoru, "Japanese Public Space as Defined by Event," in *Public Space in Asia Pacific Cities*, edited by Pu Miao (Kluwer Academic Publishers, 2010) 118. A recent iteration of a similar idea can be found in Onodera Yasushi, "Restoration of New Public Spaces," in *Hiroba: All About Public Spaces in Japan*, edited by Kuma Kengo and Jinnai Hidenobu.

CHAPTER 8
A TOKYO MODEL OF EMERGENT URBANISM

136 POPS in Japanese corresponds to *kōkai-kūchi* [公開空地] or *yūkō-kūchi* [有効空地]. Kōkai-kūchi is the name used in the *Comprehensive Design System* [総合設計制度] of the Building Standards Law. Yūkō-kūchi is used in the Urban Planning Law. Besides detailed legal procedures, both terms refer to essentially the same type of space.

137 Mori Building Co., "Vertical Garden City," Mori Building Co. Website, Accessed 15 Aug., 2020, https://www.mori.co.jp/en/urban_design/vision.html.

138 Urban researcher Ohno Hidetoshi characterizes them as islands, and he includes not only the inner-city large-scale redevelopments but also the large shopping malls built across regional Japan. See Hidetoshi Ohno, *Fiber City: A Vision for the Shrinking Megacity, Tokyo 2050* (Univ. of Tokyo Press, 2016).

139 Arita Eriko, "Tokyo's 'heat island' keeps breezes at bay: Waterfront wall of high-rises insulates asphalt jungle from cooling effect," *The Japan Times*, Aug. 18, 2004, https://www.japantimes.co.jp/news/2004/08/18/national/tokyos-heat-island-keeps-breezes-at-bay/

140 Criticism of POPS has grown recently, as studies of their actual usage produce lackluster results. In many cases, POPS appear to be cynically used as a means to obtain extra FAR, with no clear use or contribution to urban space: see Nagaoka Atsushi, Kojima Katsue, Negami Akio, Katsuya Uozaki, "Tokyo-to sōgō-sekkei seidō ni yotte umidasareta kōkai kūchi no jittai ni kan suru kenkyū," *Reports of the City Planning Institute of Japan*, no. 2 (2004): 35–39. There is also the danger that POPS administrators might ban some activities that they are not actually entitled to forbid: Saito Naoto, Soshiroda Akira, Tsutsumi Takashi, "Kōkaikūchi, yūkōkūchi no keikaku konseputo to riyōjittai ni kan suru kenkyū," *Journal of the City Planning Institute of Japan*, No. 43-3 (2008): 223–28. Also, critics argue that the current system does not include measures to guarantee the actual publicness of POPS—see Izumiyama Rui, Akiyama Hiroki, Kobayashi Masami, "Toshin-bu ni okeru 'minyūchi no kōkyō kūkan' no katsuyō manejimento ni kan suru kenkyū," *Journal of Architecture and Planning*, vol. 80, no. 710 (2015): 915–22.

141 Large construction companies are known in Japan as *zenekon*, a portmanteau of 'general contractor.'

142 In English we can find a critique of redevelopments and specifically of Roppongi Hills in Roman Adrian Cybriwsky, *Roppongi Crossing: The Demise of a Tokyo Nightclub District and the Reshaping of a Global City* (Univ. of Georgia Pr., 2011). In social research see Nakazawa Hideo, "Tokyo's 'Urban Regeneration' as the Promoter of Spatial Differentiation: Growth Coalition, Opposing Movement and Demographic Change." *The Chuo Law Review*, vol. 121, no. 3-4 (Aug. 2014) 1–31; and Kohama Fumiko, "Gentrification and Spatial Polarization in Eastern Inner-city Tokyo: The Restructuring of the Kyōjima Area in Sumida Ward." Bulletin of the Graduate School of Humanities and Sociology, vol. 33 (2017): 15–42.

143 For instance, *Daiba 1-chōme Shōtengai*, inside the Decks shopping mall in Odaiba, or the new "Shibuya Yokochō," located in the newly built shopping mall that has replaced the former Miyashita Park.

**EMERGENT TOKYO:
DESIGNING THE
SPONTANEOUS CITY**

ORO Editions
Publishers of Architecture,
Art, and Design
Gordon Goff: Publisher

www.oroeditions.com
info@oroeditions.com

Published by ORO Editions

Copyright © 2024 Jorge Almazán.

All rights reserved. No part of this
book may be reproduced, stored in
a retrieval system, or transmitted in
any form or by any means, including
electronic, mechanical, photocopying
or microfilming, recording, or
otherwise (except that copying
permitted by Sections 107 and 108 of
the U.S. Copyright Law and except by
reviewers for the public press) without
written permission from the publisher.

You must not circulate this book in
any other binding or cover and you
must impose this same condition on
any acquirer.

Authors: Jorge Almazán + Studiolab
Book Design: neucitora
Managing Editor: Jake Anderson

10 9 8 7 6 5 First Edition

ISBN: 978-1-951541-32-3

Color Separations and Printing:
ORO Editions Inc.
Printed in China.

ORO Editions makes a continuous
effort to minimize the overall carbon
footprint of its publications. As
part of this goal, ORO Editions, in
association with Global ReLeaf,
arranges to plant trees to replace
those used in the manufacturing of
the paper produced for its books.
Global ReLeaf is an international
campaign run by American Forests,
one of the world's oldest nonprofit
conservation organizations. Global
ReLeaf is American Forests' education
and action program that helps
individuals, organizations, agencies,
and corporations improve the local
and global environment by planting
and caring for trees.